0 3 MAY 2018

D0541419

90710 000 333 247

The Literary Agenda

Readers' Liberation

JONATHAN ROSE

OXFORD
UNIVERSITY PRESS

Great Clarendon Street, Oxford, OX2 6DP,
United Kingdom

Oxford University Press is a department of the University of Oxford.
It furthers the University's objective of excellence in research, scholarship,
and education by publishing worldwide. Oxford is a registered trade mark of
Oxford University Press in the UK and in certain other countries

© Jonathan Rose 2018

The moral rights of the author have been asserted

First Edition published in 2018

Impression: 1

All rights reserved. No part of this publication may be reproduced, stored in
a retrieval system, or transmitted, in any form or by any means, without the prior
permission in writing of Oxford University Press, or as expressly permitted by law, by
licence or under terms agreed with the appropriate reprographics rights organization.
Enquiries concerning reproduction outside the scope of the above should be sent to
the Rights Department, Oxford University Press, at the address above

You must not circulate this work in any other form
and you must impose this same condition on any acquirer

Published in the United States of America by Oxford University Press
198 Madison Avenue, New York, NY 10016, United States of America

British Library Cataloguing in Publication Data
Data available

Library of Congress Control Number: 2017944011

ISBN 978–0–19–872355–4

Printed in Great Britain by
Clays Ltd, St Ives plc

Links to third party websites are provided by Oxford in good faith and
for information only. Oxford disclaims any responsibility for the materials
contained in any third party website referenced in this work.

London Borough of Richmond Upon Thames	
RTR	
90710 000 333 247	
Askews & Holts	
809 ROS	£14.99
	9780198723554

Series Introduction

The Crisis in, the Threat to, the Plight of the Humanities: enter these phrases in Google's search engine and there are 23 million results, in a great fifty-year-long cry of distress, outrage, fear, and melancholy. Grant, even, that every single anxiety and complaint in that catalogue of woe is fully justified—the lack of public support for the arts, the cutbacks in government funding for the humanities, the imminent transformation of a literary and verbal culture by visual/virtual/digital media, the decline of reading...And still, though it were all true, and just because it might be, there would remain the problem of the response itself. Too often there's recourse to the shrill moan of offended piety or a defeatist withdrawal into professionalism.

The Literary Agenda is a series of short polemical monographs that believes there is a great deal that needs to be said about the state of literary education inside schools and universities and more fundamentally about the importance of literature and of reading in the wider world. The category of "the literary" has always been contentious. What *is* clear, however, is how increasingly it is dismissed or is unrecognized as a way of thinking or an arena for thought. It is skeptically challenged from within, for example, by the sometimes rival claims of cultural history, contextualized explanation, or media studies. It is shaken from without by even greater pressures: by economic exigency and the severe social attitudes that can follow from it; by technological change that may leave the traditional forms of serious human communication looking merely antiquated. For just these reasons this is the right time for renewal, to start reinvigorated work into the meaning and value of literary reading for the sake of the future.

It is certainly no time to retreat within institutional walls. For all the academic resistance to "instrumentalism," to governmental measurements of public impact and practical utility, literature exists in and across society. The "literary" is not pure or specialized or self-confined; it is not restricted to the practitioner in writing or the academic in studying. It exists in the whole range of the world which is its subject-matter: it consists in what non-writers actively receive from writings when, for example, they start to see the world more imaginatively as a result of reading novels and begin to think more carefully about human personality. It comes from literature making available much of human life that would not otherwise be existent to thought or recognizable as knowledge. If it is true that involvement in literature, so far from being a minority aesthetic, represents a significant contribution to the life of human thought, then that idea has to be argued at the public level without succumbing to a hollow rhetoric or bowing to a reductive world-view. Hence the effort of this series to take its place *between* literature and the world. The double-sided commitment to occupying that place and establishing its reality is the only "agenda" here, without further prescription as to what should then be thought or done within it.

What is at stake is not simply some defensive or apologetic "justification" in the abstract. The case as to why literature matters in the world not only has to be argued conceptually and strongly tested by thought, it should be given presence, performed and brought to life in the way that literature itself does. That is why this series includes the writers themselves, the novelists and poets, in order to try to close the gap between the thinking of the artists and the thinking of those who read and study them. It is why it also involves other kinds of thinkers—the philosopher, the theologian, the psychologist, the neuroscientist—examining the role of literature within their own life's work and thought, and the effect of that work, in turn, upon literary thinking. This series admits and encourages personal voices in an unpredictable variety of individual approach and expression, speaking wherever possible across countries and disciplines and temperaments. It aims for something more than intellectual assent: rather, the literary sense of what it is like to feel the thought, to embody an idea in a person, to bring it to being in a narrative or in aid of adventurous reflection. If the artists refer to their own works, if other thinkers return to ideas that have marked much of their working life, that is not their vanity nor a failure of originality. It is what the series has asked of them: to speak out of what they know and care about, in whatever language can best serve their most serious thinking, and without the necessity of trying to cover every issue or meet every objection in each volume.

Philip Davis

A Very Brief Preface

This book distills and explains a field of research that scarcely existed thirty years ago. Back then most scholars who thought about the problem (and not many did) believed that the history of ordinary readers was unrecoverable. We of course had access to volumes of popular books, newspaper, and magazines, but it seemed very difficult to pin down who exactly read them, and practically impossible to discern how readers responded to what they read.

In 1986 Robert Darnton published his manifesto "First Steps Toward a History of Reading," and though it appeared in a little-known Australian journal, it would have an enormous long-run impact.[1] Since then a new academic field has been built from the ground up. The sources for studying reading experiences, once thought not to exist, turned out to be quite plentiful, once historians did some serious searching. Common readers left behind correspondence, diaries, memoirs, and marginalia. Librarians kept borrowing-rosters, booksellers noted what their customers wanted, sociological surveys of reading go back as far as eighteenth-century Scotland, and in some countries secret policemen closely monitored what the masses were reading. Readers of both sexes and all races organized book clubs and kept minutes. Those sources supplied the raw material for a burgeoning body of scholarly books and articles.

We now have enough specialized studies to proceed to the next step: assembling them, like a mosaic, to create a broad narrative history of reading. That is what this book attempts to do, for the benefit of the general reader. And this story has a central theme: that reading can be and has been the most fundamental expression of human freedom, even in repressive societies. That becomes apparent when one looks beyond the censors and inquisitors and examines reading as it is experienced by readers.

Parts of this volume were previously published in the *Autism File*, and are reproduced here with the kind permission of the editors.

This book is dedicated to Flora. May she someday be free to read.

Note

1. Reprinted in Robert Darnton, *The Kiss of Lamourette: Reflections in Cultural History* (New York and London: W. W. Norton, 1990), 154–87.

Contents

Contents

1
Wrestling with the Author

Even if the Old Testament is the word of God, many of the characters in that story had an exasperating fondness for arguing with the author—and winning. Abraham sharply questions His plan to destroy Sodom, and makes Him promise to spare the city if fifty righteous men can be found, eventually bargaining Him down to ten. When God instructs Moses to liberate His people, Moses at first pleads a lack of eloquence, but evidently he's a good enough talker to persuade the Boss to assign him Aaron as an assistant. And Job quite rightly questions why he should be the innocent victim of what seems an incredibly cruel wager. Jacob wrestles with an angel, who turns out to be the Deity undercover. In spite of a dislocated hip, Jacob wins both the match and a new title: God renames him Israel, which literally means "He who struggles with God." (That explains a lot about Israel today.)

This orneriness carried over to the Talmud, which carries on interminable and detailed debates over the interpretation of reading matter. The Bar Mitzvah likewise requires offering a new and original take on a classic text, an excellent preparation for careers in academia, the law, or revolutionary movements. You can trace this kind of damnably independent reading at least as far back as the destruction of the Second Temple in Jerusalem. Rabbi Yochanan ben Zakkai, a key figure in the transition to rabbinic Judaism, was celebrated in the Babylonian Talmud for his omnivorous reading, which was by no means limited to theology: "Scripture, Mishna, Talmud, Halacha, Aggadah, Biblical grammar, scribal traditions, deductive logic, linguistic connections, astronomical calculations, gematriot [numerology], incantations for angels, incantations for demons, incantations to palm trees, proverbs of washerwomen, proverbs of foxes," not to mention legal treatises and chariot-repair manuals. The premise behind his reading—polymathic, multidisciplinary, ranging freely across high to low culture—is that all of it had educational value that could be shared with other readers: "That I may cause those that love me to inherit substance, and that I may fill their treasuries." In that sense the first-century Judean rabbi resembled the New York Jewish intellectuals of the twentieth century. Or, to take the analogy imagined by Amos Oz and Fania Oz-Salzberger in *Jews and Words*, the reader today who consumes "Tolstoy and Toni Morrison with his morning coffee while skimming two news sites on his electronic device and perusing the small print on his breakfast cereal package." That is how they explain the apparent contradiction of fractiousness and community among the Jews—who constantly argue over reading, but argue with each other and over the same readings. In conclusion, they invite their own readers to "Try to replace the word *Jew* in this book with *reader*. In many places you'd be surprised how well it works."

But, they also emphasize, "You don't have to be a rabbi (or a Jew) to belong to that club."[1] Certainly not. Radically independent reading has a very long and cross-cultural history, and its intellectual consequences have been so enormous and various that I can only sketch them briefly here. But every revolution begins with liberated reading.

Philobiblon, by the English bishop Richard de Bury, was a foundational text for all future generations of booklovers. It celebrated books as "liberal and free," which "give to all who ask" and "enfranchise all."[2] He wrote that shortly before the Black Death, which (in addition to transforming everything else) called into existence a new reading public. A third of Europe's population had been wiped out, and the resulting labor shortage boosted wages and opened up opportunities for economic mobility. As their disposable income grew, the survivors often spent it on books.[3] But now there was a shortage of scribes (many had died, and others stepped into the posts vacated by deceased clergy), and the resulting bottleneck created a demand for a new book-production technology, which was eventually figured out by Johannes Gutenberg. Perhaps because the upheavals of their time had shaken their faith in church and state, readers became decidedly more questioning. "And right as sight serveth a man to se the heighe strete," proclaimed *Piers Plowman*, "right so lereth lettrure lewed men to reason"—"And just as sight enables a man to see the high street, so letters teach ignorant men to reason."[4] And not just men: in the same spirit, we find Christine de Pisan criticizing and rejecting a misogynist tract by Matheolus. As Laurel Amtower concluded, Christine "demonstrates a viewpoint that was widely taking hold among readers of the later Middle Ages: that the individual has both the ability and the duty to engage texts analytically and to question or doubt those opinions that may turn out to be dangerous or false."[5]

Janet Coleman observed that, "By the latter part of the fourteenth century, that period of the great flowering of literature in English, numerous commentators, speaking hyperbolically for or against the English, noted how the country seemed dominated politically and economically...by the professions that required their practitioners to possess the skills of literacy that, in effect, made them England's legislators: in Parliament, in the marketplace, in the law courts."[6] Even Geoffrey Chaucer had to defer to those assertive readers:

> For my words, here and in every part,
> I speak them and invite correction
> by you that have experience of love's art,
> and allow it all to your discretion
> to increase or make a diminution
> of my language: and that I you beseech.[7]

The Lollard movement aimed to break the clerical monopoly on interpreting the Latin Bible by translating it into English, thus empowering the common man—and sometimes the common woman. Chaucer's Wife of Bath may well have been a Lollard, the first to appear in a literary work. True, he never uses the word: an explicit endorsement of Lollardy would have been dangerously heretical. But she is suspiciously well versed in Scripture and puts her own raunchy spin on it, quoting it to rebut celibate priests and defend female sexual autonomy, including the objectification of men. Marginal comments by Renaissance readers suggest that this was one of the most popular of Chaucer's stories, that he was admiringly read as a proto-Protestant, and that one in five annotators were women.[8]

Ecclesiastical authorities tried to suppress the Lollards, but as Anne Hudson notes, "The number of surviving Lollard books, amazingly high in view of the persistent persecution, points to the[ir] ... failure."[9] And even those books may understate the appeal of the movement, given that Lollards (like the surviving readers in Ray Bradbury's

Fahrenheit 451) often memorized biblical texts, thus becoming "walking books." This was necessary partly to evade prosecution for possessing vernacular bibles, and partly because many Lollards (women especially) were illiterate. In fifteenth-century Norwich Margery Baxter invited other women to her home, where her husband read aloud from a Lollard book and the women discussed it. Liberated reading was possible even for those who could not read.[10]

There was a clear correlation between literacy and heresy in the pre-Protestant movements that sprung up throughout Catholic Europe before Martin Luther. The Waldensians were a reformist sect that emerged in Lyons late in the twelfth century. A Catholic cleric in Passau was astonished and disturbed by their sheer literary energy:

> All of them, men and women, big and small, learn and teach incessantly, day and night. An artisan who works during the day learns and teaches at night. Such is their eagerness to learn that they scarcely have time to pray... If one of them makes excuses, saying he cannot learn, they say to him "Learn just one word each day and after a year you will know three hundred; in this way you will make progress"... The lukewarmness of our doctors should make them blush with shame for not spreading the truth of the catholic faith with the same zeal as the faithless Waldensians show in spreading their errors and unbelief![11]

Because the Bible was loaded with contradictions and ambiguities, it was literary dynamite, a constant incitement to independent reading, as historian Christopher Hill recognized:

> The Bible could mean different things to different people and different times, in different circumstances. It was a huge bran-tub from which anything might be drawn. There were few ideas in whose support a Biblical text cannot be found. Much could be read into and between the lines.

Of course, classical literature was also full of subversive ideas, but since only educated gentlemen could read it, it was not perceived as much of a threat to the established order. But anyone with basic literacy could and did read Scripture, and Catholics like Thomas More predicted (more or less correctly) that this would lead to spiritual anarchy. Having authorized publication of an English Bible, Henry

VIII was soon appalled to find it "disputed, rhymed, sung and jangled in every alehouse and tavern"—popular seminar rooms where no clergymen were watching. Others complained (again accurately) that Bible reading was inciting women to preach and servants to talk back to their masters. In the long run it led to the Puritan Revolution and John Milton's *Areopagitica*.[12]

Even before the English Bible authorized by Henry VIII was published (in 1539), he tried to restrict reading it. A royal proclamation of 1538 forbade scribbling notes in the margins. (Readers scribbled anyway, and ever since marginalia has been a popular method of talking back to authors.) Five years later Parliament banned Bible reading by laboring-class men and non-aristocratic women, but that too was difficult to enforce.[13]

The Puritans were delighted by all this reading and disputation. John Foxe's *The Acts and Monuments of the Christian Church*, popularly known as the *Book of Martyrs*, was the number three bestseller in Elizabethan England, after the Bible and the Book of Common Prayer. And Foxe relentlessly drove home the lesson that nothing would "debilitate and shake the high spire of ... Papacy so much as reading," that indeed God used "Printing, writing, and reading to convince darkness by light, error by truth, ignorance by learning."[14] But now (1583) that Protestantism was securely established in England, he admitted that he hesitated to write for such a critical audience:

> I perceived how learned this age of ours is in reading of books, neither could I tell what the secret judgements of readers would conceive, to see so weak a thing, to set upon such a weighty enterprise, not sufficiently furnished with such ornaments able to satisfy the perfection of so great a story, or sufficient to serve the utility of the studious: and the delight of the learned.[15]

Just as twentieth-century comics used balloons to convey speech, Foxe's *Book of Martyrs* used banderoles to communicate the dying words of Mary Tudor's victims—but in some cases the banderoles were left blank, effectively inviting the reader to take charge and insert his own words. Foxe himself explicitly endorsed this kind of interpretive freedom ("Whereof let every reader use his own judgment..."), and the marginalia written into innumerable copies of the book (often by women) suggest they took him up on his offer.[16]

Cecile Jagodzinski argues that the proliferation of books after William Caxton introduced printing to England (1476), combined with the need to conceal heretical religious views, encouraged the growth of private reading, which in turn "bred a new sense of personal autonomy, a new consciousness of the self." By the seventeenth century male readers could think more independently about politics, and male and female readers alike could think more freely about religion. Thus, "the concept of privacy as a personal right, as the very core of individuality, is connected in a complex fashion with the history of reading." We tend to associate Catholicism with hierarchy and orthodoxy, and Protestantism with subversive reading, but in Elizabethan England their positions could be reversed. The Mass was banned in 1559, and by 1585 Catholic priests were virtually defined as traitors. As Catholic churches were shuttered and devout Catholics were forced underground, the latter could only continue to practice their faith through private reading. In a preface to his 1586 translation of Luis de Granada's *Memorial de la vida Christiana*, Richard Hopkins wrote: "Now this is the thing (good Christian reader) which I have so many years desired: to wit, to see some book that should treat particularly how to form a perfect Christian, and that might contain a brief sum of all such things as do appertain unto the profession of the heavenly life." Books became surrogate priests, and were in some ways an improvement on them, for they were "neither tedious for length, (because we may leave them of when we list,) neither do they leave us with a greedy appetite by reason of their briefness, for that it is in our own power to continue the reading of them so long as we mind to take profit thereby."[17]

The individual reader, Protestant or Catholic, was now in control. Kevin Sharpe concludes that writers in the age of Shakespeare might not have been entirely happy about such a demanding clientele, but they had to accept it as a condition of doing literary business. As Francis Bacon put it in *The Advancement of Learning*, "the true office of history [is] to represent the events themselves together with the counsels and to leave the observations and conclusions thereupon to the liberty and faculty of every man's judgement." John Hayward protested that "men will not be readers only but interpreters, but wrestlers, but corrupters and depravers of that which they read"— and note that he drew no distinction between interpretation and depravity. On the plus side, authors enjoyed the same hermeneutic freedom: as Montaigne wrote, "I have read in Livy a hundred things that another man has not read in him."[18] And the King James Bible strove to achieve theological consensus by offering (in marginal notes) alternative translations of ambiguous passages. Acknowledging that uncertainty might appear to undermine scriptural authority, but the translators assured readers that "it hath pleased God in his divine providence, here and there to scatter words and sentences of that difficulty and doubtfulness," so that they could figure it all out for themselves.

In Francis Beaumont and John Fletcher's zany comedy *The Knight of the Burning Pestle* the audience hijacks the play, creates the characters, and directs the plot. Tired of kings and princes, they want solid tradesmen like themselves. Why can't the hero be a grocer for a change? Everyone working in the literary marketplace had to come to terms with the new order of consumer sovereignty, giving the public what it wanted—or, in the words of another dramatist, "as you like it." And most troubling of all, readers had insufferantly individual and divergent tastes. "No book so ill but some will both read it and praise it; & none again so curious, but some will carp at it," sighed Robert Greene. "Well, so many heads, so many wits." "He that writes, had need to have the Art of a skillful Cook," complained Thomas Dekker, for "A thousand palates must be pleased with a thousand sauces: and one hundred lines must content five hundred dispositions." Robert Burton had the same difficulty getting a fix on the readers for his *Anatomy of Melancholy*: "So many men, so many minds." George Chapman felt that, "at least, in mine own writing, I might be reasonably & conscionably master of mine own meaning," but the author had lost control: "Let the writer mean what he list, his writing notwithstanding must be construed...to the intendment of the Reader." Giles Fletcher simply threw up his hands and let the reader of his poem *Licia* decide what the heroine was supposed to symbolize: "It may be she is Learning's image, or some heavenly wonder...it may be some College; it may be my conceit, and portend nothing: whatsoever it be, if thou like it, take it."[19] Or, if you prefer, write it yourself: court records tell us that a favorite popular recreation in Jacobean England involved composing and publicly posting salacious ballads about local bawds, cuckolds, bastards, and dirty vicars, often obscenely illustrated. (Four hundred years later, this would be called cyberbullying.)[20]

So far professional authors all assumed that their readers would be men, but that would change in or around 1630. There were no references to female readers in the first folios of Ben Jonson (1616) and William Shakespeare (1623), but the prefatory matter to the first of Beaumont and Fletcher (1647) presumed that it would be read in "Ladies Closets" and guaranteed, "Here's that makes *Women Pleas'd.*" In *The Coronation* (1635), James Shirley assured his audience of "noble Gentlewomen" that they were "first within my thoughts... As free, and high Commissioners of Wit." And in *The Court Beggar* (*c.*1639), centuries before women won the vote, Richard Brome asked the "Ladyes" to exercise their "suffrages [for] th' humble Poet. 'Tis in you to save / Him, from the rigorous censure of the rest."[21] Writers now realized that women were often on top, and in fact the contents of gentlewomen's libraries indicates that they did read plays, sometimes from a proto-feminist perspective. Unable to attend a revival of Jonson's *The Alchemist* in London, Ann Merricke sighed, "I must content my selfe here, with the studie of Shackspeare, and the historie of woemen, All my countrie librarie." Of the eighty-two First Folios held by the Folger Shakespeare Library, at least ten are inscribed by women, one of whom copied out Lady Chudleigh's verse:

> Wife an[d] seruant are the same
> And only differ in the name...
> Value you[r] selues and Men despise...[22]

The initial spark that set off the English Revolution was a book resisted by readers—in the first instance, by a woman of the lower classes. In 1637 Charles I tried to impose the Anglican Book of Common Prayer on the Presbyterian Scots, but when the Dean of Edinburgh attempted to use it in a service, Jenny Geddes (a streetseller) allegedly threw a stool at him. That act of literary criticism led in turn to a riot in the cathedral, two small wars with England, and (by 1642) an English civil war between Puritan Parliamentarians and Anglican Royalists. Of course, that conflict had many long-term causes, the most important of which was a century of free Bible reading and the theological turmoil that generated. The collapse of pre-publication censorship in 1641 unleashed a deluge of radical political and religious pamphlets, many penned by uneducated men, some even by women. Now, at least for a while, everyone was free to read competing polemics from all points on the ideological compass.

In 1649 King Charles was executed and (perhaps equally revolutionary) the first English translation of the Koran was published. Suddenly here was another holy scripture, which millions considered to be the word of God, but one that presented a very different version of events from the King James Bible. Readers then had to decide which text was more plausible, an existential question that profoundly troubled John Bunyan: "How can you tell but that the Turks have as good Scripture to prove their Mahomet the Saviour, as we have to prove our Jesus is?" That, and even more so the internal contradictions of the Christian scriptures, led radical Quakers and Ranters to reject the Bible altogether—and in some cases, to burn it. This was an extreme measure, but it could have been the inevitable conclusion of the independent reading that the English Bible inspired—and theological conservatives had always warned that reading would end in this.[23]

By 1700 the English monarchy had been re-established (twice), and Lord Shaftesbury proclaimed that reader sovereignty was as right and secure as parliamentary supremacy: "Of all the artificial relations formed between mankind, the most capricious and variable is that of author and reader." And it was clear to him that no "author should assume the upper hand, or pretend to withdraw himself from that necessary subjection to foreign judgment and criticism, which must determine the place of honor on the reader's side. 'Tis evident that an author's art and labour are for his reader's sake alone." For it was "no small absurdity to assert a work or treatise, written in human language, to be above human criticism or censure...There can be no scripture but what must of necessity be subject to the reader's narrow scrutiny and strict judgment." A worshipful veneration of any author was "mere enthusiasm"—and in 1700 "enthusiasm" was the dirtiest word in the vocabulary of an English gentleman, a chilling allusion to the Puritan fanaticism that had led to civil war and regicide. Shaftesbury affirmed that only the Bible should be read as an authoritative text: "But should the record, instead of being single, short, and uniform, appear to be multifarious, voluminous, and of the most difficult interpretation, it would be somewhat hard, if not wholly impracticable in

the magistrate to...prevent its being variously apprehended and
descanted on by the several differing geniuses and contrary judgments
of mankind." The Muslims are "barbarous" because they dogmatically
"leave their sacred writ the sole standard of literate performance," and
thus "they discourage and in effect extinguish all true learning, science,
and the politer arts, in company with the ancient authors and languages,
which they set aside." In contrast, Christianity (or at least the Church of
England) relied not on an uncritical reading of the Bible alone, but on
a broad and comparative reading of all the literature of antiquity: that
is, the kind of education a gentleman would acquire at university. Thus
"our common religion and Christianity, founded on letters and
Scripture"—and not just Scripture—will flourish "whilst readers are
really allowed the liberty to read—that is to say, to examine, construe,
and remark with understanding." Social stability would be ensured by
encouraging "criticism, examinations, judgments, literate labours, and
inquiries," by asserting "the reader's privilege above the author."[24]

And indeed, the British Enlightenment relied upon a voracious and
independent reading public. Even in small towns, the professional
classes created their own subscription libraries and book clubs, which
commonly stocked Adam Smith's *Wealth of Nations* and David Hume's
History of England. These societies encouraged freewheeling (but polite)
debate and discussion. The diary of Thomas Turner, a shopkeeper who
patronized a circulating library in Tunbridge Wells, reveals the activity
of an active judgmental mind: here he "prodigiously admire(s) the
beauties" of *Paradise Lost*, there he responds to Gilbert Burnet's *History
of the Reformation of the Church of England*, "which I esteem a very impartial
history, as the author has everywhere treated his subject with moderation
and coolness, which is in my opinion always a sign of learning and
virtue." As David Allan has shown, this revolution in reading may have
begun among male elites, but it spread to their wives and daughters
and down the social scale to the artisan and servant classes.[25]

Motivated by *noblesse oblige* and an instinct for sociability, gentlemen
in eighteenth-century rural Scotland commonly lent out books from
their private libraries—to other gentlemen, often to gentlewomen, to
doctors and other professionals, and sometimes to local artisans. So
even if book-ownership was limited and bookshops were only to be
found in major cities, the works of the Enlightenment were widely
diffused throughout Scottish society.[26]

The Statistical Account of Scotland (http://stataccscot.edina.ac.uk/
static/statacc/dist/home) may be the world's first broad sociological
survey, a compilation of parish profiles reported by Presbyterian
ministers around 1790, and it confirms that the reading revolution
envisioned by Lord Shaftesbury had spread to much of rural Scotland.
A generation earlier the people of Swinton and Simprin had been
"plain unpolished farmers, scarcely distinguishable from their hynds
[laborers], either in dress, information, or mode of living." But now
they had developed a "laudable literary curiosity and taste for belles
lettres," and even their farmhands aimed "to imitate them, giving
their children as much reading, writing, and figures, as they can
spare time for." In Carsefairn, the minister was impressed to find
modest home libraries containing "some of the best authors in the
English language." In Auchterderran, even "the vulgar" were reading
"Puritanic and abstruse divinity," as well as more secular topics, and
did not hesitate "to form opinions, by reading, as well as by frequent
conversation, on some very metaphysical points connected with
religion." In Wigtown:

> servility of mind, the natural consequence of poverty and
> oppression, has lost much of its hold here; and a spirit of inde-
> pendence, in the progress of opulence, has arisen, especially
> among the more substantial part of the people. An attention to
> publick affairs, a thing formerly unknown among the lower
> ranks, pretty generally prevails now. Not only the farmers, but
> many of the tradesmen, read the newspapers, and take an interest
> in the measures of government.

And the minister of Montquhitter in Aberdeenshire agreed that an
older, simpler, and more credulous oral culture had been abandoned
for the cynical sophistication of Lord Chesterfield's *Letters to His Son*
(published in 1774):

> Books, trade, manufacture, foreign and domestic news, now
> engross the conversation; and the topic of the day is always
> warmly, if not ingeniously discussed. From believing too much,
> many, particularly in the higher walks of life, have rushed to the
> opposite extreme of believing too little; so that, even in this
> remote corner, skepticism may justly boast of her votaries.

Today we worry that hypertext undermines the ability to read long sustained narratives, encouraging readers to hop, skip, and jump, but there is evidence of similar patterns in eighteenth-century England. Edward Gibbon fondly remembered that, when illness temporarily liberated him from the demands of schoolwork, "reading, free desultory reading, was the employment and comfort of my solitary hours." Jan Fergus has actually quantified desultory reading by studying the records of circulating libraries, and counting the number of multi-volume novels that were borrowed out of sequence or only in part: one-sixth of all loans and one-third of all borrowers followed this pattern. Samuel Richardson, author of *Clarissa* (seven volumes), elicited this kind of reading more than other authors, and Dr Johnson may have put his finger on the reason: "If you read Richardson for the story, your impatience would be so much fretted that you would hang yourself."[27]

We have a roster of the books Rugby School students borrowed from a circulating library between 1779 and 1784, and here we may glimpse the early precursors of the boys who perused *Playboy* by flash-light under the blankets. Normally a boy would charge his borrowings to an account that his parents paid. But if he didn't want them to know what he was reading he could pay cash—and that was the usual practice for Henry Fielding's *Tom Jones* and Ann Skinn's equally sexy novel *The Old Maid* (1771).[28]

Certainly by the 1760s, American women (Abigail Adams, for instance) were active readers of history, philosophy, travels, science, and Richardson's *Pamela*. In sparsely settled colonies where printed matter was scarce, they formed reading circles and shared books, and in the towns they took advantage of circulating libraries. Some conduct books tried to herd women into more restricted domestic roles. But Eliza Haywood's very popular *The Female Spectator*—the first periodical published by and for women—urged them to read widely and exercise their minds.[29]

The *English Woman's Journal* (founded 1858) was Britain's first true feminist paper, and here too the editors' first priority was to encourage the habit of questioning reading among their subscribers. Book reviews offered opinions, but habitually concluded that readers should judge the volume for themselves. And those readers were further advised to check the claims made by male-dominated periodicals (that is, every other paper published at the time). When *Blackwood's Magazine* claimed that the example of the Brontë sisters proved that it was relatively easy for women to find paid work, the *English Woman's Journal* told readers where they could find hard data on female employment, marital status, pauperism, and emigration.[30]

In eighteenth-century America, the proliferation of newspapers consistently outpaced the growth in population, until by 1775 there were thirty-eight papers in the colonies. After his 1753 appointment as deputy postmaster-general for North America, Benjamin Franklin vastly improved the postal service between the colonies, with free exchange of newspapers, creating an efficient continental media network that would swing into action when the Stamp Act was imposed in 1765. It taxed (among other things) newspapers, pamphlets, and advertisements—that is, reading—and it set off a firestorm that would not be quenched until independence had been achieved. In the *Boston Gazette*, John Adams thundered that America had been founded by Puritans who "were more intelligent and better read" than Anglican prelates, and were persecuted "for no other crime than their knowledge and their freedom of inquiry and examination." The Puritans' reputation as narrow-minded bigots he dismissed as a groundless stereotype: "To many of them the historians, orators, and philosophers of Greece and Rome were quite familiar; and some of them have left libraries that are still in being, consisting chiefly of volumes in which the wisdom of the most enlightened ages and nations is deposited." Liberty, they believed, could only be preserved through "knowledge diffused generally through the whole body of the people." And from the start they had invested heavily in literacy education: "A native of America who cannot read and write is...as rare as a comet or an earthquake." For:

> liberty cannot be preserved without a general knowledge among the people, who have a right...an indisputable, unalienable, indefeasible, divine right to that most dreaded and envied kind of knowledge, I mean, of the characters and conduct of their leaders...And the preservation of the means of knowledge among the lowest ranks, is of more importance to the public than all the property of all the rich men in the country...None of the means of information are more sacred, or have been cherished with more tenderness and care by the settlers of

America, than the press...[But] the jaws of power are always opened to devour, and her arm is always stretched out, if possible, to destroy the freedom of thinking, speaking, and writing...Let us dare to read, think, speak, and write...In a word, let every sluice of knowledge be opened and set a-flowing...But it seems very manifest from the Stamp Act itself, that a design is formed to strip us in a great measure of the means of knowledge, by loading the press, the colleges, and even an almanac and a newspaper, with restraints and duties.[31]

Once independence was won, the founders realized that they would have to create a free and informed reading public. European monarchists granted that democracy might work in small communities where everyone knew everyone else, such as ancient Athens or the Swiss cantons, but in the new United States, where the population was widely dispersed, voters would lack information about other parts of the country. The young republic proposed to solve that problem through low postal rates that subsidized the distribution of newspapers to readers, and free delivery of newspapers exchanged between editors. In 1791 Congressman Elbridge Gerry proclaimed that, "wherever information is freely circulated, there slavery cannot exist; or if it does, it will vanish as soon as information has been generally diffused." (Of course, there were slaves in the United States, but given that few of them could read, one might argue that they proved Gerry's point.) He concluded that "the House ought to adopt measures by which the information, contained in any one paper within the United States, might immediately spread from one extremity of the continent to the other; thus the whole body of the citizens will be enabled to see and guard against any evil that may threaten them."[32]

It sounds like a remarkable anticipation of the Internet, and indeed technological innovation can be a response to and fulfillment of long-cherished human desires. But there was a crucial difference: postal subsidies only benefited the owners of newspapers, who decided which information would (or would not) be shared. Most of the papers in Massachusetts supported the Federalist Party, and that imbalance convinced William Manning, a farmer and minuteman veteran who passionately backed Thomas Jefferson's Republicans, that the American experiment had gone terribly wrong. As he saw it, "the Many" (those who worked with their hands) were being exploited and betrayed by "the Few" (those who worked with their heads, or not at all). Merchants had secured a trade treaty allowing Britain to dump her cheap manufactured goods and put Americans out of work. Treasury Secretary Alexander Hamilton had rigged the new financial system to run up the national debt and benefit rich creditors at the expense of everyone else. Money was pouring into expensive colleges and private academies, while public schools were underfunded. President John Adams appeared to be provoking a war with France. You couldn't even trust the doctors, who were forcing midwives and Indian herbalists out of business, though their alternative medicine was both cheaper and more effective.

In 1797 Manning penned "The Key of Libberty," a polemic so radical that even Boston's sole Republican newspaper declined to publish it. "I am not a Man of Larning my selfe for I neaver had the advantage of six months schooling in my life," Manning introduced himself, "& I am no grate reader of antient history...But I always thought it My duty to search into & see for my selfe in all maters that consansed [concerned] me as a member of society...& I have bin a Constant Reader of Publick Newspapers." He argued that the exploiter class included not only merchants, physicians, lawyers, clergymen, and government officials, but also "all in the literary walkes of Life"—that is, those who produced the printed matter that the common man consumed. Let's remember that the most influential and classic work of journalism in the era was *The Federalist Papers*, serialized in New York newspapers a decade earlier. The Few, wrote Manning, "imploy no printers, but those that will adhear strictly to their viues [views] & interests, & use all the arts & retrick [rhetoric] hell can invent to blackguard the Republican printers & all they print, & strive to make the people believe falsehood for trut[h]s & trut[h]s for falsehood." Manning concluded that, as the newspapers could not "be red with confidence as to their truth, and as newspaper knowledg is ruined by the few," the Many should create their own periodicals and freely exchange them.[33]

Thus "The Key of Libberty" may have been not only the first denunciation of what would later be called the "mainstream media"; it also seems to have originated the idea of an alternative press. Manning's radical populism and profound distrust of elites survives almost intact today in the website *Infowars*: both are based on the theory that the key to the class struggle lies not so much in ownership of the means of production but control of the conduits of information. A similar strategy was employed by the London Corresponding Society, founded in 1792 as Britain's first working-class political organization. It printed and circulated agitational tracts among its 3,500 members, until the government banned it in 1799.

The alternative press lay far in the future, but in the early American republic the Many were clearly creating their own literary culture. In *Reading Becomes a Necessity of Life: Material and Cultural Life in Rural New England, 1780–1835*, William Gilmore investigated a Vermont backwater which had fewer than thirty college men out of a population of almost 17,000, mainly small farmers and laborers. They supported ten lending libraries, two debating societies, a lyceum, and lecture series. Their home libraries commonly stocked the Bible and Noah Webster, but Gilmore also found Homer, Virgil, Cicero, Dr Johnson, Sir Walter Scott, John Bunyan, Benjamin Franklin, Oliver Goldsmith, Laurence Sterne, and John Locke.

What is striking about early American libraries is that most of them were established and run not by the government, philanthropists, or employers, but by their readers. The Davies Project at Princeton University[34] has compiled records of nearly 10,000 American libraries before 1876 (that is, before Andrew Carnegie). The geographical distribution was very uneven: the eleven states that joined the Confederacy had fewer libraries (808) than Massachusetts (1,141). Outside of Michigan and Indiana, which maintained exceptionally good networks of tax-supported free libraries, there were just 399 public libraries in the country, plus another six supported by wealthy individuals. But if we add up all the independent athenaeums, lyceums, book clubs, and library societies, the total comes to 2,942. That doesn't count 127 specifically for women, 132 for young men, and thirty-six juvenile libraries run by parents. The YMCA had 190 libraries, and fraternal organizations another 123. There were fifty-six libraries for millworkers, railroad employees, and apprentices, usually created by their employers, but also 235 more independent mechanics' and workingmen's libraries, and thirty-four mercantile libraries set up by clerks. Four scientific libraries were sponsored by the government, twenty-two by colleges, but another ninety-eight by self-governing scientific societies. Fifteen agricultural libraries were administered by state governments, seventeen by colleges, but 326 by the farmers themselves. There were eighteen foreign-language libraries for immigrants (mainly German) and thirty-nine for volunteer fire companies. And for nearly every college library (507 in all) there was a competing student society library (495 total) which offered the kind of contemporary literature that most college libraries did not stock. Two examples (which survive to the present day) were the Whig and Cliosophic societies at Princeton, where students hosted crackling debates about fiction, poetry, philosophy, and historical writing—infinitely livelier and more fun than their tedious classes in Greek and Latin.

After 1876 this spirit of voluntarism would be expanded further by the two foundational leaders in the American public-library movement. First, Andrew Carnegie would supply bricks, mortar, and even blueprints for library buildings, but local communities and librarians had to pay for and select the books on the shelves. No less critical was Melvil Dewey's decimal system of classification: the old system of having librarians guard and fetch books from closed stacks gave way to user-friendly open stacks where readers could find books on their own—a method pioneered by Carnegie himself. The first generation of public librarians diligently kept out improper books and tried to restrict the circulation of light fiction. But by the 1920s the winds of liberalism were sweeping through American society, and second-generation librarians were more inclined to give the public what they wanted.

If you have noted that so far a great many of these independent readers were female, Iris Parush may have an explanation. She has argued that Jewish women in nineteenth-century Eastern Europe enjoyed the "benefit of marginality." That is, "in certain historical situations the marginalized space that a society allocates to its disparaged or neglected social groups provides these groups with degrees of freedom and latitude that—paradoxically—grant them non-negligible advantages over the preferred elites." In this case, the rabbis expected men to master Hebrew, the Torah, and the Talmud and strongly discouraged the reading of secular books. But these strictures did not apply to women, who were free to devote themselves to modern languages and literature. In 1898 the Yiddish writer Sholem Aleichem observed that "Daughters of Israel, educated girls, have all read Shakespeare, Goethe and Schiller, Pushkin and Lermontov, Turgenev,

Tolstoy and the rest of the authors of Russia and authors of foreign lands." That broad exposure to literature, and the dreams and discontents it inspired, may help to explain why so many Jewish women in Czarist Russia were drawn to revolutionary movements.[35] One can see a parallel in Victorian Britain, where many upper-middle-class women could freely explore their fathers' libraries while their brothers had Greek and Latin thrashed into them in oppressive (and very expensive) public schools. Because they were barred from other professions but could read anything they wanted, Victorian women did wonderful things in the realm of authorship.

Scrapbooks allowed readers to take complete artistic control and create their own bricolage, combining text and image. In the United States they often took the form of highly idiosyncratic anthologies of poetry clipped from newspapers, back when every local newspaper published local poets.[36] As a hobby, scrapbooking really took off during the Civil War, when Northerners and Southerners alike assembled their own histories of the conflict, reflecting their respective biases. Confederates naturally liked to clip reports of happy slaves proclaiming their loyalty to their masters.[37]

They didn't realize that some former slaves were starting their own scrapbooks. In 1854 *Frederick Douglass's Paper* pointed to a *New York Tribune* article that mentioned black soldiers who had fought in the American Revolution: "Colored men! Save this extract. Cut it out and put it in your Scrap-book." At a time when histories and historians of African-Americans scarcely existed, Douglass was urging his readers to do it themselves. Here was a workable method for writing "unwritten histories," a phrase used by a number of black journalists. Because there were few black newspapers, most of the clippings inevitably came from white-owned papers, but even there you could find accounts of black achievements, if you looked hard enough. Of course there were also reports of attacks on black achievers. But either way, you could assemble an African-American archive with nothing more than scissors, paste, and basic reading literacy. You didn't have to be a fluent writer. It wasn't even necessary to buy a scrapbook. Joseph W. H. Cathcart was a janitor in a Philadelphia office building, where he could pick up cast-off government reports. Starting in 1856, he pasted African-Americana onto their pages—a total of more than 130 volumes. It was an ingenious use of very limited resources.[38]

After its publication in 1852, black newspapers were filled with responses to *Uncle Tom's Cabin*—and they were very mixed. At first black readers welcomed the novel as an ideological superweapon against slavery, but after some reflection they began to have doubts about Harriet Beecher Stowe. She appeared all too sympathetic to the idea of shipping former slaves back to Africa. And (anticipating James Baldwin's criticisms a century later) readers found Uncle Tom far too submissive and pious. Men like him were no threat to the slave system. "Uncle Tom must be killed," demanded a letter to the editor of the *Provincial Freeman*.[39]

If you think the letters column was a site where readers talked back to editors, wait till you see the letters that editors *didn't* publish. In his study of manuscript letters sent to the *Chicago Tribune* and *Chicago Herald* between 1912 and 1917, David Nord showed how radically individualistic reader response could be—except that in many cases it was very difficult to tell what the readers were responding to. The correspondents included publicity-seekers ("We are two young athletic women and we expect to walk from Chicago to New York in the very near future") and crackpots ("I am that messiah that the Jews are looking for") who wrote with no apparent reference to anything published in the papers. Others began by mentioning a specific article, but then veered off onto totally unconnected personal obsessions. Reactions to coverage of the First World War were more coherent, but equally oppositional: the *Chicago Tribune* was variously damned as pro-German or pro-Allied, depending on the reader. And some responses to discourses embedded in the newspaper were of a type not generally anticipated by poststructural theorists: "If the officers of my union would find me Guilty of useing any part of your scabby paper in my toilet, I would be subject to a $100 fine at the next meeting."[40]

That kind of obstreperous reading could blossom in what appeared to be inhospitable cultures. The Meiji Restoration (3 January 1868), which began the modernization of Japan, was not reported in any Japanese newspapers, simply because they did not yet exist. Togukawa Japan announced current events in broadsides (about 500 of them covered the 1854 intrusion of Matthew Perry's fleet), but except for a few Western-language papers aimed at foreigners and summaries of the foreign press, the first experiments in modern journalism were attempted shortly after the Restoration. And very early on, those papers made clear their intended audiences: "high and low" readers, "women and children," "even a farmer." In reality, outside the cities, illiteracy was common and political passivity the norm. "What could be done with this country of ours, where there were so many people as ignorant as this!" protested one pioneering editor. "People themselves invited oppression." Some found the Western idea of the newspaper difficult to grasp, like the merchant who, having already bought one copy, wondered "why should I take it every day?" And the new Meiji regime almost immediately imposed press controls. But the reading habit caught on quickly throughout the country: village groups clubbed together to buy and discuss newspapers, and in tearooms women read them aloud to customers. Beginning in 1874, the *jiyū minken undo* (People's Rights Movement) agitated for parliamentary government and freedom of expression, and the press was the motor behind the movement. As one editor argued, national independence could only be secure if the Japanese people "develop a free and independent temperament." In *On Liberty*, John Stuart Mill had argued that "barbarians" could not be entrusted with freedom, and Japanese journalists drew from that premise the corollary that their country could only preserve its autonomy with a liberated press and unshackled readers. As one paper reported, the agitation was fueled by reading-rooms where "newspapers and periodicals from all over the country [are] piled high as a mountain." Liberal editor Fukuzawa Yukichi was stunned to find common readers devouring newspapers "like birds let out of a cage one day a week," and that the new reading culture had created a new "understanding of freedom and rights that, in its turn, had generated a mysterious life force." He noticed that his own editorials went viral, inciting debate "through all the Tokyo newspapers, even unto the provincial press, until enthusiasts from the provinces began to come up to Tokyo to present petitions for the opening of the Diet...My whim has unexpectedly shaken the whole country." "Readers and reporters felt a common bond as they worked together toward a common destiny," concludes journalism historian Yamamoto Taketoshi; "it was one of the happiest periods in press history." And this politically aware reading public extended down the social pyramid, even to peasants and women. "I have perused massive quantities of historical documents," concludes Irokawa Daikichi, "but in no period of Japanese history have I encountered evidence of the same kind of enthusiasm for study and learning that existed in mountain farming villages in the 1880s."[41]

By 1900 Japan, like the Western countries, had a mass-circulation press, and one of its most effective circulation-boosting techniques was to solicit and publish postcards from readers expressing opinions about the issues of the day. They received thousands, largely from urban workers, thrilled by this very new opportunity to express themselves.[42] And Japanese journalists, like their American counterparts, were publishing stories about human interest, new technology, poverty, labor unrest, taxes, streetcar-fare hikes, corrupt politicians, exploitive capitalists, and ever-popular success stories. The difference between the two cases was that, in a generation, Japan had created a newspaper press from scratch, and those papers had transformed a deferential feudal society into one where the people were loudly demanding their democratic rights. "Never since the dawn of world history has the growth of the individual been so respected and material happiness so sought-after as in present-day Japan," one paper reported, and the breathless exaggeration was understandable, given that something like a revolution had taken place.[43]

In dealing with that unrest, the Japanese government sometimes resorted to censorship, but shrewdly concluded that cooptation would be more effective. Liberal papers could be bought off with subsidies: the contemptuous term for this kind of cooptation was *kanka seraru*, "officialization," just as the label *officiales* is today applied by Cuban dissidents to bloggers who feign independence but in fact don't stray far from the government line.[44] Starting in the late 1870s, officials set up clubby press rooms offering tea and press releases, from which more troublesome journalists could be excluded. Today it would be called "access journalism" or "embedded journalism," and certainly it gave favored reporters inside scoops, but Yamamoto Taketoshi more accurately called it *kyosei hodokoshimono*—"emasculation charity." The Shunshūkai (Spring and Autumn Club) was a schmoozing venue for the whole Japanese establishment—business leaders, government men, and journalists—where, according to one newspaperman, editorialists "stand at attention, like a group of soldiers...repeating tirelessly, Your Excellency, Your Excellency." Japan had been making remarkable progress toward democracy and modernity, but largely because journalists failed to establish true press freedom, and allowed themselves to be seduced by imperialism, emperor-worship, and elite patronage, Japan would swerve from that path and end in catastrophe.[45]

During the long war in East Asia and the Pacific (1937–45), the Japanese government imposed censorship and propaganda on all forms of literature. But there is also evidence that younger readers especially were able to (in the words of one editor) "read behind the lines" (*kotoba no urangwa o yonde morau*). Faced with the alternatives of properly patriotic literature and fun magazines, children advised each other to tell your parents to buy one and then buy the other for yourself. The science-fiction tales of Unno Jūza were especially popular for their futuristic military technology, and a 1939 story in which Earth repels a Martian invasion was no doubt read by the censors as a paean to Japanese military prowess. But the propaganda element didn't make much of an impression on his young fans: they loved the Buck Rogers gadgetry, which inspired some of them to become scientists, doctors, or *manga* sci-fi authors. One reader thought that Unno's message was that this was "no time for the inhabitants of Earth to fight each other. We must unite ourselves to oppose a [greater] enemy from space." Some of his earlier stories predicted air-raids on Tokyo, which the military did not approve of, especially when they proved to be devastatingly accurate. During the actual bombing raids, author Komatsu Sakyō remembered, he would guiltily indulge in *manga* and low comic papers: "I would think 'Oh my goodness, what a treacherous imperial subject (*hikokumin*) I am.'" Others took refuge in rural areas, and were delighted to discover in farmhouses caches of old books and magazines, where there was no war but plenty of delicious advertisements for consumer goods that were now unobtainable.[46]

After the Nazis took power in Germany, some writers convinced themselves that they could still enjoy (in the words of Hans Carossa) "complete inner independence." In Carossa's case this was a self-serving rationalization: publicly he collaborated with the regime and was rewarded with honors and favors. But Joachim Maass tried to continue working in Germany before he left for America in 1939, long enough to get a sense of how readers were trying to preserve their souls under a nightmare regime. As he explained to a skeptical Thomas Mann (who had chosen to emigrate in 1933):

> at least a certain strata of a nation react to such pressure on their conscience by becoming subtle and sensitive listeners; people are accustomed to speaking in symbols and understanding symbols as such. And this circuitous way of speaking and writing

against power is not cowardly and ignominious, but the only true option of the mind against power: that is attested not only by justice and reason, but also by great and eternally honorable names in intellectual history such as Tacitus.

Nazi censorship was absurdly arbitrary and inconsistent, banning Erich Kästner's innocuous children's book *Emil and the Detectives* while permitting most classic and modernist literature, much of which could be read subversively. For Carossa, Sophocles' *Antigone* was a critique of Nazism. Another writer, Hermann Stresau, found the same kind of relevance in the brutal politics of Shakespeare's histories. "Such conditions used to be considered the long-lost past, just because the political methods are different," he observed, but "only now do we realize the childishness of thinking that kind of thing no longer exists just because one is now more 'civilized'." And in Aldous Huxley's *Brave New World* he discovered how "nightmarishly close we have come to this ironic utopia." Though it offered veiled criticism of the regime, and even predicted (metaphorically) the death camps and the destruction of Germany, Ernst Jünger's *Auf den Marmorklippen* (*On the Marble Cliffs*) was published under the Nazis, and editor Annemarie Suhrkamp found it "an extraordinary process of detoxification, from a poison that is threatening to destroy many people." Later, when the RAF was bombing Berlin, she recalled a chillingly prophetic phrase from the book: "the profundity of decay becomes evident in towering flames."

Marcel Proust, William Faulkner, Thomas Wolfe, Joyce's *Ulysses*, Steinbeck's *The Grapes of Wrath*, Sinclair Lewis, Joseph Conrad, George Bernard Shaw, and D. H. Lawrence were all widely available in the Third Reich. And as the war went from bad to worse, readers increasingly took refuge in escapist fiction. One of the top bestselling novels was Heinrich Spoerl's *Die Feuerzangenbowle* (*The Punchbowl*), in which a successful writer, who had been home-schooled, tries to recover what he had missed by enrolling in a gymnasium. Set in the Weimar period, it's a light comedy of student pranks and amusingly pedantic professors, where wartime readers could return to a carefree Germany which (if it had ever really existed) was being destroyed by Hitler and Allied bombers. In the dark hours of September 1944, publisher Karl Heinrich Bischoff explained that, "When night falls again, and most people cannot go out to the movies, they simply need something that really distracts them and gives them strength, something that is always at hand."[47]

In the Russia of Khrushchev and Brezhnev, *Literaturnaya Gazeta* reported a "reading boom" (using the English term). In 1965 about 1 billion books in Russian were printed, and more than 1.5 billion copies of magazines in all Soviet languages—respectively a threefold and sixfold increase since 1940. In the public libraries the shelves of fiction were usually *na rukakh* ("loaned out"). This was largely a function of the huge expansion of middle schools after the Second World War. In grades 4 through 10 fully 630 hours of literary study was required (about twice as demanding as German schools), much of it devoted to a nationwide standard curriculum of Russian classics. But most of what Russian readers read was neither Turgenev nor Tolstoy nor propaganda nor dissident literature. Mainly it was middlebrow quality fiction, because the regime insisted that the New Soviet Man would only be interested in that kind of book, not anything elitist or edgy or pulpy. (Imagine American literature with James Michener but no Henry James, no Allan Ginsburg, and no Judith Kranz.) Even within those limits, a remarkable degree of freedom could be achieved by post-Stalin readers, such as the machine-tool factory foreman who proudly showed off his personal library to Klaus Mehnert, and said he relied on his workmates for literary tips. When Mehnert asked about book reviews, the foreman snorted, *"Ya sam sebe retsenzent"* (I am my own reviewer), a very typical attitude among Soviet readers. With 10 million members, the All Union Voluntary Society of Book Lovers was one of the largest public organizations in the USSR (and note the significant word "Voluntary" in a command economy). As with many other classes of consumer goods, there was vast black market in Dumas, Petrarch, Byron, and Yevtushenko. These authors were not banned, but the planned economy could not respond to market signals, and therefore never produced enough of their books to meet the demand. *Komsomolskaia Pravda* reported that doctors, artists, engineers, stage directors, and even a philosophy professor had become book bootleggers.[48]

The appeal of post-Stalin literature is often attributed to its apolitical nature, but in a totalitarian society avoiding politics is itself a political stance. Escaping from ideology and dealing with human themes, these stories opened up a liberated space that their readers profoundly appreciated. The plot of Yuri Nagibin's "Gray Hair Urgently Needed" seems pedestrian—an older man falls in love with a young woman but then returns to his wife—yet it hit a nerve, especially among female readers, for whom the denouement was a disgraceful cop-out. "How did you dare to allow the man to betray his love!" they wrote the author. "He is a coward, afraid to venture forward into a new life, a measly skunk!"[49] Note the similarity in plot to *Brief Encounter*, except that where Noel Coward reaffirmed bourgeois family values, Russian readers demanded a jailbreak. Yuri Trifonov, whose father was one of those high-ranking Party men executed in the Great Purges, said that he preferred to write about losers (*neudachniki*), because they have the capacity for self-knowledge (*samoraskrytiye*). But the aim of the author, he made clear, is not to re-engineer the human soul, and he often quoted the nineteenth-century socialist exile Alexander Herzen: "We writers are not the healers, we are the pain."[50]

In glaring contrast, late Soviet readers were also devouring the obscenely violent crime novels of James Hadley Chase, whom they considered an almost canonical Western author. Cultural apparatchiks allowed the translations, because they interpreted these *noir*-ish stories as brutally honest exposés of a sick capitalist society. But for the reading public they were a bracing relief from the wholesome tepidness of Soviet literature, and Chase's criminals were existential antiheroes who refused to respect the state monopoly on violence. Chase's popularity continued to grow after the fall of Communism because, as Russia lurched from one regime to another, he always seemed to be a voice of radical liberation. Amidst the chaotic freedom of the Yeltsin era, the same thrillers could be read as tales of individual survival in a lawless world. And still later, Chase's stories appeared to have anticipated Putin's mafia state: in both, the police were essentially gangsters in uniform.[51]

Meanwhile, back in the West, left critics were writing off middlebrow and popular literature as mind-deadening commodities produced by "culture industries," though in fact they could be quite liberating for their readers. The quintessential culture industry product was the comic strip, marketed to newspapers by big syndicates. Yet they might be powerfully influenced by reader feedback: after all, they were serials that could and did change direction according to audience response, something a book normally could not do. In 1934 Milton Caniff launched *Terry and the Pirates*, a strip about American adventurers in China. He soon attracted a steady torrent of fan letters (more than

100,000, nearly a third of them from women), which he took care to preserve and respond to. Initially the strip was populated by ludicrously babbling Chinese and knockout dames in need of rescue. Caniff admitted that he derived his knowledge of China (where he had never set foot) from travel books by Pearl S. Buck and Noel Coward. But many of his readers knew the Far East at first hand, they wrote detailed letters pointing out gross factual errors—and Caniff readily incorporated their suggestions. Gradually the stereotypes faded away and the strip became starkly authentic. Newspaper readers soon found that *Terry and the Pirates* portrayed the horrors of the Sino-Japanese War more fully and accurately than the news columns. They also intervened to save one of the most deliciously campy characters ever created: the Dragon Lady, a slinky Eurasian buccaneer queen. When Caniff killed her off, hundreds of vehement protest letters forced him to resurrect her. As one Harvard fan wrote, "I'll bet I've been involved in about three hundred discussions about what...the 'dragon Lady' will do next...If you ever run out of ideas, write us—we are lousy with them." Later, the Second World War, the Cold War, and newspaper syndicates forced cartoonists to be more patriotic and blander, but before then Caniff knew who was in charge. "I didn't sell comic-strip realism to my readers," he admitted. "My readers sold realism to me."[52]

In 1955 *Puck*, a humor weekly, commissioned a remarkably sophisticated and nuanced study of reader response, surveying 700 Chicago residents for their reactions to the Sunday comics. It was a moment when intellectuals were most anxious about mass culture, and the comics seemed to be the ultimate "standardized form of entertainment and advertising. Large sections of their audience receive similar or identical Comic strips and Comic sections every weekend." The investigators therefore began with the assumption that the funny papers were "a stereotyped experience for the reader, the same for one and all...determined by the creators and publishers of the Comic sections. The Comic reader would, presumably, read the strips as the creators wish, and feel as they wish him to feel." But this, they found, was:

> far from the truth for our respondents...For the consumer and reader, the Comic experience tends to be personal, private, and

even secret, not visible to others, and only partly visible to the reader. The Comics are like an iceberg, with the important and significant part of their meaning tending to be below the surface and concealed from the public view.

Most of the people we studied appeared to be active readers of the Comics. They sought out the kinds of strips and the kinds of activity within the strips which interested them and gave them satisfaction. They selected and chose, manipulated and interpreted, in order to obtain the experience they desired from the Comics. Physically passive while reading, they tended to participate emotionally.

Well before Susan Sontag published "Against Interpretation," these readers experienced the comics intensely and immediately, and did not closely analyze or understand their own responses. Drawing on a series of interviews, the investigators found that: "The total experience people have with the Comics, the satisfactions they receive, is conscious as well as unconscious."[53]

Though few comics were "photographically realistic," in the minds of readers they authentically portrayed human motives and psychology, even when the characters belonged to some other species. *Donald Duck* was read as a kind of magic realism, inasmuch as his domestic dramas resembled what his readers experienced every day: "You see that at work; in everyday life, you see guys like that. There's no difference between the strip and everyday life. Actually, that's where cartoons come from; you can't dream them up."[54] Comics were read for humor, for cliffhanging thrills (*Brenda Starr* specialized in that), for artistry (many admired the draftsmanship of *Prince Valiant*), for psychological insight (*Mary Worth*'s relationship advice), for dramatizing the mundane (*Dennis the Menace*), for historical nostalgia, and for vicarious adventure (*Steve Canyon*). Comics could reaffirm faith in law and order (*Dick Tracy*); alternatively they could undermine military authority (*Beetle Bailey*), bosses as a class (Dagwood in *Blondie*), or gender roles (Little Iodine was admired as "a typical tomboy"). They might provide education in nature studies (*Mark Trail*), medical issues (*Rex Morgan MD*), and medieval history (*Prince Valiant* again). For immigrants, comics were excellent ESL textbooks. Men who were not comfortable in female company found refuge in *Hopalong Cassidy* and *Superman*. Before women's liberation, female readers admired Brenda Starr as the career gal who had it all: "She looks like an established girl, the ideal working girl: a good job, beautiful, men, and lots of clothes!" Sometimes they crossed gender boundaries and identified with superlatively masculine characters: "I liked [Tarzan] because...he was big, strong, handsome," reported Julie, a 21-year-old woman. "It was different and exciting. All these things used to take me outside myself. I would always put myself in each character's position. I did live it vicariously"—this at a time when most comic strip protagonists were male. And for all the enthusiastic readers of comics, there were on the other hand skeptics who objected that the superheroes were unbelievable, the women were too sexy, the talking animals were too silly, the characters were predictable, and that (contra Dick Tracy), as a matter of fact, crime often paid quite handsomely.[55]

For many, comics were relief from oppressive realities. Bertha had been raised in Zion, a planned utopian community north of Chicago, and like most utopias, it was a miserable place to be a child. The theatre, circuses, dancing, oysters, and tan shoes were all banned, and she recalled, "a neighbor got fired from his job for reading the Comics." She found liberation in marriage, but she was too old have children, so she found surrogate children in the funny papers. She was especially drawn to Dennis the Menace and Bratinella, because they broke all the rules and still enjoyed unconditional parental love.[56]

Walker, a churchgoing black father, accepted as a fact of life that he had to work harder for less, but allowed himself one pure indulgence: early Sunday mornings, before his kids awakened, he "greedily" devoured the comics in all the papers. He had grown up in the South, where food, love, and reading matter had been in very short supply. There were practically no black characters in the comics in 1955, but the investigators don't tell us whether he minded or even noticed that. They do report that "The Comics give him release from his life of labor and sober responsibility; symbolically, they give him nourishment and love," like a parent who "tells him all manner of interesting and exciting stories." You can call that escapism if you like, but Walker thought he was fully entitled to a moment's escape.[57]

A Frankfurt School critic might conclude that Dick Tracy and the Phantom offered compensatory fantasies to blue-collar workers trapped in dead-end jobs and sexually repressed marriages.[58] A feminist critic might theorize that, for the typical frustrated 1955 housewife, Brenda Starr allowed her "imaginatively to live the exciting career denied to her by marriage and children;" that Blondie's conflicts with Dagwood reconciled her to tensions with her own husband; that she imagined Mary Worth "as the mother she should have had...stepping in today...and straightening out [her] difficulties with her children and with her husband."[59] And a postmodern critic might argue that Li'l Abner deconstructs positivistic Western scientific rationality: "In Dogpatch, it is not necessary (or sensible) to be rational, planful, and cautious."[60] And in fact, among the 700 readers interviewed by this project, you could find a few who fit each of these models exactly. So all of these critics are right on target, at least as often as a broken clock. But they always tell the same time, and they don't appreciate the infinite variety of readers and reading experiences.

What distinguished Students for a Democratic Society as a radical left movement was its conviction that the revolution could be brought about through independent reading. From its launch in 1962, SDS produced a blizzard of agitational leaflets and pamphlets using cheap, do-it-yourself reproduction technologies. Their manifesto *The Port Huron Statement*, collectively authored, edited, and mimeographed by the founding members, sold more than 100,000 copies in a few years. When SDSers talked about "participatory democracy," they meant that Americans should no longer passively consume *Life*, *Look*, or the *Saturday Evening Post*, or uncritically read *Time*, *Newsweek*, or *US News and World Report*, or lazily watch the news on CBS, NBC, or ABC, all of which presented the same bland consensus. Rather, by creating their own "young people's media, we take over the media in order to take over the government." Breaking with a central Marxist dogma, they proclaimed that "the key to understanding the oppressive class structures now developing in American society is found less in the maldistribution of the nation's property than in the maldistribution of its knowledge." SDS activists never seized control of any factories or mines, but in 1968, when they occupied the office of Columbia University President Grayson Kirk, they commandeered his Xerox machine. However, "the people" SDS aimed to liberate did not really participate in what was supposed to be a media democracy. In one pamphlet, calling for "an extensive supply of literature on economic and social issues, suitable for working class readers," the naivete and condescension are now apparent. As Kristin Mathews notes, "The rhetoric in and dissemination of this print matter created two categories of print and community: one for the educated organizer and one for the 'ignorant' organized."[61]

Meanwhile, at the other end of the political spectrum, another challenge to the liberal consensus was adopting remarkably similar tactics, bypassing mainstream publishers and periodicals to reach readers directly. In 1964 John Stormer self-published *None Dare Call It Treason*, which charged that America had been betrayed by opinion-makers with Communist sympathies. It was produced and sold cheaply: 75 cents for a single copy, but as little as 20 cents when bought in bulk. Before the year was out (Barry Goldwater was running for President) 6 million copies had been distributed. Goldwater's own *Conscience of a Conservative*, first published by a dummy imprint set up by a political supporter, ultimately sold 3.5 million copies—and both books outsold *The Feminine Mystique*. As conservative editor M. Stanton Evans put it, the New Right amateur publisher works "outside the going circuits of communication" and "tilts his pen at the machinery of established discourse." As pamphleteers in the tradition of Tom Paine, "dissent is their vocation," and they were filling "the gap between what the Establishment thinks people ought to read and what they in fact want to read." (Note how closely his language resembled that used by SDS.) Conservatives had their own alternative presses, such as Henry Regnery and the Idaho-based Caxton Printers. At the grassroots level they developed a vast network of study groups and reading clubs: forty-four of them reportedly set up by one California doctor. As much as any radical commune, conservative publishers and readers disdained the profit motive in favor of disseminating literature widely and inexpensively, mainly through cheaply produced paperbacks and periodicals. "Newsletters were copied and spread around," one agitator remembered, "if you didn't have the money to order a newsletter from the Christian Anti-Communism Crusade or *Human Events*...people just shared all these things."

With their opposite numbers on the New Left, they shared a sincere democratic faith in the power of reading to enlighten the masses. In addition to disseminating right-wing polemics, they actually encouraged reading leftist literature, in order to "know your enemy." The Bookmailer, a mail-order distributor, stocked volumes defending the House Un-American Activities Committee, but also *The Cuban Story*, Herbert L. Matthews's sympathetic report on Fidel Castro, because it was confident that its readers would see through "his tortured logic which still justifies admiration for the ideals, talents and personality of Castro."[62] J. Edgar Hoover concluded his *Masters of Deceit* (sales more than 2 million copies) with an annotated bibliography of the works of Marx, Engels, Lenin, and Stalin. (Contrast that with recent calls to shut down ISIS websites, voiced by Hillary Clinton and Donald Trump, as well as legal experts Cass Sunstein and Richard Posner. Posner would make it a crime to merely *read* those sites.)[63]

The Internet has made readers more powerful than ever, whether they are bomb-throwers or bodice-rippers. Especially in genres where books are knocked out according to formula, the audience is now wholly in charge, instantly e-mailing their likes, dislikes, and instructions to writers. They can even compel the author to transition gender, whether he/she likes it or not. "Simone Scarlet" is a successful New Jersey writer of romance porn, delectably objectifying muscular male martial artists for a mainly female audience. Simone's public persona is all woman: the author page on Amazon is headed with a photo of what looks like a sexy female in kinky outfit—viewed from behind. But he is in fact a man, born and raised in an English cathedral town. "You definitely sell more books if the author's name is female," he confesses. (Things have changed since the Brontë sisters.)

> Romance writing is really formulaic. And there are rules. In one of my books, there was infidelity, and the readers told me, "Nope, no cheaters." An early cover showed a man with a beard, and readers said they were not going to read this one because beards were gross. So, OK, I removed the beard. I used to write in the third person, but readers want first-person, and they want to hear first-person from each of the main characters, in alternating chapters. So that's what I do.[64]

Postcolonial critics tend to treat the transmission of Western literature to the rest of the world as a form of cultural imperialism, but it's not quite that simple. True, newly independent nations usually remain (for an interval) dependent on literary imports from the former mother country. In 1848 Charles Dickens and Charlotte Brontë were as big as the Beatles in America, where six of the eight bestselling books were

British (*Jane Eyre*, *Wuthering Heights*, *Dombey and Son*, *Vanity Fair*, Macaulay's *History of England*, and Grace Aguilar's *Home Influence*) and just one was American (poetry by John Greenleaf Whittier). In fact, the nineteenth century saw the creation of a global literary emporium, where readers everywhere could promiscuously enjoy writers from everywhere else. Swedes read Washington Irving and James Fenimore Cooper. Brazilian women read Portuguese versions of German fashion magazines, which included local authors such as Machado de Assis and Artur Azevedo. French schoolchildren were assigned *Tom Sawyer*, and German radicals loved Walt Whitman, though in both cases some of their anarchic energy was lost in translation. Jewish immigrants in New York read Yiddish translations of *Don Quixote*, *Die risen Guliver's*, *Di kamelyandame* (*Dame aux camélias*), and *Di shklaveray* (*Uncle Tom's Cabin*). Cigar-workers in Cuba and Florida traditionally hired a *lector* to read to them while they worked, and some of their favorite selections were Victor Hugo, Rudyard Kipling, Schopenhauer, Peter Kropotkin, Karl Marx, and Alexandre Dumas (after which the Monte Cristo cigar was named).[65] The novel as a genre had been unknown in India until Indians discovered Thackeray and Jules Verne, and then they began writing their own, at first in native languages and then in English. Once Japan opened up to the world and created newspapers, they serialized fiction by Zola, Dickens, Boccaccio, Nathaniel Hawthorne, and Wilkie Collins. In 1863 Western literature accounted for a third of the inventory at the Bazunov bookstore in St Petersburg, and its influence on the Russian intelligentsia was enormous.[66]

Literatures—and readers—do not flourish in isolation. They both need cross-fertilization to achieve real intellectual and national independence. In colonial Ghana there were dozens of literary clubs devoted mainly to English literature, organized by clerks, teachers, and lower-level civil servants. "You were supposed to be civilised in those days if you talked literature," one member recalled. "In other words, your horizons extended beyond the confines of your country"—or in this case, the confines of a remote rural district where there was nothing to do after work. Shakespeare and Dickens were standard readings, but the clubs had their own idiosyncratic definitions of what constituted a classic. In one case it included Emma Severn's *Anne Hathaway*, *Wuthering Heights*, *Hiawatha*, *Treasure Island*, *The Prisoner of Zenda*, *The Pilgrim's Progress*, and *Animal Farm*. Members seriously discussed the moral issues raised, and applied them directly to their own situation in Ghana. "Was it relevant to you?" was the inevitable question asked. As Stephanie Newell concludes, these readers did not "simply set out unconditionally to assimilate the imported cultural models in a show of deference to the British master-culture." They were training themselves to become an intellectual class independent of both African chiefs and colonial officials, an essential step toward political and cultural self-rule.[67]

In England *Pilgrim's Progress* had always been an inspirational text, first for religious dissenters and later for working-class radicals, and its effects on African readers were no less subversive. It was translated into dozens of African languages, and many of the translators were black. Episodes like the imprisonment of Christian and Hopeful by Giant Despair could easily be read as allegories of imperialism, and how to resist it. And because missionaries distributed it throughout the continent, it became a foundational common text for African revolutionaries and early African authors.[68]

In the final third of the twentieth century, Western readers were beginning to pay attention to African writing. The problem, Pascale Casanova explains, is that, long after the end of formal colonialism, Westerners still own the means of book production. Publishers and critics in New York, London, and Paris decide which African authors are rewarded with publication, publicity, and prizes.[69] As Kole Omotoso pointed out in 1973:

> One side effect of a foreign audience is that this audience can take only a few "phenomenal" African writers at one time. There can only be one Achebe at a time and his way of writing also becomes the way African literature must be written. If another writer attempts to do something else, he upsets the foreign audience and there is an end. If our audience was home based, then we could have any number and variety of writers because, except there would be deliberate attempt to court trouble, the sky is wide enough for two birds to fly in peace!

But at the time, Africa mostly lacked domestic publishing and distribution networks. A few European firms (notably Heinemann) invested in lists of African fiction, but they were mainly aiming at the school-text market, their remoteness from African authors made communication difficult, and Europeans remained the ultimate gatekeepers. However, the digital revolution now at last enables the creation of a truly independent African reading community. Through Kindle, on-demand publishing, Facebook, and listservs, African authors can directly reach African audiences, and African readers can discuss among themselves African literature without going through European intermediaries. It may be that the most practical means of publishing African books is through mobile telephones, a method that has already enjoyed some success in South Africa.[70]

After 1945, there was a sharp reaction against the wartime regime of censorship in Japan. In 1954 the Japan Library Association issued a "Statement on Intellectual Freedom in Libraries," which affirmed the unbridled right to collect and loan any materials, guaranteed the privacy of users, and opposed "any type of censorship categorically." That in turn directly inspired a pop-culture phenomenon, *Library War* (*Toshokan Sensō*), which began in 2006 as a series of bestselling novels by Hiro Arikawa, and then was successively remade into *manga*, an *anime* television series, and both *anime* and live-action films. They are all set in a near-future Japan, where the central government has imposed a Media Betterment Act, allowing their agents to confiscate any books they judge harmful or subversive. But the librarians fight back—literally. They organize a Library Defense Force which engages government troops in surreal gunfights in the stacks. And it's all dead serious: the commander of the library militia solemnly quotes Heine: "Where they burn books they will burn people." His librarians are action heroes, and they seem to be more formidable soldiers than Japan's actual Self-Defense Forces. So you could say there is a kind of militarism in *Library War*, but this time it is directed against censorship, and the "Statement on Intellectual Freedom in Libraries" (rather than the Emperor) becomes an object of worship—a complete reversal of what prevailed during the Second World War.

It's different in Russia. After an interval of intellectual freedom and economic turmoil under Boris Yeltsin (very much like Weimar Germany), we have seen a retreat to autocracy, xenophobia, political thuggery, and Stalin nostalgia. But in reaction to that, there is also emerging a twenty-first century reincarnation of the old Russian intelligentsia, who in some ways resemble Western twentysomething hipsters, only far more hungry for literature. Book fairs and lectures on Elizabethan theater attract huge crowds. Russia has its own crime writers in the mold of James Hadley Chase, but now they are being outsold by popular science books. The old phrase "internal exile" is coming back into fashion, as readers once again try to carve out a personal space for free minds. "We can't win" against Putin, says Yulia Shakhnovskaya, head of the Moscow Polytechnic Museum, "but that does not mean we should stop resisting, so we try to grow a garden in the middle of hell." A favorite author of the new literati is Sergei Dovlatov, a Soviet dissident they are too young to remember. As the dissident poet and exile Joseph Brodsky explained it, Dovlatov "belonged to that generation which took the idea of individualism and the principle of autonomy of human existence more seriously than anyone, anywhere."[71]

Starting in 1966, the Great Cultural Revolution destroyed the Chinese public library system, but underground groups devoted to reading proscribed books proliferated. (They managed to get hold of limited editions of this literature, which normally only high officials were allowed to read.) Often they studied Marx, Engels, Lenin, and Trotsky, which shocked them into realizing how far Mao had strayed from original Marxist ideals. Their favorites included Hayek's *The Road to Serfdom*, Solzhenitsyn's *One Day in the Life of Ivan Denisovich*, Sartre's *Nausea*, Camus's *The Stranger*, Osborne's *Look Back in Anger*, Salinger's *The Catcher in the Rye*, Beckett's *Waiting for Godot*, and William L. Shirer's *The Rise and Fall of the Third Reich*. The parallels in the last of these were all too obvious.[72]

Chinese Internet dissidents today naturally read critics of state power: Friedrich Hayek, Karl Popper, Nelson Mandela, Václav Havel, George Orwell. (Several versions of *Animal Farm* and *Nineteen Eighty-Four* have long been freely available in the PRC—including, amazingly, translations into Tibetan. Evidently the censors were mollified by the assurance that Orwell was only writing about Russia and Britain.)[73] But one can also read more orthodox texts in ways that officialdom may not have anticipated. *The President is Unreliable* is a guide to the American political system by a Chinese couple writing under the name Lin Da, who try to explain how the executive, legislative, and judicial branches often disagree with each other. "The same 'government' is almost simultaneously delivering different information." They grant that this can be "very confusing" to more conservative

Chinese readers, who are used to a leadership that speaks with one voice, and they may conclude that the American system is hopelessly chaotic and not a model to follow. But for the dissidents it is liberating to discover that the US Constitution is capable of multiple readings, and that Washington has no reliable narrator. They also like to quote Hu Feng's poem "Time Has Begun," which celebrated the founding of the People's Republic of China—but which could also be a call for yet another revolution. "Every book is not revolutionary," concludes one blogger, "but if you keep reading it in a certain way, it will become revolutionary."[74]

Notes

1. Amos Oz and Fania Oz-Salzberger, *Jews and Words* (New Haven and London: Yale University Press, 2012), 21, 204. Babylonian Talmud, Sukkah 28a.

2. *The Love of Books: The Philobiblon of Richard de Bury*, trans. E. C. Thomas (New York: Cooper Square, 1966), 12.

3. Laurel Amtower, *Engaging Words: The Culture of Reading in the Later Middle Ages* (New York: Palgrave, 2000), ch. 1.

4. A. V. C. Schmidt, *Piers Plowman: A New Translation* (Oxford: Oxford University Press, 1992), 129.

5. Amtower, *Engaging Words*, 1–2.

6. Janet Coleman, *Medieval Readers and Writers* 1350–1400 (New York: Columbia University Press, 1981), 14.

7. Geoffrey Chaucer, *Troilus and Cressida*, modernized by A. S. Kline (https://www.poetryintranslation.com), stanza 191.

8. Alison Wiggins, "What Did Renaissance Readers Write in Their Printed Copies of Chaucer?" *Library* 9 (Mar. 2008): 3–36.

9. Anne Hudson, "'Laicus litteratus': The Paradox of Lollardy," in *Heresy and Literacy, 1000–1500*, ed. Peter Biller and Anne Hudson (Cambridge: Cambridge University Press, 1994), 233.

10. D. H. Green, *Women Readers in the Middle Ages* (Cambridge: Cambridge University Press, 2007), 166–78.

11. Alexander Patschovsky, "The Literacy of Waldensianism from Valdes to *c.* 1400," in *Heresy and Literacy, 1000–1500*, ed. Peter Biller and Anne Hudson (Cambridge: Cambridge University Press, 1994), 131.

12. Christopher Hill, *The English Bible and the Seventeenth-Century Revolution* (London: Penguin Press, 1993), 5–6, 15–16, 40.

13. Kevin Sharpe, *Reading Revolutions: The Politics of Reading in Early Modern England* (New Haven and London: Yale University Press, 2000), 329.

14. The Acts and Monuments Online (https://www.johnfoxe.org/), 1583 edn., 731–2.

15. Ibid., 15.

16. John N. King, *Foxe's Book of Martyrs and Early Modern Print Culture* (Cambridge: Cambridge University Press, 2006), 200–3, 243, 320.

17. Cecile M. Jagodzinski, *Privacy and Print: Reading and Writing in Seventeenth-Century England* (Charlottesville and London: University Press of Virginia, 1999), 26–36.

18. Quoted in Sharpe, *Reading Revolutions*, 40–3.

19. All quoted in John Kerrigan, "The Editor as Reader: Constructing Renaissance Texts," in *The Practice and Representation of Reading in England*, ed. James Raven, Helen Small, and Naomi Tadmore (Cambridge: Cambridge University Press, 1996), 125–37.

20. Adam Fox, "Popular Verses and Their Readership in the Early Seventeenth Century," in *The Practice and Representation of Reading in England*, ed. James Raven, Helen Small, and Naomi Tadmore (Cambridge: Cambridge University Press, 1996), 113–15.

21. Sasha Roberts, "Engendering the Female Reader: Women's Recreational Reading of Shakespeare in Early Modern England," in *Reading Women: Literacy, Authorship, and Culture in the Atlantic World, 1500–1800*, ed. Heidi Brayman Hackel and Catherine E. Kelly (Philadelphia: University of Pennsylvania Press, 2008), 46–51.

22. David Scott Kastan, "Performances and Playbooks: The Closing of the Theatres and the Politics of Drama," in *Reading, Society and Politics in Early Modern England*, ed. Kevin Sharpe and Steven N. Zwicker (Cambridge: Cambridge University Press, 2003), 179–80.

23. Hill, *English Bible*, 230–48.

24. Anthony Ashley Cooper, Earl of Shaftesbury, *Characteristics of Men, Manners, Opinions, Times, etc.* (London: Grant Richards, 1900), 2:296–307.

25. David Allan, *A Nation of Readers: The Lending Library in Georgian England* (London: British Library, 2008), 50–1, 108, 217–26.

26. Mark Towsey, '"The Talent Hid in a Napkin': Castle Libraries in Eighteenth-Century Scotland," in *The History of Reading*, Volume 2: *Evidence from the British Isles, c. 1750–1950*, ed. Kate Halsey and W. R. Owens (Basingstoke: Palgrave Macmillan, 2011), 15–31.

27. John Fergus, *Provincial Readers in Eighteenth-Century England* (Oxford: Oxford University Press), 108–17.

28. Ibid., 183–8.

29. Kevin J. Hayes, *A Colonial Woman's Bookshelf* (Knoxville, Tenn.: University of Tennessee Press, 1996).

30. Beth Palmer, "Reading Langham Place Periodicals at Number 19," in *Reading and the Victorians*, ed. Matthew Bradley and Juliet John (Farnham: Ashgate, 2015), 48–52.

31. John Adams, "A Dissertation on the Canon and Feudal Law," in *The Works of John Adams* (Boston: Charles C. Little & James Brown, 1851), 3:448–64.

32. Michael Warner, *The Letters of the Republic: Publication and the Public Sphere in Eighteenth-Century America* (Cambridge, Mass.: Harvard University Press, 1995), 127–32.

33. William Manning, *The Key of Libberty* (Billerica, Mass.: Manning Association, 1922), 3, 6, 37, 61–3.

34. <https://daviesproject.princeton.edu/databases/index.html>.

35. Iris Parush, *Reading Jewish Women: Marginality and Modernization in Nineteenth-Century Eastern European Jewish Society*, trans. Saadya Sternberg (Waltham: Brandeis University Press, 2004), esp. xiii, 3–7, 14–18, 91, 154–71, 186–9, 202.

36. Mike Chasar, *Everyday Reading: Poetry and Popular Culture in Modern America* (New York: Columbia University Press, 2012).

37. Ellen Gruber Garvey, *Writing with Scissors: American Scrapbooks from the Civil War to the Harlem Renaissance* (Oxford: Oxford University Press, 2013), ch. 3.

38. Ibid., ch. 4.

39. Marva Banks, "*Uncle Tom's Cabin* and Antebellum Black Response," in *Readers in History: Nineteenth-Century American Literature*, ed. James L. Machor (Baltimore and London: Johns Hopkins University Press, 1993), 209–27.

40. David Paul Nord, *Communities of Journalism: A History of American Newspapers and Their Readers* (Urbana and Chicago: University of Illinois Press, 2001), ch. 11.

41. Irokawa Daikichi, *The Culture of the Meiji Period* (Princeton: Princeton University Press, 1985), 107. James L. Huffman, *Creating a Public: People and Press in Meiji Japan* (Honolulu: University of Hawaii Press, 1997), 21–3, 37–50, 59–60, 73–4, 79, 84–5, 100–4, 120–1, 135.

42. Huffman, *Creating a Public*, 233–4.

43. Ibid., 330–6.

44. Ibid., 136–8.

45. Ibid., 347–58.

46. Sari Kawana, "Reading Beyond the Lines: Young Readers and Wartime Japanese Literature," *Book History* 13 (2010): 154–84.

47. Jan-Pieter Barbian, *The Politics of Literature in Nazi Germany: Books in the Media Dictatorship*, trans. Kate Sturge (New York: Bloomsbury, 2013), 357–67.

48. Klaus Mehnert, *The Russians and Their Favorite Books* (Stanford: Hoover Institution Press, 1983), 7–31.

49. Ibid., 68.

50. Ibid., 89.

51. Birgitte Beck Pristed, "Glasnost Noire: The Soviet and Post-Soviet Publication and Reception of James Hadley Chase," *Book History* 16 (2013): 329–63.

52. Jennifer Hayward, *Consuming Pleasures: Active Audiences and Serial Fictions from Dickens to Soap Opera* (Lexington, Ky.: University of Kentucky Press, 1997), 19, 95–131.

53. Advertising Research Foundation, *The Sunday Comics: A Socio-Psychological Study with Attendant Advertising Implications* (New York: Puck, 1955), 23–5.

54. Ibid., 28.

55. Ibid., 50–77, 87–93, 162.

56. Ibid., 168.

57. Ibid., 165.

58. Ibid., 140–4.

59. Ibid., 152–4, 166.

60. Ibid., 163.

61. Kristin Mathews, "The Medium, the Message, the Movement: Print Culture and New Left Politics," in *Pressing the Fight: Print, Propaganda, and the Cold War*, ed. Greg

Barnhisel and Catherine Turner (Amherst and Boston: University of Massachusetts Press, 2010), 31–49.

62. Laura Jane Gifford, "The Education of a Cold War Conservative: Anti-Communist Literature of the 1950s and 1960s," in *Pressing the Fight: Print, Propaganda, and the Cold War*, ed. Greg Barnhisel and Catherine Turner (Amherst and Boston: University of Massachusetts Press, 2010), 50–67.

63. Erik Eckholm, "ISIS Influence on Web Prompts Second Thoughts on First Amendment," *New York Times*, 27 Dec. 2015.

64. Kelly-Jane Cotter, "Sex on the Beach," *Morristown Daily Record* (10 July 2016): M5.

65. Gary R. Mormino and George E. Pozzetta, "'The Reader Lights the Candle': Cuban and Florida Cigar Worker's Oral Tradition," *Labor's Heritage* 5 (Spring 1993): 4–27.

66. For a survey of this literary internationalization, see Jonathan Rose, "The Global Common Reader," in *The Victorian World*, ed. Martin Hewitt (London and New York: Routledge, 2012), 555–68.

67. Stephanie Newell, *Literary Culture in Colonial Ghana: How to Play the Game of Life* (Bloomington, Ind.: Indiana University Press, 2002), ch. 1.

68. Isabel Hofmeyr, *The Portable Bunyan: A Transnational History of* The Pilgrim's Progress (Princeton: Princeton University Press, 2004).

69. Pascale Casanova, *The World Republic of Letters*, trans. Malcolm DeBevoise (Cambridge, Mass.: Harvard University Press, 2007).

70. Joyce B. Ashuntantang, "The Publishing and Digital Dissemination of Creative Writing in Cameroon," in *The Book in Africa: Critical Debates*, ed. Caroline Davis and David Johnson (Basingstoke: Palgrave Macmillan, 2015), 245–66.

71. "Special Report: Russia," *Economist* (22 Oct. 2016): 13–15.

72. Song Yongyi, "A Glance at the Underground Reading Movement during the Cultural Revolution," *Journal of Contemporary China* 16 (May 2007): 325–33.

73. Michael Rank, "Orwell in China: Big Brother in Every Bookshop," *Asia-Pacific Journal* 11 (June 2014): 2.

74. Emily Parker, *Now I Know Who My Comrades Are: Voices from the Internet Underground* (New York: Farrar, Straus & Giroux, 2014), 65–7.

2

Student Power

In 1916 Columbia University dropped its Latin requirement for admissions, effectively opening its doors to the striving sons of immigrants. Thus (in a word) it became the first Ivy League school to deal with the issue of diversity. In the same year, Professor John Erskine proposed what became the General Honors course, Columbia's celebrated core curriculum of Great Books. Much later that program would come under fire for not including enough female and non-Western authors—but measured against the standards of its time, it was strikingly democratic, inclusive, and anti-authoritarian. The students who were now entering, educated at public schools, lacked the common classical training of prep-school boys, so Erskine aimed to teach them a shared body of literature that was far more broad and accessible. It took the Classics Department a year to get through Herodotus in the original: General Honors covered him (in translation) in a week. And Erskine's definition of "Great Book" was clearly flexible: he envisioned that the reading list would be revised from year to year, and at first it was. The aim was not to follow a rigid canon, but to create the basis for a common conversation. And so it did: the early cohort of students included young men who would go on to shape intellectual discourse in mid-century America: Lionel Trilling, Jacques Barzun, Clifton Fadiman, Whittaker Chambers, Joseph Mankiewicz (future screenwriter and director), and Leon Keyserling (later Harry Truman's top economic advisor), with Mark Van Doren and Mortimer Adler serving as instructors. Early in his teaching career, Erksine explained his liberation pedagogy:

> A college course in literature should provide for two things—the direct contact of the student's mind with as many books as possible, and the filling in of any gaps in his sympathy with what he reads. Almost all the great books were intended for the

average man, and the author contemplated an immediate relation with his audience. There is room for the annotator or teacher only when time has made the subject remote or strange, or when the reader's imagination is unable to grasp the recorded experience...If the student's task is to read great books constantly, the teacher's part [is] to connect the reading with the pupil's experience...

And Erskine knew what his most adventurous students were reading: he had been an early contributor to the *Smart Set*. In its glory days, when it was edited by H. L. Mencken and George Jean Nathan (1914–24), the *Smart Set* published all the excitingly new writers: F. Scott Fitzgerald, Eugene O'Neill, Aldous Huxley, Sherwood Anderson, Theodore Dreiser, Sinclair Lewis, Dashiell Hammett, Dorothy Parker, Djuna Barnes, Anita Loos, two of James Joyce's *Dubliners* stories, as well as erotic fiction by Willa Cather and Edna St Vincent Millay. As such, the magazine appealed to snidely intelligent minds. Edmund Wilson described it as a "sort of central bureau to which the young looked for tips to guide them in the cultural confusion," and Anita Loos confirmed that Mencken was "a 'matinee idol' on every college campus." How could they not love him, when he confirmed what they all knew: that what the typical college "combats most ardently is not ignorance, but free inquiry; it is devoted to forcing the whole youth of the land into one rigid mold." (A later cohort of students would call this "conformity," and still later "political correctness," and in each generation it represented a healthy adolescent skepticism.) Mencken and Nathan finally went too far—they were fired for a lampoon of the recently deceased President Warren G. Harding—but amongst the coming generation they won immortality as martyrs for the cause of debunking hooey. Racy, iconoclastic, militantly anti-Puritan, and adventurously literary, the *Smart Set* was in some ways an anticipation of *Playboy*, only coed. In fact, Mencken and Nathan did once put on their cover (March 1922) a tarted-up flapper who may or may not have been naked. (*Playboy*'s cover girls were usually more wholesome.) And much like Hugh Hefner, Mencken respected the autonomy of the reader, who does not "want to be told precisely what to think about the subject being discussed." The function of the critic was not to arrive at settled conclusions but to communicate personal fascinations, for anything he "finds interesting is very apt to seem interesting to all persons of taste and education."[1]

Erskine expected his students to do heavy reading and write frequent response papers, but like Mencken, he respected and cultivated their individuality. "In a sense," he explained, "the students gave the course; I criticized their presentations." And because he recognized that literary criticism was an art rather than a science, he eventually replaced critical class essays with creative-writing assignments, asking students to respond to the assigned texts with their own poems, stories, and plays. "The creative habit of mind, no matter how modestly exercised, is the surest of all protections against pedantry": and he practiced what he preached, writing middle-brow fiction like *The Private Life of Helen of Troy* (the number-one bestseller of 1926). Occasionally he published something scholarly in the *PMLA*, but for the most part he left behind the academic ghetto and wrote for general audiences in *Reader's Digest* and the *Saturday Evening Post*.

Erskine's objective was not to train graduate student clones of himself who would copy his methods and parrot his ideology, but to encourage autonomous thinking among undergraduates. Each General Honors seminar was taught by a team, who would inevitably disagree: thus students would learn that there was no one correct reading, though they might be inspired by watching two minds at work in different directions.[2]

Meanwhile, across Broadway, a Barnard undergraduate was working out her own libertarian approach to academic literary criticism. Louise Rosenblatt was editor of the student newspaper, the *Barnard Bulletin* (succeeding her roommate, Margaret Mead), and she laid out her theories of reading in a series of editorials published in 1923 and 1924. "Authoritarianism no longer holds full sway in matters of intellect," she proclaimed, at the high tide of post-war modernism. "New attitudes in politics, in economics, in art, in education, are manifesting themselves. New values are seeping into the thought of the time." Barnard was hosting liberal speakers like Roger Baldwin, Bertrand Russell, and Franz Boas. Rosenblatt herself invited John Dewey to a luncheon seminar, where he said that true intellectual freedom required more than just an absence of censorship, it was a muscle that needed to be trained and exercised: " 'Self-expression' can come only as the result of intellect and effort."

Though Columbia and Barnard were opening their doors to students who were not WASPs (Rosenblatt was the daughter of Jewish immigrants), she saw that the whole purpose of this diversity could be defeated by balkanization, where ethnic or ideological sects holed up in their own enclaves and no real dialogue took place. There seemed to be, she editorialized, "a tacit agreement between members of different groups to refrain from any inquiry into one another's ideas... we have a large number of small group standards. Each group... engages in its own activities and is usually indifferent to—if not contemptuous of—the ideas and standards of the other groups." There was also increasing division along disciplinary lines: "Students come to college, acquire knowledge in various fields, and keep the types of information isolated in separate compartments of the mind, without ever correlating them, or realizing their interrelationships." That might not bother anyone who conceived of college as "a place where experts are trained for the punctiliously accurate administration of our complex industrial machinery," but Rosenblatt saw that such an education would never prepare students to question the system:

It is not enough that the college student be made an effective part of the machine, an eliminator of friction in the industrial world. He should be able to comprehend the machine in its entirety, to understand the significance of his relationship to other men, and above all, to enjoy and appreciate all that our culture may offer. The college of liberal arts should develop people who can live more fully, and with greater intensity of appreciation, than if they had not been members of a college for four years.

Rosenblatt, then, saw the beginnings of problems that weigh down higher education today: the "insulation of ideas" and overconfidence in "the omnipotence of 'systems'" (what would later be called "theory"). And in 1978, when the "new ethnicity" was becoming fashionable in literature departments, she worried "that membership in the group may impose its own kind of rigid conformity upon the individual."[3]

Rosenblatt secured a doctorate in comparative literature from the Sorbonne, returned to Barnard to teach, and then in 1938 published *Literature as Exploration*. As the title implied, reading for her was not a science that aimed to arrive at a "correct" interpretation of the text, but an open-ended process of individual growth. And the reader was at the center, more than the text or the instructor:

> The reader counts for at least as much as the book or poem itself; he responds to some of its aspects and not others; he finds it refreshing and stimulating, or barren and unrewarding. Literature is thus for him a medium of exploration. Through books, the reader may explore his own nature, become aware of potentialities for thought and feeling within himself, acquire clearer perspective, develop aims and a sense of direction. He may explore the outer world, other personalities, other ways of life. Liberated from the insularity of time and space, he may range through the wide gamut of social and temperamental alternatives that men have created or imagined.
>
> We need to find out what happens when specific human beings, with their interests and anxieties, participate in the emotional and intellectual life that books make possible. We need to know what human insight, what knowledge, what habits of mind, will enable our students to attain ever richer literary satisfactions, and to derive attain ever richer literary satisfactions, and to derive from them the equipment to embark on increasingly fruitful explorations of literature—and of life.[4]

Both today and in the 1930s, critics debated whether literature should be judged as a work of art (what some call "formalism") or as a statement about social justice (what others call "propaganda"). Rosenblatt was firmly opposed to making "literature merely a handmaiden of the social studies or a body of documents illustrating moral points or sociological generalizations. The Victorians demonstrated the sterility of seeking in literature only moral lessons" when they ranked Charlotte Yonge over George Eliot.[5] On the other hand, she told literature teachers that they could not ignore "the fact that we are dealing, in the liveliest terms, with subjects and problems usually thought of as the province of the sociologist, the psychologist, the philosopher or historian."[6] Art for art's sake was divorced from reality, but the literature of social significance was often dull agitprop. Because in fact most readers experienced literature as both an aesthetic and a political experience, because life itself is both aesthetic and political, these critical dimensions could not be divorced, and had to be studied together. Literature used art to illuminate social issues "with an immediacy and emotional persuasiveness unequalled by practically any other educational medium." What would the student reader find more memorable: "statistics about New England's shipping or Melville's *Moby Dick?*... the provisions of the Fourteenth Amendment or Mark Twain's Huck Finn and Nigger Jim?"[7]

The role of the teacher, then, was to encourage each student to explore the text from all possible angles, and to encourage a conversation among students about their differing responses, without favoring one critical approach over another. The instructor would also provide historical context and explain how the societies that produced *The Iliad, King Lear,* and *Uncle Vanya* were very different from our own. (Rosenblatt had absorbed much anthropology from Franz Boas and Margaret Mead.)

A later generation of critics would argue that reading experiences are conditioned by race, class, and gender, and Louise Rosenblatt took all three into account when she discussed Walter White's *Fire in the Flint,* Dreiser's *An American Tragedy,* and Ibsen's *A Doll's House.* You could hardly avoid these issues in 1938, when the newspapers were full of Joe Louis, Josef Stalin, and Eleanor Roosevelt. She granted that, "in spite of personal differences, human beings are a part of particular social systems and tend to fall into groups age, sex, profession, nation, race"—and she knew "how pervasive these forces of social conditioning are." So identity politics was already an issue in literature departments in 1938.

However, Rosenblatt also realized that hundreds of social forces (not just three) shaped our sense of identity. Religion, philosophy, psychology, family life, urban/rural upbringing, illness/disability, politics, artistic taste, and any number of other factors influence reader response, and the permutations were endless, to the point where no two students could be pigeonholed into exactly the same category. Yes, on average, some groups are less advantaged than others, but students aren't averages: the experiences of members of the same racial or ethnic group can vary enormously. And in a crucially important sense all students are unique: no two of them have read exactly the same books. Therefore, the teacher of literature cannot generalize about reader response. There is simply no alternative to treating students as individuals. And that had radical implications for pedagogy:

> There is no such thing as a generic reader or a generic literary work; there are in reality only the potential millions of individual readers of the potential millions of individual literary works. The novel or play or poem exists, after all, only in interactions with specific minds. The reading of any work of literature is, of necessity, an individual and unique occurrence involving the mind and emotions of some particular reader. We may generalize about similarities among such interactions, but we cannot evade the realization that there are actually only innumerable separate responses to individual works of art.

Of course, there were certain basic facts that the teacher could impart to the class: "facts about the conditions under which literary works were written; facts about the social, economic, intellectual history of the age in which they were written; facts about the way contemporary readers responded or did not respond to them; facts about the author and his life; facts about the literary traditions which he inherited; facts, even, concerning the actual form, structure, and method of the work." But once the discussion shifted from historical background to criticism, the teacher could no longer rely on lecture notes or theoretical formulas, and she would not "have a systematic, nearly packaged, unchanging body of information to impart." Rather, she "must be constantly aware of the living and unstereotyped nature of the reading experience, made up as it will be of many complex elements in a never-to-be-duplicated combination." She would have to speak to the personal reading experiences of each student, and moderate a conversation in which all students shared their responses. The aim of that conversation would not be to arrive at any consensus about the meaning or value of the work, which would be both pointless and impossible. Instead, each reader would learn something far more true and valuable: an understanding of the unique minds of other readers. And that would make a real intellectual community out of a diverse student body, at once breaking down barriers and training genuinely free thinkers, achieving the goal that Rosenblatt had set out in her undergraduate editorials.[8]

Rosenblatt never argued for an anything-goes theory of criticism, nor did she believe that every unexamined response to literature was equally valid. The student had to begin by evaluating the work on his own terms, but that was only the first step: then the teacher had to guide him to "a critical awareness of his own reactions," involving both "increased self-knowledge" and "a keener and more adequate perception of all that the work offers." Thus the student would learn to read critically both literature and himself.[9] Too often literature classes were "spectator sports," where "The students sit on the sidelines watching the instructor or professor react to works of art."[10] Like Erskine, she envisioned the teacher as a moderator and facilitator: the hard work of criticism had to be done by the students themselves.

Rosenblatt did believe that some reading was "misreading," for instance the young woman who thought Anna Karenina was too self-centered to see that her husband really did love her but couldn't articulate his feelings. "There are people like that, with very warm hearts and intense affections, who are unable to let others know it," the student explained. "Why, my own father is like that!" And yet one has to wonder: did this woman see something that Tolstoy didn't? Did Rosenblatt fail to pursue her theory of independent reader response far enough?[11]

"Just as the author is creative," she concluded, "so the reader also is creative." Even "the same book will have a very different meaning and value to us at different times in our lives or under different circumstances."[12] While authorial intention was certainly worth exploring, it did not necessarily override reader responses. "College freshmen have been known, very disconcertingly, to sympathize more than Shakespeare intended with Lear's unfilial daughters," and that wasn't a mistake, if it helped the students to work through their adolescent rebellion.[13] Rosenblatt was aware that:

> until quite recently... English literature was not a "subject" for organized study and teaching. Yet it was a vital and absorbing interest to many, perhaps because it was not a subject upon which had been elaborated a whole superstructure of traditional teaching practice. If the student turned to English literature, it was because he felt its personal value. He read with a free spirit, not because the academic powers decreed a knowledge of it necessary. We are not arguing a return to the old scholastic curriculum, of course; it possessed its own stultifying routines. Yet our aim should certainly be not to overlay with a dull film of

routine the living sense of literature which was at least possible
when there was no organized study of English literature.
Unfortunately, it sometimes seems that it would be much better
if students were turned loose in a library to work out for themselves some personal approach to literature.[14]

She was familiar with an experiment conducted at the Ohio State
University School in the 1930s, where seventh-through-ninth graders
were allowed to choose and discuss their own reading. Their selections
were remarkably sophisticated, and matured with time. The sev-
enth-grade favorites included Mark Twain, Jules Verne, Arthur Conan
Doyle, Robert Louis Stevenson, and Louisa May Alcott, and by the
ninth grade they had graduated to *The Merchant of Venice* and *David
Copperfield*. Overall, adult books accounted for about a third of fiction
read by boys and nearly half read by girls, and the proportions rose
sharply with age. When the same opportunities were given to tenth-
through-twelfth graders, some of their most popular choices were
Austen's *Pride and Prejudice*, Pearl S. Buck's *The Good Earth*, Samuel
Butler's *Erewhon*, Willa Cather's *Death Comes for the Archbishop*, Conrad's
Lord Jim, Dickens's *A Tale of Two Cities*, George Eliot's *Silas Marner*, Hans
Fallada's *Little Man, What Now?*, Oliver Goldsmith's *The Vicar of
Wakefield*, Knut Hamsun's *Hunger*, Hardy's *Far from the Madding Crowd*
and *Tess of the d'Urbervilles*, Victor Hugo's *Les Misérables*, Aldous
Huxley's *Brave New World*, Thackeray's *Vanity Fair*, Turgenev's *Fathers
and Sons*, Sigrid Undset's *Kristen Lavransdatter*, Voltaire's *Candide*, Edith
Wharton's *Ethan Frome*, Oscar Wilde's *The Picture of Dorian Gray*,
Chekhov's *The Cherry Orchard*, Goldsmith's *She Stoops to Conquer*, Ibsen's
A Doll's House, Eugene O'Neill's *Strange Interlude*, Pirandello's *Six
Characters in Search of an Author*, Shakespeare's *As You Like It* and *Hamlet*,
Sheridan's *School for Scandal*, J. M. Synge's *Riders to the Sea*, Gertrude
Stein's *The Autobiography of Alice B. Toklas*, the poems of Emily Dickinson
and François Villon, Housman's *A Shropshire Lad*, FitzGerald's *The
Rubaiyat of Omar Khayyám*, Virgil's *Aeneid*, and Whitman's *Leaves of
Grass*. And none of these students had yet set foot in college.[15]

   Literature as Exploration (which went through four editions, and has
never been out of print) was inspirational to any number of literature
teachers in high schools and colleges, but Rosenblatt won little recognition in the rarified world of academic criticism. She kept jargon to

a minimum, the philosophers she cited were American (William James, C. S. Peirce, John Dewey) rather than French, and she published mostly in journals devoted to pedagogy rather than theory. She did develop a theory of literature, but it amounted to saying: Don't theorize, focus on the student. Her methods might work brilliantly in the class-room, but they were not suited to the bureaucratic structures of research universities, where faculty—whether they taught chemistry, economics, sociology, or English—were expected to publish monographs that arrived at definitive conclusions. New Criticism, Marxism, Freudianism, Leavisism, deconstruction, feminism, New Historicism, postcolonialism, queer theory, critical race theory, ecocriticism, and so on all offered professors formulas for the industrial production of journal articles, but Rosenblatt devolved that power to students, and made criticism anarchic, artisanal, and amateur.[16]

Mortimer Adler was more radical still, especially as an angry young man. He seems to have spent much of his undergraduate career telling the Columbia philosophy faculty (John Dewey especially) that they were all wet. He became convinced that all the growing and hardening bureaucratic structures of the modern university—departments, spe-cialized research, committees, PhDs—would have to be dynamited to clear the way for real education.

In addition to teaching for General Honors, Adler served an apprenticeship (1926–8) with the People's Institute, an adult-educa-tion program for working-class New Yorkers of all ethnicities. He found these students highly receptive to Descartes and Shakespeare, sometimes "as good as my Columbia groups," and the experience convinced him that the great books could be an emancipating force for anyone, within or outside the university. By engaging with funda-mental questions that the best minds had grappled with over the centuries, readers could learn to decide for themselves what constituted the good life and a just society, and become thinking actors in a partici-patory democracy.[17]

In alliance with Robert Hutchins, its bright young president, Adler went to the University of Chicago and created a liberal stud-ies program based largely on the great books, in face of entrenched faculty opposition. One has to grant that sometimes Adler spoke of his colleagues as Stalin spoke of the kulaks: "Until the professors and their culture are liquidated, the resolution of modern problems will not begin," he thundered. "Democracy has more to fear from the mentality of its teachers than from the nihilism of Hitler." As he later laid out in his autobiography, *Philosopher at Large*, Adler's objective was far more revolutionary than anything today's "tenured radicals" would dare contemplate:

> ... (1) there should be no vocational training of any sort; (2) there should be no electives, no majors or minors, no specialization in subject matter; (3) there should be no division of the faculty into professors competent in one department of learning rather than another; (4) no member of the faculty should be unprepared to teach the course of study as a whole; (5) no textbooks or manuals should be assigned as reading material for the students; (6) not more than one lecture a week should be given to the student body; (7) there should be no written examination.[18]

What Adler wanted was a radically free encounter between readers and literature, and you could say he achieved that in *How to Read a Book*. It was the number-two non-fiction bestseller of 1940, and it would ultimately be translated into French, German, Italian, Spanish, Swedish, and Japanese. In June 1946, flush with post-war optimism, he addressed the American Library Association convention and called for "a universal adult education program involving 60,000,000 men and women." His Great Books Foundation, launched in 1947, set up pilot seminars in several American cities, attracting more than 50,000 students.[19]

For a sense of which books these groups studied, we can look to those set up in Washington, DC between 1945 and 1949. At a time when the city was still strictly segregated, 10 percent of the participants were black. "Matter of fact, this is the first time I ever sat at the same table with a Negro," confessed one white Southerner. And the groups did confront racial issues: several of them studied the 1947 *Report of the President's Committee on Civil Rights*. Given that Washington was a one-factory town, the groups tended to focus on politics, broadly speaking. The single most-studied volume was Plato's *Republic* (adopted by 48 groups), followed by the *Apology* and *Crito* (32 each), Aristotle's *Politics* (18) and *Ethics* (15), Thucydides's *Peloponnesian War* (23), Thomas Aquinas's *On the Law* (14), Machiavelli's *The Prince* (21), Hobbes's *Leviathan* (30), Locke's *Second Treatise on Civil Government* (15), Rousseau's *Social*

Contract (27), Smith's *Wealth of Nations* (15), the Declaration of Independence (40), *The Federalist Papers* (30), *The Communist Manifesto* (16), the works of Friedrich Engels (12), and Thorstein Veblen's *Theory of the Leisure Class* (15).

There was less interest in the drama (Aeschylus, Aristophanes, Euripides, Sophocles, Shakespeare, Ibsen, Shaw), still less in science or the novel. The reason was, quite simply, that the world was in a crucible. America was preparing for returning GIs, Europe had to be reconstructed, the New Deal might be either expanded or cut back, the Cold War and the Red Scare loomed, the United Nations and the atomic bomb had transformed world politics. How could you not ask fundamental questions about human society and how it might be reshaped? So Ruth Benedict's *Patterns of Culture* was studied in twenty groups, because it offered "a useful... theory of social organization" illustrated by a comparative study of cultures ("one of which sounds like a caricature of Veblen's *Leisure Class*"). The most discussed novelist (far ahead of Cervantes, Dostoevsky, and Flaubert) was James T. Farrell, who "dramatize(d) the impact of social forces upon individual experience."[20]

On 15 April 1952, at a much-publicized banquet at the Waldolf Astoria, Adler celebrated the publication of his encyclopedic fifty-four-volume *Great Books of the Western World*. For $249.50 it anthologized exactly 102 "great ideas," and to qualify for inclusion an author had to deal with at least twenty-five of them. In contrast to the reading lists of the Washington pilot groups, the series was inflexible and excluded twentieth-century authors, stopping at Sigmund Freud. It was a not a great success at first, selling a miserable 138 sets in all of 1953. Only aggressive door-to-door sales tactics saved the series, boosting sales above 40,000 sets by 1960. Reviewers were at best ambivalent, seeing the educational value of what Adler had done, but always demanding to know why he had included certain authors and not others. That kind of criticism is inevitable with such canonizing projects, and Adler had left himself vulnerable by conveying the impression that these fifty-four volumes were *The* Great Books of the Western World. In fact, as he privately admitted, canons do evolve over time, and the editorial choices for this series involved a lot of subjectivity and editorial dickering.[21] Adler, who once hurled Molotov cocktails at campus bureaucracies, had bureaucratized the classics. Marshall

McLuhan saw that all too clearly: "May we not ask how this approach to the content and conditions of human thought differs from any other merely verbal and mechanized education in our time?"[22]

Nevertheless, by 1957–8 there were almost 2,000 Great Books groups in the United States, averaging about a dozen members each. One study found that, compared with the American adult population, Great Books readers were much more likely to be college graduates (60 vs. 5 percent), PhDs (5 vs. 0.1 percent), and Jewish (15 vs. 3 percent). Of the men, 85 percent were professionals or managers, and just 5 percent were blue-collar. And compared with other middle-class Americans, Great Books readers were considerably less likely to have working-class fathers: that is, they did not represent the upwardly mobile.[23]

If the Great Books program had an ideological impact, it tended to move participants toward libertarianism, broadly defined. They became more sympathetic to free-thinking religious movements (mysticism, atheism, agnosticism, liberal Protestantism, Reform Judaism) and less sympathetic to more orthodox faiths (Thomism, mainstream and fundamentalist Protestantism, Orthodox Judaism, Christian Science). In the wake of the New Deal and McCarthyism, they became more concerned about both the growth of big government and the erosion of civil liberties.[24] One mother of five, not college-educated but restive in a strict Dutch Calvinist family, was exposed to Sophocles's *Antigone*, Tolstoy's *The Death of Ivan Ilyich*, Dostoevsky's *The Brothers Karamazov*, Nathanael West's *Miss Lonelyhearts*, and Milton's *Areopagitica*. Dostoevsky made her realize how scary moral freedom can be: "Each person has to go the way themselves. That's why no priest or rules or anything will do it for you." She first thought that Nathanael West had written "a vile book," but then Milton convinced her that, "Really, you learn something from everything you read, and this is enough reason to read indiscriminately, more or less, based on your own desires." All that subverted her religious faith to the point where her marriage was under strain and she suffered a nervous breakdown. Her husband blamed the Great Books, and of course he was right.[25]

In another study of similar groups in the Los Angeles area, nearly half of all participants, and more than half of those without a college degree, reported that the experience had inspired them to read more books, more challenging books, and a broader range of books.[26] When asked to check off their reasons for joining, the top answers all involved intellectual emancipation: "To learn what the greatest minds in history have to say about the basic issues of life" (64 percent), "Reacquainting myself with a cultural background which had become rusty" (44 percent), "Improving my ability to analyze and criticize arguments" (42 percent), "Escaping the intellectual narrowness of my occupation" (42 percent). As a motive, socializing was well down the list, and acquiring skills useful at work was virtually at the bottom. "Escaping the intellectual narrowness of being a housewife" was checked by 30 percent, a remarkable total given that 35 percent of the whole sample were housewives: the Great Books were another possible solution to the problem identified by Betty Friedan.[27] And fully 97 percent of participants felt satisfied with or positively enthusiastic about the program.[28]

A 1962 market study found that though most owners of *Great Books of the Western World* had read at least some of the volumes, only 1 percent had read them all, and 18 percent had read none. It seemed to confirm what critics like Dwight Macdonald had suspected: that the owners belonged mainly to the culturally insecure lower middle class, aware of the gaps in their education and anxious to fill them, but lacking confidence in their own judgment, and too ready to "appeal to authority" and stick to "accepted values." They were limited by a "factual bent," and looked to the fifty-four volumes to provide "*the* answers to questions"—which had never been Adler's goal. He had always encouraged critical readings. Of course (he granted) Aristotle was a sexist, but you couldn't criticize him intelligently if you didn't read him, and on many other issues he was still an indispensable philosopher.[29]

The heroic flaws of *Great Books of the Western World* were clear: it was set in stone, monumental, and focused on the past. But when Adler made the classics relevant to contemporary issues and respected the autonomy of the reader, he found a much more receptive audience. Starting in 1958 he wrote a popular weekly newspaper column, "Great Ideas from the Great Books." Readers sent in queries about current front-page controversies—war, sex, racism, loyalty, nationalism and internationalism, Communism, the welfare state, technology and automation, divorce, censorship, women's rights—and Adler would (in a few hundred words) point them to classics that confronted these questions.[30] And then, in December 1963, he published "How to Read a Book Superficially" in *Playboy*.

It was an absolutely brilliant stroke. Reading had always been Hugh Hefner's other great passion. The early issues of *Playboy* had serialized *Fahrenheit 451*. As an employee benefit, Bunnies could take advantage of a college tuition program (seriously). And in his very first issue he had famously dedicated his magazine to the highbrow bachelor who enjoyed "mixing up cocktails and an hors d'oeuvre or two, putting a little mood music on the phonograph and inviting in a female acquaintance for a quiet discussion on Picasso, Nietzsche, jazz, sex." But if the lady spied the ponderous *Great Books of the Western World* on her host's shelves, she might mark him down as a hopeless square and call it an evening. Adler had to make the classics hip, and he did that by relating them to books *Playboy* subscribers had actually read. They might think that "the works of Homer, Virgil, Dante and Shakespeare [are] practically unreadable," but, he assured them, "The truth is that these books are actually fully as readable as *Captain Horatio Hornblower*, *The Caine Mutiny*, the Inspector Maigret mysteries and *The Catcher in the Rye*. The knack lies in knowing how to read them." Don't reverentially analyze every word: you'll get bogged down and give up. Instead, read a classic as you would a contemporary book. Get the gist of it. Skim where necessary. Skip the parts that are boring (all that business about the Masons in *War and Peace*) or repetitive (how many times does Homer have to tell us that the dawn is "rosy-fingered"?). Don't worry if you can't always follow Plato's logic or lose track of all those Russian characters: you can reread later, and you will learn more from each reading. Shakespeare's language might seem intimidatingly archaic, but in fact it "is not much more difficult than that of grasping any other English local dialect, such as the speech of Faulkner's rural Southerners or Sillitoe's provincial British workingmen." And surely, anyone who wasn't fazed by the gross language of *The Naked and the Dead* could figure out what Iago meant when he insinuated that "an old black ram is tupping your white ewe." (*Playboy* readers took pride in being cool about obscenity and interracial sex.) "*Playboy's* patron monk" Rabelais, who was "most delightfully and wholesomely" randy, also offered "a distillation and presentation of Renaissance learning"—exactly the editorial balance that Hefner was striving to achieve. Throughout, Adler shrewdly flattered his *Playboy* readers, addressing them as men of the world who were educated but irreverent, intellectual but never pedantic, independent thinkers who, in an age of conformity, reached their own conclusions about everything, including the classics. And he spoke to a skeptical younger generation on their own terms. Yes, he asserted, the great books are in a sense timeless and universal, "But we must start from where we are and with what we are—with our present age, experience and insight—and let these works and writers communicate to us here and now."[31]

The term "egghead" had always suggested a deficit of masculine oomph: for example, Gary Cooper as the effete lexicographer in *Ball of Fire*, not to mention Adlai Stevenson. But in or around 1961 all that changed, thanks largely to Hugh Hefner, Mortimer Adler, and John F. Kennedy. The President surrounded himself with Harvard men, and inevitably some of his own erotic charisma rubbed off on them. The New Frontier had its own great-books seminar, codenamed "Hickory Hill University," which met weekly at the home of Attorney General Robert F. Kennedy. Mortimer Adler spoke there on the question of whether the Declaration of Independence made America a Christian country, to an audience of the most powerful men in the government: Douglas Dillon (Treasury Secretary), Robert McNamara (Defense Secretary), Newton Minow (chair of the Federal Communications Commission), Edward R. Murrow (head of the US Information Agency), Pierre Salinger (White House press secretary), Walt Rostow (chief policymaker at the State Department), Walter Heller (chairman of the Council of Economic Advisors), and David E. Bell (director of the Budget Bureau).[32] Clearly, smart had become sexy.

Great Books of the Western World had been published at precisely the moment in history when it became obsolete. The expansion of higher education produced a new and growing class of readers who simply didn't need it. Thanks to the quality paperback revolution, they could order classic literature *á la carte* from Penguin or New American Library or Doubleday Anchor books, which offered far cheaper prices and much greater variety. So even if Adler's prepackaged upper-case Great Books had disappointing sales (slowing to a trickle in the 1970s), the more broadly defined lower-case great books were enjoying an unprecedented boom. By working the more intellectual TV talk shows (Dick Cavett, William F. Buckley, Bill Moyers) Adler was still able to sell 50,000 copies of *Aristotle for Everybody* (1978).[33]

When Adler brought out a revised and expanded edition of *Great Books of the Western World* in 1990, he was slammed on all sides for failing to add any black authors. His response was cranky, but that was probably a function of old age. In fact he had always used the classics to address issues of racial injustice, and in 1969 (before it was academically fashionable) he had brought out a three-volume anthology, *The Negro in American History*.

And exactly when the traditional canon was being challenged on campus, college great-books programs were proliferating. There had only been one such program in the 1920s (Columbia's), two more founded in the 1930s (notably St John's of Annapolis), and another nine in the 1940s, including some prestigious institutions (Yale, Chicago, and the universities of Wisconsin and Michigan). Another fifteen were launched in the 1950s, fourteen in the 1960s, but then the real surge began: thirty-four new programs in the 1970s, fifty-one in the 1980s, thirty-four in the 1990s. In 1994 great-books college instructors started their own professional organization, the Association for Core Texts and Courses, which as of 2001 listed 177 such programs in colleges throughout the United States. Some of them are conservative Catholic and Christian institutions, but others are notoriously liberal (New York University, Reed College, Simon's Rock College, University of California at Santa Cruz), and some serve highly diverse inner-city student bodies (Brooklyn College).[34] Evidently the general dismantling of college requirements in the 1960s and the "assault on the canon" spurred many academics to reassert the importance of a foundation of common readings. True, their syllabi are now more likely to include Frederick Douglass, Black Elk, and Lady Murasaki. But any traditional institution, confronted by revolutionary pressures, can preserve and revitalize itself by making timely reforms, and the Great Books idea offers a classic illustration of that political principle.

In the January 1966 issue of *Playboy* Mortimer Adler and Clifton Fadiman wondered aloud what would be "The Great Books of 2066."[35] In addition to making their own guesses, they reported the results of an advertising supplement that asked readers of the *New York Times* and the *Chicago Tribune* which twentieth-century authors would prove most enduring. In descending order, they listed George Bernard Shaw, Albert Einstein, T. S. Eliot, James Joyce, Jean-Paul Sartre,

Ernest Hemingway, Albert Camus, William Faulkner, Eugene O'Neill, Thomas Mann, Arnold Toynbee, and Franz Kafka.

It wasn't very scientific, but it probably represented the views of sophisticated urban newspaper readers at the time. What it did not reflect was the tastes of a younger and edgier generation. For them, Hugh Hefner was constructing a still newer and more radical canon. From the start, the *Playboy* Interviews assumed they were addressing serious readers, usually running close to 10,000 words, and often interrogating famous authors: Bertrand Russell, Vladimir Nabokov, Henry Miller, Jean-Paul Sartre, Arthur M. Schlesinger, Arnold Toynbee, Norman Mailer, John Kenneth Galbraith, and Marshall McLuhan, all before the end of the 1960s. Though there was some overlap with the preferences of readers of the *New York Times* and *Chicago Tribune*, *Playboy* pushed the boundaries much farther, including interviewees who were militantly black (Malcolm X, Martin Luther King, Dick Gregory, Eldridge Cleaver) or theatrically gay (Jean Genet, Truman Capote, Allen Ginsberg, Gore Vidal). *Mad* magazine wondered aloud when Hefner would run a nude centerfold of Ayn Rand—who was in fact interviewed in March 1964. And if you were also interested in women's minds, you could read fiction by Nadine Gordimer, Doris Lessing, Anne Sexton, and Joyce Carol Oates. (Oates was thoroughly nonplussed when feminists excoriated her for publishing in that venue.) In the 1960s a majority of male American college students regularly read *Playboy*—and a 1971 survey found that fully a quarter of its readers were female, which when you think about it is not so astonishing. Rather than purchase it at a newsstand, they probably borrowed the magazine from their boyfriends, brothers, and husbands. It offered brainy women a range of exciting new writers, as well as egalitarian discussions of female sexuality in the "Playboy Advisor" column.[36] These young readers of both sexes probably read the magazine with greater engagement than what they were assigned in English classes, and at that formative age the magazine communicated a much more expansive and modern sense of what constituted great books and who wrote them. And many of these students would go on to become literature professors, publishers, and critics themselves. In that sense, *Playboy* had an indispensable role in starting the process that would later be called "opening up the canon." Feminists really should be more generous in acknowledging the debt they owe to Hugh Hefner.

Even as an ageing establishmentarian in the 1960s, Adler publicly sympathized with campus rebels' critique of contemporary higher education. He agreed that the "megaversity" had increasingly abandoned the kind of liberal education that studied the best books and posed fundamental questions about everything, instead churning out the technocrats and specialists that industrial capitalism demanded. He regretted that professors were rewarded less and less for teaching and challenging undergraduates, and more and more for publishing irrelevant scholarship. So he was not inclined to condemn SDS for organizing its own "free universities."[37] They probably reminded him of his early work with the People's Institute. And after all, he had occupied and liberated the University of Chicago, thirty years before another generation of firebrands did that at Columbia.

Notes

1. Sharon Hamilton, "'Intellectual in Its Looser Sense': Reading Mencken's *Smart Set*," in *Middlebrow Literary Cultures: The Battle of the Brows*, ed. Erica Brown and Mary Grover (London: Palgrave Macmillan, 2012), 134–8.

2. Katherine Elise Chaddock, *The Multi-Talented Mr. Erskine: Shaping Mass Culture through Great Books and Fine Music* (New York: Palgrave Macmillan, 2012), 44–6, 86–98.

3. This biographical account is drawn from Gordon M. Pradl, "Reading Literature in a Democracy: The Challenge of Louise Rosenblatt," in *The Experience of Reading: Louise Rosenblatt and Reader-Response Theory*, ed. John Clifford (Portsmouth, NH: Boynton/Cook, 1991), 23–46.

4. Louise M. Rosenblatt, *Literature as Exploration* (New York: D. Appleton Century Co., 1938), vi–vii.

5. Ibid., 36.

6. Ibid., 4–5.

7. Ibid., 8–9.

8. Ibid., 32–7.

9. Ibid., 89.

10. Ibid., 72.

11. Ibid., 93–4.

12. Ibid., 43–4.

13. Ibid., 47.

14. Ibid., 85.

15. Lou L. LaBrant and Frieda M. Heller, *An Evaluation of Free Reading in Grades Seven to Twelve, Inclusive* (Columbus, Ohio: Ohio State University, 1939), 18–20, 28, 61–3.

16. Carolyn Allen, "Louise Rosenblatt and Theories of Reader Response," in Clifford, *Experience of Reading*, 15–22.

17. Tim Lacy, *The Dream of a Democratic Culture: Mortimer J. Adler and the Great Books Idea* (New York: Palgrave Macmillan, 2013), 22–4.

18. Daniel Born, "Utopian Civic-Mindedness: Robert Maynard Hutchins, Mortimer Adler, and the Great Books Enterprise," in *Reading Communities from Salons to Cyberspace*, ed. DeNel Rehberg Sedo (Basingstoke and New York: Palgrave Macmillan, 2011), 81–100.

19. Lacy, *Dream of a Democratic Culture*, 34–5.

20. John Walker Powell, *Education for Maturity* (New York: Hermitage House, 1949), 42, 115, 122, 213–14, 234–9.

21. Lacy, *Dream of a Democratic Culture*, chs. 2–3.

22. Marshall McLuhan, *The Mechanical Bride* (Corte Madera: Gingko Press, 2002), 43.

23. James A. Davis, *A Study of Participants in the Great Books Program* (n.p.: National Opinion Research Center, 1960), Part A.

24. Ibid., 97–102.

25. Philip H. Ennis, *Adult Book Reading in the United States* (Chicago: National Opinion Research Center, 1965), 27–32.

26. Abbott Kaplan, *Study-Discussion in the Liberal Arts* (n.p.: Fund for Adult Education, 1960), 56–7.

27. Ibid., 30.

28. Ibid., 42.

29. Lacy, *Dream of a Democratic Culture*, 91–7.

30. Mortimer Adler, *Great Ideas from the Great Books* (New York: Washington Square Press, 1969).

31. Mortimer Adler, "How to Read a Book Superficially," *Playboy* 10 (Dec. 1963): 115, 122, 196, 199.

32. "Random Notes in Washington: Fall Term at Hickory Hill U.: Robert Kennedy's Seminars Make Scholars Students," *New York Times* (23 Sept. 1962): 11.

33. Lacy, *Dream of a Democratic Culture*, 166.

34. Listed on <http://www.coretexts.org/college-great-books-programs/>.

35. Mortimer Adler, "The Great Books of 2066," *Playboy* 13 (Jan. 1966): 137, 224–8.

36. Carrie Pitzulo, *Bachelors and Bunnies: The Sexual Politics of Playboy* (Chicago: University of Chicago Press, 2011), ch. 6.

37. Lacy, *Dream of a Democratic Culture*, 119–20.

3

Up from Middlebrow

The Chinese had a word for it—*wanbao quanshu*. It's a bibliographic term, which literally means "complete compendia of myriad treasures," but an alternate translation might be "middlebrow." These were encyclopedic works that distilled and summarized sophisticated science, history, and politics in cheap, accessible, illustrated guidebooks. Their audience (as a 1933 survey of Shanghai bookstalls confirmed) was neither the educated elite nor the impoverished peasantry, but an intermediate semi-educated class of shop-clerks, apprentices, house-wives, workers, and prostitutes. Very few readers had thoroughly mastered the Chinese vocabulary of 50,000 characters, but many more, without much difficulty, had learned 2,000 basic terms, enough to read popular newspapers and *wanbao quanshu*. The latter commonly ran the subtitle *wanshi buqiuren* ("myriad matters you won't need to ask"), which underscored their mission: self-education. They had titles like *Riyong wanshi baoku choushi bixu*, which could be rendered "Treasury of all daily things necessary for social relations" or (more idiomatically) "How to win friends and influence people."

Wanbao quanshu were the contemporaneous counterparts of H. G. Wells's *The Outline of History* and Will Durant's *The Story of Philosophy*. They flourished in Republican-era China, the same time frame that Joan Shelley Rubin identified as the heyday of American middlebrow culture. In societies where a wide gap opens up between elite and pulp literature, where literacy is growing but access to higher education is still restricted, where modernizing forces arouse both optimism and anxiety, middlebrow bridges those divides and makes sense of rapid change.

Those conditions certainly prevailed in China, the United States, and Great Britain in the first half of the twentieth century, but not only then. Middlebrow has a very long history: *wanbao quanshu* can be traced back to the seventeenth century.[1] And how about eighteenth-century Europe? Two generations ago historians studied the High

Enlightenment of Voltaire and Rousseau, one generation ago Robert Darnton discovered a Low Enlightenment of Grub-Street hacks and smut-mongers, and now a team of young scholars at Radboud University in the Netherlands are creating the database MEDIATE: Middlebrow Enlightenment: Disseminating Ideas, Authors and Texts in Europe (1665–1820). They are finding that most readers in this period learned about the Enlightenment not from *philosophes* or pornographers, but from popularizers, whose easy guides to modern thought were neither forbidden nor particularly subversive.[2]

We have seen a similar middlebrow turn in English departments. They always studied great books, and over the past fifty years they increasingly turned their attention to pulp fiction, porn, and comics (pardon me, "graphic novels"). But they ignored the vast territory in between until 1992, when Joan Shelley Rubin published *The Making of Middlebrow Culture*, one of those very rare monographs that actually deserves to be called "groundbreaking." That opened the door to a new wave of scholarship, which now gives us a sense of what the emerging literary landscape of the middlebrow looks like.

Let's begin with late nineteenth-century America, and run through our checklist of preconditions hospitable to middlebrow culture. A large gap between high literature and popular literature? That was certainly the case where the genteel tradition coexisted with dime novels. In the pages of the *Nation*, E. L. Godkin turned up his nose at the "chromo-civilization" and "pseudo-culture" offered by more popular magazines.[3] Rising levels of literacy combined with restricted access to higher education? That held true for all American subgroups, including blacks, Indians, women, and immigrants. Rapid and often disorientating modernization? That summed up what both the big cities and small frontier towns were coping with.

Now let's establish a baseline definition of middlebrow. Which authors and books do we mean? Here we have an invaluable historical resource illuminating a classic case-study. The borrowing records for the Muncie (Indiana) Public Library from 1891 to 1902 have been preserved and keyboarded into the "What Middletown Read" database, where books are searchable by author and title, and borrowers are broken down by sex, race, and occupation. Muncie would later be the subject of Robert and Helen Lynd's pioneering sociological investigation *Middletown: A Study in Modern American Culture* (1929). Muncie is

sometimes characterized as a "typical American town," but of course
such a thing never existed, not in a country so vast and various. It was,
however, Midwestern, far from any major literary centers, neither a
big city nor a small rural town (population 24,000 in 1910). And it was
the kind of community that would be eviscerated by Sinclair Lewis. If
middlebrow literature was anywhere, it was here.

At the public library, the most frequently borrowed author was
Horatio Alger: a total of 9,230 loans, which put him far ahead of
Mark Twain (877), Charles Dickens (672), Walter Scott (658), William
Shakespeare (268), Henry James (208), and Jane Austen (179). Overall,
62 percent of borrowers were white-collar and 37 percent blue-collar,
and both classes tended to borrow the same number and types of
books, with a few telling exceptions. As in Britain, Shakespeare was
something of a proletarian hero, and was borrowed somewhat
more frequently by the working classes. Moreover, the proportion of
borrowers who were children varied inversely with income, ranging
from 24.5 percent for the upper-middle classes up to 57.3 percent
for unskilled workers. For young people growing up in economic
poverty and (probably) book-poor homes, the public library was an
indispensable and well-used resource.

Muncie newspapers did cover literary affairs, including some fairly
edgy authors. In 1898 there were reports on Richard Le Gallienne,
"Leader of the Decadents," and Émile Zola's defense of Captain
Dreyfus. But neither author could be found in the stacks of the
Muncie Public Library. Nor did it stock Oscar Wilde, Walt Whitman,
Jean-Jacques Rousseau, Voltaire, Rabelais, Gustave Flaubert, Guy de
Maupassant, Emily Dickinson, *Moll Flanders*, *Tom Jones*, *Frankenstein*, or
Dracula. There was no Karl Marx, though Edward Bellamy's socialist
utopia *Looking Backward 2000–1887* was available and borrowed
eighty-three times. *Jude the Obscure* was not on the shelves; *Tess of the
D'Urbervilles* was, but evidently no one disturbed it.

So far it appears that Muncie was sleepy and complacent, and that
Sinclair Lewis had it right. But was there a ferment not immediately
visible in the library registers? The "What Middletown Read" database
enabled Frank Felsenstein and James Connolly to track directly the
connection between reading and social activism among the members
of the Woman's Club of Muncie. The link was fairly obvious when
they borrowed the social fiction of Charles Dickens or Elizabeth

Gaskell, or Bellamy's *Looking Backwards*, or Bertha von Suttner's pacifist novel *Ground Arms!* The library books most frequently borrowed by club members tended to be books with a message, such as Helen Hunt Jackson's *Ramona* (which exposed the injustices done to American Indians) and *Les Misérables*. The connections were made explicit in club lectures, as when one presenter discussed the role of female social activists in *Tom Jones*, *Bleak House*, and Mrs Humphry Ward's *Marcella*.[4]

And this was very typical. By 1906 it seemed that every American town of any size had a ladies' literary society, self-organized and democratically governed. In that year there were an estimated 50,000 to 100,000 women's clubs of all types, and most of them had a literary focus,[5] filling a vacuum of books. Outside of the big northeastern cities, there were few proper bookstores. In 1895–6 Houston had just six, and all of them carried a range of merchandise besides books (stationary, typewriters, jewelry). Public libraries were equally scarce (in 1887 there were only twenty in the Southern and western states) and women's clubs ultimately took the initiative in establishing three out of four Carnegie libraries in the nation. At a time when few women attended college and most states did not permit them to vote, members presented and discussed papers on current affairs and history, they acquired research and writing skills, and they entered into the arena of social activism. They also became a driving grassroots force behind the Progressive movement, discussing issues such as child labor, immigration, and expanded higher education for women. But their main focus was classic and contemporary literature (at the time, of course, Charles Dickens and Robert Browning were contemporary). These reading groups led straight to intellectual freedom and political emancipation—"a democracy of brains," as one clubwoman put it.[6]

Beyond that, Katherine West Scheil has uncovered more than 500 Shakespeare clubs across America, largely in small towns, and most of them organized by women. These were grassroots institutions of higher self-education, where there were no professors and all students were on an equal footing. Remarkably, they did with Shakespeare everything that professional academics do today. They staged their own productions. They closely analyzed the texts, and tried to discern the nuanced meanings of Elizabethan English. They read critical studies of Shakespeare, and they edited their own journals, which published their own scholarship and criticism. They situated the plays in their historical context, related them to modern literature, and performed interdisciplinary studies that connected Shakespeare with (for instance) art history. They assigned themselves homework: essays, study questions, syllabi, and oral presentations. They systematically accumulated their own archives, providing today's scholars with all the source materials they need to write the history of the movement. All this intellectual exercise (as a Tuscaloosa club boasted) developed "the latent executive talent" of the pre-suffrage generation of American women: "Many ladies, too timid at one time to speak in any gathering, can now conduct the exercises according to parliamentary rules, with the greatest ease and dignity." These clubs engaged women of all classes and backgrounds (three of the eight groups in Topeka were African-American), but they flourished especially in small towns and on the frontier, where (along with other chores) women had to make their own cultural life.

Today, when most academic literary criticism only colors inside the lines drawn by a few superstar "theorists," one has to be impressed by the intellectual independence of these clubwomen. They often made a point of reading the plays first, doing their own hermeneutics, and only then consulting the critics—who (as some Topeka women noted) "seldom escaped minor criticism from us." In 1886 the popular journal *Shakespeariana* advised, "be sure that you are exercising your power to make your own product," which resonated with women who were still making their own clothes, jams, and home remedies.[7]

After studying hundreds of these clubs, Katherine Scheil reported, "I have found no evidence of members being chastised for dissenting opinions." Given that she teaches at a university in the early twenty-first century, you can understand her surprise. The minute books of these Progressive-era women's clubs are filled with references to "argument" and "heated debate," and apparently no one complained to the dean that any of this was "offensive," "inappropriate," or "hurtful." (Happily, there were no deans.) Had these women attended an actual college, then or now, they would have found bureaucratic machinery in place for restricting academic freedom, responding to pressure from alumni, contributors, or students. But these societies were absolutely self-governing, answerable to no one other than their members,

who clearly valued above all else freedom of expression, which means
a lot to readers who can't vote and haven't been encouraged to
voice their opinions. *Shakespeariana* realized that its readers would be
shy about asserting themselves in the public sphere, and gave them a
vigorous push:

> Agreement and opposition both will have their use in giving you
> new light and fresh suggestions. Discuss it as freely as you can.
> Let not the tongue-tied spirit of man hamper you, and never
> decline your turn in the conversation. Never think you have not
> facts enough for the purpose, others have no better than you
> and your book furnishes. Dare to speak as you feel and you will
> find not only that you have unlocked hidden stores of your own
> but of your author's and of other peoples, and the inspiration
> of conversation may begin for you in your club.

Once they broke through that barrier, these women brought to their
discussions an exhilaration rarely found in college classrooms today.
"From the outset, Shakespeare [was] something dynamic, inexhaustible,
and 'worth while'," reported a club in Woodland, California. "There
was no limit as to the time spent on any suggestive point or passage;
often six or seven weeks would be occupied in the study of one play."[8]
The question-and-answer sessions gave even the women of Zanesville,
Ohio, a license to explore sex in fairly graphic language (and in 1878!):
What did "gelded" mean? And what was this business in *Much Ado
About Nothing* about "Hercules in the smirched, worm-eaten tapestry,
where his codpiece seems as massy as his club"?[9] There were certainly
discussions of controversial issues surrounding race (several clubs
were organized by black women) and gender (when studying *The
Taming of the Shrew*, though in free debate you could argue the case for
either Katherine or Petruccio). Feminist literary criticism didn't begin
in the 1970s: favorite readings in Victorian Shakespeare clubs included
Anna Jameson's *Characteristics of Women* (1832), Mary Cowden Clarke's
The Girlhood of Shakespeare's Heroines (1850–2), and Helen Faucit
Martin's *On Some of Shakespeare's Female Characters* (1885).[10] In 1897 one
lecturer indicted the dramatist for "criminal injustice in placing his
heroines in every play at a disadvantage," and radically argued that
"the whole structure of Shakespeare's dramas rests upon the disen-
franchisement of those heroines whom he is falsely supposed to idealize."

(The audience responded with stormy applause and shouts of "Down with Shakespeare!")[11] Middlebrow has been labeled commercial, conformist, bowdlerized, unchallenging, and ever striving for a bland consensus, but there was none of that in these clubs.

The women's literary clubs declined very rapidly after 1920, rendered obsolete by their own successes. The battles for female suffrage, progressive reform, public libraries, and higher education for women had all been won. America was becoming a coed nation, where men and women mixed more readily in social and professional circles, and all-female clubs were something your mother did. No one with pretensions to literary sophistication would want to be one of the bourgeois club ladies in Helen Hokinson's *New Yorker* cartoons. But perhaps what really killed the women's literary club was a single shot, right between the eyes, fired by Sinclair Lewis. In *Main Street* he reproduced what purported to be the minutes of a typical Midwestern clubwoman's lecture:

> Mrs. Ole Jenson said that Shakespeare was born in 1564 and died in 1616. He lived in London, England, and in Stratford-on-Avon, which many American tourists loved to visit, a lovely town with many curios and old houses worth examination. Many people believed that Shakespeare was the greatest playwright who ever lived, also a fine poet. Not much was known about his life, but after all that did not make so much difference, because they loved to read his numerous plays...

It was a caricature that bore little resemblance to reality. In fact the literary clubs had helped to create a vast new reading public. When Robert and Helen Lynd were investigating Muncie in 1925, they found that while the old reading circles had practically disappeared, Middletowners were reading more than ever. Nearly half the population now held library cards, as opposed to just 20 percent in 1910. In 1924 there were 6.5 annual per capita book loans, compared to 0.85 in 1890. (With the onset of the Depression that figure would leap again, to 12.2 loans by 1933.) And magazine reading had exploded: in 1924 one in six Muncie households subscribed to the *Saturday Evening Post*, which in 1890 had a nationwide sale of just 33,000.

So why all the complaints that middlebrow was creating a nation of Babbitts? In the 1910s and 1920s a host of new periodicals had sprung up to publish and champion literary modernism. For the hardcore avant-garde there were little magazines like the *Dial* and the *Little Review*. For fashionable sophisticates (and those who wished to be) there were larger-circulation journals like *Vanity Fair*, the *New Republic*, and the *New Yorker*. And for sniggering iconoclasts, there was H. L. Mencken's *Smart Set* and *American Mercury*. The *raison d'être* of these magazines was to certify that their readers were highbrows and to securely distance them from what Mencken called "boobs" and Harold Ross (of the *New Yorker*) called "the old lady in Dubuque," and still others called "middlebrow." The very success of *Main Street* (the top fiction bestseller of 1920) suggested that there was a huge reading public that wanted to escape the taint of middlebrow, even if *Main Street* was itself the great American middlebrow novel.

The explanation behind this apparent contradiction may lie in the fact that, while all categories of literature were booming, middlebrow reading was swamping highbrow reading. In 1890 the *Saturday Evening Post* had three times the circulation of the *Atlantic*. By 1925 the ratio was more than 40 to 1, though the readership of the *Atlantic* had multiplied twelve times over. In Middletown there were only about fifteen subscribers to the *New Republic* and almost 2,000 (one-in-five households) for the *American Magazine*. So while there was much more reading overall, in the era of Sinclair Lewis, Midwestern intellectuals had some reason to feel that they had become a small and beleaguered minority.[12] But they could find consolation and support in magazines like the *New Republic*, which hadn't existed a few years earlier.

Yet the *American Magazine* was preaching a gospel of middlebrow self-education, obviously aimed at subscribers who knew little about literature but wanted to read more and better books. Amidst ads for the Harvard Classics (which sold 350,000 sets in twenty years), it published H. G. Wells and F. Scott Fitzgerald, John Erskine on "What Education Means to Me" (October 1928), William Lyon Phelps on "Cashing in on the Classics" (December 1930), Will Durant on "How to Widen Your World" (March 1931), and an explanation of Sigmund Freud ("How It Feels to Be Psychoanalyzed," May 1925). It wasn't Greenwich Village, but one of the most successful ventures in middlebrow culture would germinate in the precincts of Washington Square Park.

Will Durant began as a teacher at a Greenwich Village anarchist school, and then lectured at the Labor Temple, and adult-education center on the Lower East Side, where his audience was mainly radical Jewish immigrants. He joined forced with Emanuel Haldeman-Julius, the socialist publisher of the Little Blue Books. This series of pulp pamphlet-sized paperbacks offered a mix of self-help, how-to, pop sexology, very light reading ("Best Jokes of 1930"), guides to self-education, and a vast range of classic reprints, all selling for 5 cents each. Haldeman-Julius was called "the Henry Ford of literature," and his booklets were indeed a marvel of mass cultural production, selling at least 300 million copies in the 1920s and 1930s. Haldeman-Julius published eleven of Durant's lectures as Little Blue Books, and then suggested that they be spliced together in a hardcover volume. It was titled *The Story of Philosophy*, which became one of several middlebrow non-fiction works that scaled the *Publishers Weekly* annual bestseller list in the 1920s. Others included H. G. Wells's *The Outline of History* (1921), Hendrik Van Loon's *The Story of Mankind* (1922), James Harvey Robinson's *Mankind in the Making* (1922), J. Arthur Thompson's *The Outline of Science* (1922), and Claude Bowers's *Jefferson and Hamilton* (1926). Each of them took subjects normally handled by academics and made them understandable to a mass audience. But they did not, as many critics feared, crowd out more serious literature. On the same *Publishers Weekly* list can be found books that would have passed muster in Bloomsbury and Greenwich Village: John Maynard Keynes's *The Economic Consequences of the Peace* (1920), Lytton Strachey's *Queen Victoria* (1922), George Bernard Shaw's *Saint Joan* (1924), Eugene O'Neill's *Strange Interlude* (1928), and Erich Maria Remarque's *All Quiet on the Western Front* (first place in 1929).[13] In the age of Babbitt, everyone was reading more books and better books.

Nevertheless, the Book-of-the-Month Club (founded 1925) infected critics with a bad case of twentieth-century blues. Wasn't it reducing literature to a standardized product? Weren't readers surrendering their right to make their own book choices to "experts"—the BOMC judges? Would the last refuges of American individualism, the home library and the independent bookstore, fall victim to the relentless conforming pressures of a modern industrial society? Author Charles Edward Russell worried aloud that newspaper chains, big Hollywood studios, radio networks, and the BOMC might make us "a nation of automata. One hundred million Babbitts!" And across the Atlantic, intellectuals like Aldous Huxley, Ortega y Gasset, and Theodor Adorno were still more fearful of "culture industries" and "Americanization."

But did that actually come to pass? Harry Scherman, one of the entrepreneurs behind the BOMC, pointed out that the very highbrow magazines that criticized his venture themselves produced a predictably standardized editorial mix for their readers, whether it was the Boston brahminism of the *Atlantic* or Mencken's snarkiness in the *American Mercury*. The BOMC offered a variety of book options, and its monthly newsletters tailored recommendations to the various tastes of its subscribers, suggesting (like your neighborhood bookseller) that a particular selection might appeal to some readers more than others. BOMC judge Henry Seidel Canby gave up teaching in Yale's English department because it was too stuck on dead authors and too rigid about canonization. He refused to rule out the possibility that "a vital pictorial art [might] come from the comic strip, or a new literature from the *Saturday Evening Post*." And he was just plain tired of producing "articles that only scholars could understand, which no one, not even scholars read." (That rut did not begin with deconstruction.) Canby wanted to shift attention to readers and connect them with literature that spoke to their personal interests. "The best book is worth nothing at all if it never finds a reader," he proclaimed. "Good reading is a highly personal experience, whose quality depends upon the taste, the intellect, the imagination, and the sensitivity of the individual reader. Still he has to get the books. I find too little in histories of literature and criticism of how books get to readers."[14]

Far from putting bookstores out of business, selection of particular titles by the BOMC (like later film and television adaptations) consistently boosted bookstore sales. And before we romanticize the old corner bookstores, bear in mind that, outside of the big metropolitan areas, they were very scarce on the ground, even in mid-sized cities. In 1928 there were about 200 general bookshops in New York, but just nine in Pittsburgh, seven in Cincinnati, and four in Newark. In many smaller towns only druggists and perhaps the local department store offered a very limited selection of books.[15] By 1942 Americans held 750,000 memberships in all book clubs—a considerable market, but in a nation of 130 million, a tiny percentage of the whole book-reading public.[16] Far from debasing popular taste, clubs made a greater variety of books available to literature-starved readers. And far from standardizing those readers, it gave them more opportunities for individual choice. A broad national survey of all classes of American readers (businessmen, students, industrial workers, farmers, housewives, postal employees, prison convicts, shop-clerks, teachers, telephone operators, waiters and waitresses), carried out in 1929–31, was able to reach no simple conclusions:

> because individual readers are so different. The same person may read all day long for several weeks on the same problem and then read nothing but an occasional newspaper for the next month. While two readers have the same eagerness to read about money matters, one may love poetry and the other may hate it. People who are fond of the same sort of reading may differ greatly in their ability to get it. If one lives opposite a large public library and the other lives on a farm, their reading habits are likely to differ widely.[17]

The investigators did find that some middleweight topics had broad readerships: "The Successful Life" and "Getting Along with Other People" appealed to the millions who were waiting for Dale Carnegie. But there were also large audiences for serious issues, such as "The Next War" and "International Attitudes," and just about everyone wanted to read about "Self-Improvement." Women were especially interested in the "Changing Status of Women" and "The Meaning of Culture," while "Adult Education" was checked off by postal clerks, machinists, farmers, factory girls, telephone operators, and housewives.[18]

Meanwhile, Britain had its own middlebrow champions. In 1897 a young journalist named William Whitten covered an essay contest on Robert Browning for the poor children of Walworth. The recently published "Penny Poets" series had made possible the cheap mass distribution of Browning's works, and the resulting essays made clear that he had connected with these slum readers. "It was while walking through the fields and leafy lanes of Dulwich that many of [Browning's] best ideas came into his head," wrote one girl, and Whitten applauded her: "Thus Browning's child-critics are doing more to bring out this fact than all the Browning societies put together."

In 1919 Whitten launched *John O'London's Weekly*, his own venture in populist criticism. His first issue was headed with a manifesto for liberated reading:

> Book Shyness. Many thousands of people suffer from it. They ask themselves vaguely and fearfully, "ought I to read Ruskin?" "ought I to read Balzac?...and Jane Austen's novels, and Hazlitt's essays?" and so on. There is, of course no *ought* about it. Right reading is self-chosen reading, and the bogeys of correctness and completeness are responsible for a great deal of shivering on the brink of literature.

The function of criticism, then, was not to lay down rules, establish canons, or promote one mode of reading over another: it was to communicate enthusiasm and help the reader to discover literature according to his own lights:

> I believe myself that a taste for good reading can be acquired by infection, that is by reading good criticism—by which term I do not mean, in this case the criticism which seeks to correct or classify literary works, but the kind which seeks to communicate the writer's enjoyment of them. When you see a man smacking his lips over a good dish, or raising a glass of wine to revel in its colour...you are apt to enjoy his enjoyment, and even by sympathy, to share it.

Whitten's tastes were catholic, but not philistine. There were appreciations of Shakespeare and Hazlitt alongside what would now be called "popular culture." Well before George Orwell subjected boys' weeklies and naughty postcards to serious analysis, *John O'London's* did something similar to *Tit-Bits* (a paper for readers with short attention spans, as the name suggests) and Charles Garvice (who knocked out romances at the rate of about one per month, and sold in the millions). Whitten granted that Garvice was a lowbrow, but he:

> novelized the day-dreams of the daughters of the people. They were innocent, sentimental day-dreams, and he added nothing to them. He simply gave them shape as stories, invented details, found backgrounds, and presented his millions of readers with something in which they saw themselves in the sunlight of love

and the starlight of luck. His stories were enormously popular, but they were read by a public which one does not take into account when discussing public taste.

Where other populist critics of the 1920s rubbished the modernists, *John O'London's* broadmindedly introduced them to the readers of trashy melodramas. Virginia Woolf's *Night and Day* was celebrated as "an achievement of outstanding distinction, an important addition to modern imaginative literature." And when Dorothy Richardson experimented with stream-of-consciousness prose in *Interim*, *John O'London's* simply explained, in plain language, the method to her madness: "Miss Richardson writes exactly as most of us think, one thing almost arbitrarily suggesting another." Yes, the method was very avant-garde, but "Progress and development absolutely depend on experiment." When modernists were trying their best to "make it difficult," Whitten had the nerve to make them seem unintimidating and user-friendly, as if to say, *If you like Charles Garvice, you might want to try Virginia Woolf.*[19]

In inter-war Britain middlebrow writers produced serious but accessible literary criticism in mid-market papers: Arnold Bennett and J. B. Priestley in the *Evening Standard*, Compton Mackenzie in the *Daily Mail*, Winifred Holtby in the *News Chronicle* and *Good Housekeeping*. And even highbrows might deign to write for the popular press, Wyndham Lewis reviewing Clive Bell on modern art in the *Daily Herald*, or D. H. Lawrence on sex in the *Weekly Dispatch*. Editors wanted provocative essays that would set everyone talking, and they paid generously. They also serialized fiction, mainly romance and crime, but not entirely: Tennessee Williams's *A Streetcar Named Desire* produced a huge circulation boost for the *Evening Standard*.[20]

At a time when British academic critics ignored American literature, Bennett immediately recognized the value of Theodore Dreiser, Sinclair Lewis, Ernest Hemingway, and William Faulkner. And some of his picks were daring. He stood up for Radclyffe Hall's *The Well of Loneliness* when other popular journalists demanded its suppression, and he recommended *Banjo* by the black American novelist Claude McKay, which has only recently been resuscitated by scholars.[21]

Middlebrow fiction is often dismissed as conventional and petty bourgeois, and one has to grant that it was never revolutionary, but it could help bring into the mainstream attitudes once considered radical. The popular detective novels published by Margery Allingham, Agatha Christie, Georgette Heyer, Ngaio Marsh, and Dorothy L. Sayers in the 1920s and 1930s introduced heroines who were not exactly feminists, but they smoked, solved mysteries, had good heads for business, and shot (or threatened to shoot) baddies. They weren't wholly androgynous, but they were boyish flappers who were no less rational than men. They were, as Melissa Schaub put it, "female gentlemen" who adopted and adapted a traditionally male code of conduct and sportsmanship. That was a gentle subversion of gender roles that even a skittish male might find oddly appealing. If the pre-war suffragettes were the shock troops who scored breakthroughs (often against furious resistance), the post-war detective writers were the infantry who occupied and secured the newly conquered territory. Mystery writing had once been a male preserve, and its takeover by women was in itself a remarkable change.[22]

Or take a still edgier issue. *The Well of Loneliness* was certainly middlebrow, all vague and gauzy, so much so that when my mother read it as a teenager she didn't realize it was about lesbianism. It was suppressed in Britain but not in the United States. No less frank about homosexuality was Rosamond Lehmann's *Dusty Answer* (1927), Evelyn Waugh's *Brideshead Revisited* (1945), and Nancy Mitford's *Love in a Cold Climate* (1949).[23] Jaime Harker has identified a whole school of "Middlebrow Queer" novels of the 1940s and 1950s: Christopher Isherwood's *The World in the Evening*, Gore Vidal's *The City and the Pillar*, William Maxwell's *The Folded Leaf*, John Horne Burns's *The Gallery*, Truman Capote's *Other Voices, Other Rooms*, Carson McCullers's *Reflections in a Golden Eye*, William Goyen's *The House of Breath*, and Charles Jackson's *The Lost Weekend*. (This last, about an alcoholic writer, suggests that he is a secret homosexual, but that theme was omitted from the Ray Milland movie version). Isherwood promoted these books, which were taken on by mainstream publishers (Random House had a particularly strong list). Cyril Connolly had warned that Isherwood would slip into a "fatal readability," and *The World in the Evening* confirmed that in the minds of the critics. "A perfectly acceptable second-grade American novel," sneered Kingsley Amis, "tops for readability, okay on human-interest quotient, a bit paunchy in regard to conflict and short on humour; general rating *Fairly Good*

Entertainment." In *Encounter*, edited by Stephen Spender (also gay), Angus Wilson (ditto) pronounced that the novel simply wouldn't meet the standards of F. R. Leavis. (What more do you need to know?) Even at the time, reviewers (regardless of their sexual orientation) recognized that these stories were formulaic and fatalistic. Isherwood complained that they always ended in "tragedy, defeat and death," and he dismissed Vidal's prose as pure "Satevepost." But they made homosexuals visible to Middle America without scaring off readers, they communicated sympathy and tolerance, and they set in motion vast long-run changes in social attitudes.[24]

Indeed, middlebrow reading was at the core of what may be the most famous account of self-education in the world of literature. When Malcolm X was committed to Norfolk Prison Colony in 1948, it was an exceptionally libertarian penal institution, with a remarkably well stocked open-stack library. And he ploughed through it all, "sometimes as much as fifteen hours a day."

He read Western and Eastern philosophers: Socrates (whom he thought borrowed ideas from the Egyptians), Spinoza (whom he imagined was black), and Kant, Schopenhauer, and Nietzsche (whom he considered proto-fascists). He read W. E. B. DuBois's *Souls of Black Folk*, Carter Woodson's *Negro History*, and J. A. Rogers's *Sex and Race*, in a deliberate effort to recover the black history that was ignored by conventional textbooks. And yet he also learned much about non-white peoples from white middlebrow writers. H. G. Wells's *The Outline of History* and Will Durant's *The Story of Civilization* were genuine attempts at writing global history: Malcolm was particularly impressed by the first volume in Durant's series, *Our Oriental Heritage* (1935). Frederick Law Olmstead's journalistic exposes of slavery "opened my eyes to the horrors suffered when the slave was landed in the United States," and Pierre van Paassen's *Days of Our Years* revealed Italian atrocities in the Abyssinian War. "The very first set of books that really impressed me" was an educational series for younger readers, *Wonders of the World*. "It's full of pictures of archeological finds, statues that depict, usually, non-European people."[25]

In the Harvard Classics "Five-Foot Shelf," perhaps the most scorned example of potted middlebrow culture, Malcolm found the most subversive text of all: *Paradise Lost*. There Satan mobilized Europeans—popes and knights, Charlemagne and Richard I—to storm heaven. That seemed to corroborate what Elijah Muhammad had said: that white men were devils. As leader of the Nation of Islam, Mr Muhammad had preached that the first humans had been black and created "a peaceful heaven on earth," but then they expelled a troublemaker named Yacub, who took his revenge by genetically engineering an evil white race, who in their turn subverted the black utopia and enslaved its inhabitants. It all sounds like a bizarre riff on Milton, though you could argue that *Paradise Lost* is itself a fairly bizarre riff.

During the Second World War, literature—middlebrow or otherwise—enjoyed an unprecedented boom. In its end-of-the-year survey, *Time* reported that "Nineteen forty-three was the most remarkable in the 150-year-old history of U.S. publishing." Total book sales jumped by about a quarter, to an estimated 300 million. Fifteen million of them were about religion, including a new Modern Library edition of the King James Version. Bibles were in such demand that some bookstores rationed them, even in godless Manhattan. Pocket Books sold 38 million paperbacks, up from 5 million in 1940, but at the other end of the market university press sales were growing apace: in October the *Columbia Encyclopedia* spiked by 1,500 percent.

"It's unbelievable. It's frightening," exclaimed Bennett Cerf of Random House. The manager of Scribner's Fifth Avenue bookstore coolly noted that it made his job much easier: "At 9 o'clock we just open the doors and jump out of the way." And *Time* hailed the arrival of what "all the carriers and custodians of U.S. culture had hoped for all their lives: a time when book-reading and book-buying reached outside the narrow quarters of the intellectuals and became the business of the whole vast literate population of the U.S." There was a huge audience for serious discussions of the shape of the post-war global order.[26] In the realm of middlebrow intellect, bestsellers included Van Wyck Brooks's *The World of Washington Irving*, Douglas Southall Freeman's *Gettysburg to Appomattox*, George Santayana's autobiography *Persons and Places*, and *Yankee from Olympus*, Catherine Drinker Bowen's biography of Oliver Wendell Holmes. Sales of Gunnar Myrdal's *An American Dilemma* were disappointing, but not because readers were reluctant to touch race issues: Lillian Smith's sensational novel of interracial sex, *Strange Fruit*, was the top fiction bestseller.[27]

If your grandfather served in the US military during the Second World War, and you've kept his memorabilia in an attic, you may well find there an Armed Services Edition book, one of more than 120 million printed (roughly eight volumes for every active duty soldier, sailor, and airman). They were cheap, compact paperbacks (production cost 6 cents each), sized to fit in a standard GI pocket. As one serviceman put it, "They are a popular as pin-up girls," and another warned that "to heave one in the garbage can is tantamount to striking your grandmother."[28] (In addition, tens of millions of standard paperbacks were sold or donated to the armed forces, perhaps as many as 50 million Pocket Books alone.)[29]

The Armed Services Editions succeeded because they represented (deliberately) a cross-section of contemporary American trade publishing. The 1,322 titles were mainly middlebrow fiction (Howard Fast, J. P. Marquand, MacKinlay Kantor), humor (James Thurber, Robert Benchley), punditry (Walter Lippmann, H. L. Mencken), popular science, accessible poetry (Carl Sandburg, Robert Frost), biography (from George M. Cohan to Joe Louis), mysteries, westerns, sports, travel and adventure, pop music (Benny Goodman, George Gershwin), *Dracula*, *Tarzan of the Apes*, and history (usually military). But mixed in were some challenging classics: *Lord Jim*, Charles Lamb's essays, Plato's *Republic*, *Jane Eyre*, *Vanity Fair* and *Henry Esmond*, *Tristram Shandy*, Lytton Strachey's *Eminent Victorians*, several Dickens novels, Shelley and Keats, Tennyson and A. E. Housman, Whitman and the Brownings, Robert Herrick and Leo Tolstoy, Eugene O'Neill's plays, *The Education of Henry Adams*, Henry James, Virginia Woolf's *The Years*, Margaret Mead's *Coming of Age in Samoa*, *The Odyssey* translated by T. E. Lawrence, stories by Aldous Huxley, and Mark Van Doren on Shakespeare.[30] You could have not only *Moby Dick*, but *Omoo* and *Typee* as well. "Hot stuff," exclaimed a Marine on reading the last of these. "That guy wrote about three islands I'd been on!"[31] A Brooklyn private who probably never would have encountered it otherwise discovered that he enjoyed *Candide*, especially Dr Pangloss. (That response was understandable, given that he was assigned to dynamite German pillboxes during the Normandy invasion, while patriotic Hollywood movies trumpeted that this was the best of all possible wars.)[32] *The Great Gatsby* had been poorly received by critics when it was published in 1925, and sold only 25,000 copies by 1942, but 155,000 copies of the Armed Services edition were distributed. Somehow the tale of too-rich Jazz Age wastrels resonated with soldiers in foxholes, and it was launched into the literary canon.[33] (Today it sells a half-million copies a year.)[34]

Lewis Gannett, the *New York Herald Tribune* book critic, found ASEs everywhere: "From hospitals in England, from Negro service units in Normandy... in the front lines and at the rear, in jeeps, in pillboxes, in planes, at bases." There was "a division where the noncoms and privates at the back of the general's war tent were all reading and discussing constantly—they had a lot of time when they were just on duty, with nothing to do except be on duty, and they wanted good books."[35] If anything, letter-writers requested more classics. One asked for Shakespeare and Bernard Shaw. Another said that the men in his unit wanted Dumas and Balzac, and "would like to get hold of *Anna Karenina* (literally)."[36]

Gatsby, and perhaps most of the ASEs, had obvious escapist appeal. Pinned down in a ditch by fearsome enemy fire, one private decided, "It was no use to stew and fret; events were completely beyond my control," so he calmed his mind with Lytton Strachey's *Queen Victoria*.[37] Betty Smith's *A Tree Grows in Brooklyn* elicited 1,500 fan letters a year from servicemen, ten times as many as she received from civilians, and Rosemary Taylor's *Chicken Every Sunday* offered heartwarming nostalgia for home.[38] Two other bestsellers appealed to the other major preoccupation of soldiers: Kathleen Winsor's *Forever Amber* (a Restoration romance verging on pornography) and Lillian Smith's *Strange Fruit* (also fairly steamy). The fact that both novels were banned in Boston was frequently cited by servicemen as a recommendation.[39] Three soldiers in a hospital ward requested *Forever Amber*, but their hands were so badly burned that they could not carry the full weight even of a paperback, so an army librarian tore the book apart and gave them a few pages at a time.[40]

Some middlebrow ASEs struck surprisingly deep psychological chords. The stories of Katherine Anne Porter elicited hundreds of letters, one of which praised her ability to recall "frightening emotions where we all... once lived—lost when rejected, content when loved, made into small witch-ridden animals when abused."[41] In May 1944 a Marine confessed to Betty Smith that *A Tree Grows in Brooklyn* had reduced him to tears. "I'm not ashamed," he wrote. While recovering from malaria, "I have read it twice and am halfway through it again...Every time I read it, I feel more deeply than I did before." As he explained, "I went through hell in two years of combat overseas... Ever since the first time I struggled through knee deep mud...carrying a stretcher from which my buddie's life dripped away in precious blood and I was powerless to help him, I have felt hard and cynical against this world and have felt sure that I was no longer capable of loving anything or anybody." But *A Tree Grows in Brooklyn* had restored his capacity for empathy: "I can't explain the emotional reaction that took place, I only know that it happened and that this heart of mine turned over and became alive again. A surge of confidence has swept through me and I feel that maybe a fellow has a fighting chance in this world after all."[42]

Beyond actual combat (which the large majority of US armed services personnel never experienced), two aspects of war were particularly hard to bear. The first was the loss of individuality. "We come from a nation and a culture that values life and the individual," observed one Marine. "To find oneself in a situation where your life seems of little value is the ultimate in loneliness."[43] The second was absolute boredom. A respite from both could be found in reading, where you could be fully engaged, intellectually alive, and (as long as you followed orders about mundane matters) absolutely free. Stationed in Alaska to stand guard against a Japanese attack that never came, Irving Howe had nothing to do but "read for the unalloyed pleasure of knowledge. I read about the Maoris and Matthew Arnold's critical thought, the Bolshevik Revolution and the decline of Rome. In nearly two years in Alaska I must have read 150 solid books, more and better ones than any time before or since."[44] Top brass made sure that the Alaska Army was well supplied with libraries, correctly anticipating that it might spend the entire war sitting and waiting.[45] In effect, Howe enjoyed a graduate fellowship in literature fully funded by the US Army, and he went on to become a leading New York intellectual.

Thus, among both soldiers and civilians, middlebrow had called into existence a vast new book-reading public. And now, thanks to the paperback revolution, literature was far cheaper. Paperback sales jumped from 40 million in 1943 to 270 million by 1952.[46] Many of them were pulp westerns and thrillers, and even better books were marred by tawdry art. (The cover of *Nineteen Eighty-Four* foregrounded

Julia's bosom rather than Winston Smith.) But more and more of them were quality paperbacks—Anchor Books, New American Library—which made classics inexpensively available for college courses and an increasingly sophisticated reading public.

Given its enormous popularity in the first half of the twentieth century, one has to ask: Who (or what) killed middlebrow? Perhaps we can answer that with a post-mortem on one of the most famous examples of the genre, Paul de Kruif's *Microbe Hunters* (1926). De Kruif started out as a productive research bacteriologist, but he also knew how to write for the *Ladies' Home Journal* and *Reader's Digest*, and in 1922 he left the lab to become a full-time author. He closely collaborated with Sinclair Lewis on *Arrowsmith*, and was rewarded with a 25 percent share of the royalties: some say he should have been listed as co-author. His next literary venture was *Microbe Hunters*, a collection of mini-biographies of twelve pioneering microbiologists. A critical reader might conclude that, like *Arrowsmith*, it was a work of middlebrow fiction. The treatment of scientific issues was simplistic, but the twelve stories were all vivid and full of human interest. Every scientist was a hero, relentlessly pushing back the frontiers of medical knowledge, overcoming enormous obstacles to win famous victories in the war against disease (the book was full of military metaphors). Where the historical record ran thin, de Kruif simply made up dialogue and stage directions. ("Then Pasteur's eyebrows cocked at them, and his thinning grey hair seemed to stiffen: 'Do the same experiment over again—no matter if it failed the last time—it may look foolish to you, but the important thing is not to leave the subject!'") *Microbe Hunters* sold a half-million copies in its first decade, inspired any number of high-school biology students, and established the template for a whole subgenre of popular science history.[47]

In 1951 the firm of Alfred A. Knopf would score an equal success for archaeology with C. W. Ceram's *Gods, Graves, and Scholars*, which explicitly followed de Kruif as a model. Ceram explained that he had "deliberately chosen for portrayal those cultures whose exploration has been richly fraught with romantic adventure"—and since he could not find any romantic adventures in Chinese archaeology, he had nothing to write about that. Regardless, *Gods, Graves, and Scholars* was selected by the Book-of-the-Month Club and became a bestseller not only in English, but in thirteen translations as well.

One would expect Knopf to repeat the de Kruif/Ceram formula, but soon Knopf editor Harold Strauss began nudging his authors in a more sophisticated direction. In 1952 he recruited University of Pennsylvania professor Harold S. Coon to write a history of anthropology for general readers, but something "somewhat more serious and scholarly...We would not expect a hopped-up, slick popularization." There should be less biography, more "controversial theories" and technical detail. "Everything should be done which will make that book more accessible to the intelligent general reader," but at the same time "nothing should be done which damages the scholarship and the authority of an important book." Coon ultimately produced *The Story of Man* (1954), which clearly broke with the de Kruif/Ceram model: it was solidly grounded in scientific literature, and anthropologists writing in professional journals treated it with respect. It also proved that a serious history of anthropology could make the *New York Times* bestseller list. When he saw an early draft of Coon's next book, *The Seven Caves*, Strauss prodded the author still further: "I do think you are sacrificing anthropology and archaeology too much. It is true that this will be primarily a human interest book, but its sense of suspense, its drama, must revolve around your discoveries" rather than personalities.

As Strauss explained to another author in 1958, "Times have changed a bit, and it is now possible to publish trade books in the field of science for the general reader with a *slightly*—I repeat—slightly— increased seriousness, and a corresponding slight decrease in sugar coating, such as details about the personal lives of the scientists." The change was more than slight, and it was driven by hard evidence of audience response. Knopf's popular-science books provoked numerous letters from readers who corrected mistakes, pointed out gaps, and alerted the authors to more up-to-date scholarship. The letter-writers were almost all lay people, and usually they were right. Thanks largely to the GI Bill and the huge expansion of higher education after the Second World War, American readers were now better informed, and they were demanding something more challenging than middlebrow.[48]

By the 1950s and 1960s, books that engaged with important political and social issues were transforming the American cultural landscape. Yale University Press assumed that David Riesman's *The Lonely Crowd*

(1950) would only interest academics and printed just 3,000 copies, but it struck a chord among general readers, sold 600,000 Anchor paperbacks, and by 2002 had almost 1.5 million copies in print. Now consider this long list of books, all published between 1952 and 1966, and think about what they had in common:

Whittaker Chambers, *Witness* (1952)
Alfred Kinsey, *Sexual Behavior in the Human Female* (1953)
James Baldwin, *Notes of a Native Son* (1955)
C. Wright Mills, *The Power Elite* (1956)
William H. Whyte, *The Organization Man* (1956)
Vance Packard, *The Hidden Persuaders* (1957)
John Kenneth Galbraith, *The Affluent Society* (1958)
Elie Wiesel, *Night* (1958)
Paul Goodman, *Growing Up Absurd* (1960)
Daniel Bell, *The End of Ideology* (1960)
Jane Jacobs, *The Death and Life of Great American Cities* (1961)
Barbara Tuchman, *The Guns of August* (1962)
Rachel Carson, *Silent Spring* (1962)
Michael Harrington, *The Other America* (1962)
Betty Friedan, *The Feminine Mystique* (1963)
Hannah Arendt, *Eichmann in Jerusalem* (1963)
Marshall McLuhan, *Understanding Media* (1964)
The Autobiography of Malcolm X (1965)
William Masters and Virginia Johnston, *Human Sexual Response* (1966)

All of these books were challenging and disturbing, each of them transformed American cultural debate, none of them was middlebrow, and yet all of them ranked among the top ten on the *Publishers Weekly* annual ranking of non-fiction bestsellers. America had created something unprecedented in history—a mass highbrow market—and that left no room for middlebrow.

Or have those obituaries been greatly exaggerated? As a popularizer of semi-serious literature, Oprah Winfrey has been compared to Arnold Bennett, and has been subjected to the same kind of highbrow dismissal.[49] In fact the selections of Oprah's Book Club (OBC) were not all tearjerkers, and most of them were favorably assessed by the *New York Times Book Review*.[50] Oprah's endorsement could sell hundreds of thousands of books, almost 2 million in the case of her first selection, Jacquelyne Mitchard's *The Deep End of the Ocean*. *US News & World Report* found that heretofore book-club members had been "mostly college-educated, white, suburban couples, particularly in the West," but Oprah was reaching "blue-collar urban women from the South and Northeast." Barnes and Noble was pleased to report that "Seventy-five percent of the people who buy the Book Club title are buying something else, too... They shop, they browse, and then they come back." Thanks to her, fiction shot to the top of the *Publishers Weekly* bestseller list, which had heretofore been dominated by self-help, religion, health, and computer manuals.[51]

So where Oprah's detractors accused her of pandering to middlebrow tastes, her defenders countered that she was calling a new book-reading public into existence. Business economist Craig Garthwaite has subjected these claims to rigorous statistical analysis, and found that they were both wrong. True, an OBC endorsement reliably boosted sales of a selected title by 700,000 to a million copies, but there was no overall increase in sales for the publishing industry as a whole. In the weeks immediately following an OBC selection, there was a significant decrease in sales of mystery, action, and romance titles, but an increase in sales of classics. OBC, then, was not creating new book customers, it was stealing existing customers: regular book buyers who would have read something else if Oprah had never existed.

But even if we aren't buying more books, Oprah had arguably inspired us to read better books. Her selections were generally more complex and artistic than the mystery/action/romance novels they displaced. And by introducing her readers to quality contemporary and classic fiction, she may have broken down their resistance to reading classics, a genre which generally enjoyed a boost in sales. Bear in mind that overall book sales can actually be depressed by increasing sales of classics: since they are longer, more difficult, and take more time to read, they can crowd out trashier books, an obvious problem when OBC recommended *Anna Karenina* and *Great Expectations*.

The evidence also suggests that readers followed Oprah's suggestions not out of slavish celebrity-worship but because they found her a genuinely reliable guide to reading. An OBC endorsement immediately boosted sales of a given title into the stratosphere, but then weekly sales declined only gradually. Twenty-six weeks after the endorsement, sales were still nearly five times what they had been the week before the endorsement. This suggests a literary multiplier effect: those who watched OBC broadcasts enjoyed the books and then recommended them to their friends, many of whom were not regular Oprah watchers. Moreover, selection by OBC boosted sales of other titles by the same author, though here the surge peaked about twelve weeks after the broadcast. All this indicates that, like Book-of-the-Month Club judges, Oprah instinctively recognized the kind of books her audience enjoyed.[52]

And like Henry Siedel Canby, she emphasized that her readings were not academic readings: "If we were reading this in English class, our English teacher would be talking about the levels of confession for everybody. And I'd be like: did she know that that was supposed to be part of the theme of the book?"[53] In fact, her one conspicuous failure came when she tried to follow the collegiate model of literary analysis. The January 1998 selection, Toni Morrison's *Paradise*, was opaque and baffling, and instead of the usual round-table debate in a television studio, the discussion was moved to a Princeton classroom, where Morrison assumed the authoritative professorial role of explaining (or not explaining) the book. The audience was vocally frustrated, and the ratings were very low.

We also recall the 2001 brouhaha when Oprah selected Jonathan Franzen's *The Corrections*. Franzen suggested that he was "solidly in the high-art literary tradition" and she wasn't, and found himself disinvited from her program. What's significant here is that, in the ensuing debate, the media almost unanimously sided with Oprah.

Far from commodifying literature, Oprah never personally profited from the books she promoted. Novelist Jacquelyne Mitchard described her as "utterly independent; there's no way to buy her. No one has enough money in the world to buy her...She makes her selections based on her honest opinion of what she thinks is best for her audience." One PR agent complained that, though an OBC endorsement would be worth a king's ransom to any publisher, angling for one was a waste of effort: "People tell you to write these wonderful letters, but it doesn't matter. They run their show like Fort Knox. They do what they want to do." And in fact Oprah's operation was far more independent than the general run of literary reviews, dependent as they are on publishers' advertising.[54]

Plenty of critics have taken issue with Oprah's selections. John Steinbeck is all very well, but why *East of Eden*? It seems a highly idiosyncratic choice: a gripping story to be sure, but hardly a classic. And that, for Oprah, was precisely the point. Even though journalists described her second book club as devoted to the "classics," she avoided that term. She described them as "great books," but not "*the* Great Books." In fact she had only shifted her focus from contemporary to older novels, but throughout she made clear her sole criterion for selection: she chose books that spoke to her. Robert James Waller's *The Bridges of Madison County* was a sentimental romance, but she read it in one sitting, broke down in tears, and phoned the author. "I know it wasn't literature," she granted, "I just loved the idea of the story. Give me that, OK? Just give me that."[55]

That personal passion, which she dramatically broadcast in her programs, gave her authenticity in the eyes of her readers. The first priority of any classroom teacher is to convince his students that the book before them is worth reading: bloodless dissection and formulaic criticism won't accomplish that, but wild enthusiasm will. It doesn't matter if you're under-theorized as long as you're over the top. In this sense Oprah echoed Hugh Hefner, when he said that he edited the kind of magazine he wanted to read. If you're so inclined, you can fault them both for an unhealthy obsession with women's bodies, whether via centerfolds or dieting. But their genuine book lust is vastly more important.

Notes

1. Joan Judge, "In Search of the Chinese Common Reader: Usable Knowledge and Wondrous Ignorance in the Age of Global Science," unpublished paper. See also Liu Ts'un-yan, ed., *Chinese Middlebrow Fiction from the Ch'in and Early Republican Eras* (Hong Kong: Chinese University Press, 1984).
2. <http://mediate18.nl/>.
3. E. L. Godkin, "The Chromo-Civilization," in *Reflections and Comments 1865–1895* (New York: Charles Scribner's Sons, 1895), 199–205.
4. Frank Felsenstein and James J. Connolly, *What Middletown Read: Print Culture in an American Small City* (Amherst and Boston: University of Massachusetts Press, 2015), ch. 6.
5. Joseph F. Kett, *The Pursuit of Knowledge Under Difficulties: From Self-Improvement to Adult Education in America, 1750–1990* (Stanford: Stanford University Press, 1994), 153–6.
6. Elizabeth Long, *Book Clubs: Women and the Uses of Reading in Everyday Life* (Chicago and London: University of Chicago Press, 2003), 34–58.

7. Katherine West Scheil, *She Hath Been Reading: Women and Shakespeare Clubs in America* (Ithaca and London: Cornell University Press, 2012), 1–36.

8. Ibid., 38–40.

9. Ibid., 50–2.

10. Ibid., 32–9.

11. Ibid., 54–7.

12. Robert S. Lynd and Helen Merrell Lynd, *Middletown: A Study in American Culture* (New York; Harcourt Brace Jovanovich, 1957), 229–42, 290–1. Robert S. Lynd and Helen Merrell Lynd, *Middletown in Transition* (New York: Harcourt, Brace, 1937), 569.

13. <www.booksofthecentury.com>.

14. Janice A. Radway, *A Feeling for Books: The Book-of-the-Month Club, Literary Taste, and Middle-Class Desire* (Chapel Hill and London: University of North Carolina Press, 1997), 194–242, 264–79.

15. Douglas Waples, *People and Print: Social Aspects of Reading in the Depression* (Chicago: University of Chicago Press, n.d.), 113.

16. "Design for Giving," *Saturday Review of Literature*, 7 Feb. 1942.

17. Douglas Waples and Ralph W. Tyler, *What People Want to Read About* (Chicago: American Library Association and University of Chicago Press, 1931), xvii.

18. Ibid., chs. 2–3.

19. Jonathan Wild, "'A Strongly Felt Need': Wilfred Whitten/John O'London and the Rise of the New Reading Public," in *Middlebrow Literary Cultures: The Battle of the Brows, 1920–1960*, ed. Erica Brown and Mary Grover (Basingstoke: Palgrave Macmillan, 2012), 98–111.

20. Adrian Bingham, "Cultural Hierarchies and the Interwar British Press," in *Middlebrow Literary Cultures: The Battle of the Brows, 1920–1960*, ed. Erica Brown and Mary Grover (Basingstoke: Palgrave Macmillan, 2012), 55–68.

21. John Shapcott, "Aesthetics for Everyman: Arnold Bennett's *Evening Standard* Columns," in *Middlebrow Literary Cultures: The Battle of the Brows, 1920–1960*, ed. Erica Brown and Mary Grover (Basingstoke: Palgrave Macmillan, 2012), 82–97.

22. Melissa Schaub, *Middlebrow Feminism in Classic British Detective Fiction: The Female Gentleman* (Basingstoke and New York: Palgrave Macmillan, 2013), esp. ch. 3.

23. Nicola Humble, "The Queer Pleasures of Reading: Camp and the Middlebrow," in *Middlebrow Literary Cultures: The Battle of the Brows, 1920–1960*, ed. Erica Brown and Mary Grover (Basingstoke: Palgrave Macmillan, 2012), 218–30.

24. Jaime Harker, *Middlebrow Queer: Christopher Isherwood in America* (Minneapolis: University of Minnesota Press, 2013), ch. 1.

25. Malcolm X, *The Autobiography of Malcolm X* (New York: Ballantine, 1992), 181–2, 198–219.

26. "The Year in Books," *Time* (20 Dec. 1943).

27. "The Year in Books," *Time* (18 Dec. 1944).

28. Molly Guptill Manning, *When Books Went to War: The Stories that Helped Us Win World War II* (Boston and New York: Houghton Mifflin Harcourt, 2014), xiv–xv, 75.

29. John Jamieson, *Books for the Army: The Army Library Service in the Second World War* (New York: Columbia University Press, 1950), 1–2, 286.

30. A complete bibliography is in Manning, *When Books Went to War*, 202–32.

31. Ibid., 161–2.
32. Jamieson, *Books for the Army*, 159.
33. Manning, *When Books Went to War*, 81.
34. Deirdre Donahue, "'The Great Gatsby' by the Numbers," *USA Today* (7 May 2013).
35. Manning, *When Books Went to War*, 89–90.
36. Ibid., 119–20.
37. Ibid., 127–8.
38. Ibid., 105–10.
39. Ibid., 123–5.
40. Jamieson, *Books for the Army*, 88.
41. Manning, *When Books Went to War*, 103–4.
42. Ibid., xi–xii.
43. Ibid., 43–4.
44. Irving Howe, *A Margin of Hope: An Intellectual Autobiography* (New York: Harcourt Brace Jovanovich, 1984), 95.
45. Jamieson, *Books for the Army*, 100–4.
46. Manning, *When Books Went to War*, 191.
47. William C. Summers, "*Microbe Hunters* Revisited," *International Microbiology* 1: 65–8.
48. Beth Luey, "'Leading the Public Gently': Popular Science Books in the 1950s," *Book History* 2 (1999): 218–53.
49. Kathleen Rooney, *Reading with Oprah: The Book Club that Changed America* (Fayetteville, Ark.: University of Arkansas Press, 2005), 23–5.
50. Ibid., 69, 78.
51. Ibid., 120–3.
52. Craig. L. Garthwaite, "Demand Spillovers, Combative Advertising, and Celebrity Endorsements," *American Economic Journal: Applied Economics* 6(2014): 76–104.
53. Long, *Book Clubs*, 204.
54. Rooney, *Reading with Oprah*, 124–5.
55. Ibid., 145, 199–200.

4

Dreamers of the Ghetto

Not only was my mother not a reader, but I remember being in the back hallway when I was about nine—I'm going to say this without crying—and my mother threw the door open and grabbed a book out of my hand and said, "you're nothing but a something-something bookworm. Get your butt outside! You think you're better than the other kids. And I'm not taking you to no library!" I was treated as though there was something wrong with me because I wanted to read all the time.[1]

(Oprah Winfrey)

This chapter does not pretend to offer a complete history of the African-American common reader. It only sketches in a few outlines of a much bigger story. But when that history is written, it will inevitably have to confront this painful contradiction. The woman who did more than any contemporary American to promote reading was raised by a mother who hated books.

For an explanation, we might begin by looking to Frederick Douglass's classic autobiography. Once he realized that most slave-owners feared black literacy, "I understood the pathway from slavery to freedom," and determined, "at whatever cost of trouble, to learn how to read." He developed strategies to acquire literacy surreptitiously, offering bread to poor white boys in return for reading lessons. And in *The Columbian Orator*, an anthology of great speeches, he found inspirational literature that spoke directly to his condition, in particular Sheridan's philippics for Catholic emancipation. However, later he fell into the hands of a more brutal master, who completely (but temporarily) broke his desire to read: "My natural elasticity was crushed, my intellect languished, the disposition to read departed, the cheerful spark that lingered about my eye died; the dark night of slavery closed in upon me; and behold a man transformed into a brute!"[2] In another slave narrative, Leonard Black testified that when he bought something to read, his master "made me sick of books by beating me like a dog...He whipped me so very severely that he overcame my thirst for knowledge, and I relinquished its pursuit," at least until he escaped from bondage.[3]

So there were two possible and polar opposite responses to the terror campaign against black readers. One was to acquire literacy at all costs and by any means necessary. "I do begrudge your education," admitted a black steamboat steward as he served lunch to a white college student. "I would steal your learning if I could."[4] But others internalized the whippings and developed a fear of and aversion to books. These are both legacies of slavery, and they both survived far beyond the slave era.

In the 1930s, interviews carried out by the Federal Writers Project with former slaves suggested that no more than 5 percent of them were literate. But another study found that as many as 20 percent of newspaper advertisements for runaway slaves in Kentucky specified that they could read. Apparently literate slaves were less acquiescent, more restless, better equipped to navigate the outside world, and more willing to make a run for it.[5] Several Southern states banned literacy education for slaves, and stories circulated about fearsome punishments for breaking that taboo: whippings, amputations of fingers, even executions. The laws weren't always enforced, and the horror stories were sometimes exaggerated, but still they were powerful deterrents to literacy. Sarah Fitzpatrick, who had been an Alabama house servant during the Civil War, recalled that quite a few slaves were literate, but "de kep' dat up deir sleeve, dey played dumb lack dey couldn't read a bit till after surrender."[6] Slaves sometimes taught reading to each other, or taught themselves with Noah Webster's blue-back speller. They borrowed (or occasionally stole) books from their masters. Some learned at Sunday school, and some masters wanted slaves who could study their Bible, read novels aloud at night, and handle basic correspondence. And free blacks in both the South and North organized their own schools—a total of forty-four in Philadelphia, compared with just twelve that were provided for black pupils by white patrons.[7]

As one Mississippi slaveholder recalled, "there ent one of my niggers but what can read; read good too—better'n I can at any rate." When asked how they learned, he explained simply, "Taught themselves. I b'lieve there was one on 'em that I bought, that could read, and he taught all the rest."[8] Father Josiah Henson, as an ex-slave, did not doubt that literacy was the basic key to his freedom:

> It was, and has ever been since, a great comfort to me to have made this acquisition; though it has made me comprehend better the terrible abyss of ignorance in which I had plunged all my previous life. It made me also feel more deeply and bitterly the oppression under which I had toiled and groaned; but the crushing and cruel nature of which I had not appreciated, till I found out, in some slight degree, from what I had been debarred. At the same time it made me more anxious than before to do something for the rescue and elevation of those who were suffering the same evils I had endured and who did not know how degraded and ignorant they really were.[9]

In Reconstruction there was surge of black literacy instruction conducted by the Freemen's Bureau, but it was also largely a self-help effort. The Northern Methodists often recruited illiterate black preachers, but the African Methodist Episcopal Church required full literacy in their clergy. Not only was that skill essential to exercising the franchise: only the ability to read labor contracts would prevent the reimposition of slavery under another name.[10]

Black Americans reduced their adult illiteracy rate from 93 percent in 1865 to 23 percent in 1920, agitating relentlessly for the expansion of public education. Though they didn't have the wealth or influence of white women's clubs, black women's clubs worked to create and expand libraries for their communities. Inspired by Booker T. Washington's *Up from Slavery*, Andrew Carnegie invested in libraries for black colleges, though only about 7 percent of his library grants went to the Southern states.[11]

To say that African-Americans have a rich oral culture and musical culture is obviously true, but it may be something of a backhanded compliment, implying that they don't have a reading culture. Not until the unexpected 1992 success of Terry McMillan's *Waiting to Exhale* did mainstream publishers fully wake up to the existence of a large black book-buying public. But Elizabeth McHenry excavated a long history of black literary clubs, going back to the 1820s. The stated objectives of the Colored Reading Society of Philadelphia (founded 1828) were, quite simply, "a liberal education" and the "cultivation of taste." Through "the study of belle lettres"—meaning the ancient classics and "our best English writers"—the members worked to "discipline the mind itself, to strengthen and enlarge its powers, to form habits of close and accurate thinking, and to acquire a facility of classifying and arranging, analyzing and comparing our ideas on different subjects." That may strike us today as exceedingly genteel, but in this time and context it was a radical affirmation of equality and self-determination. All of the black literary societies, setting their own reading agendas and drawing on their own resources, set out to acquire the intellectual skills necessary to act and speak as free citizens—the very skills that whites had denied them. One member of the Female Literary Association (also based in Philadelphia) proclaimed that she learned rhetoric from Demosthenes, whose "eloquence was more dreaded...than all the fleets and armies of Athens." You can see why that might appeal to a black audience in a slave-owning nation.[12] But reading was not just a means to achieving freedom: it was freedom itself. "We must do just what white men do," demanded Frederick Douglass. "It must no longer be...white editor, and black street cleaner."[13] As one black paper proclaimed in 1837, a free reader could do and experience everything that a slave could not:

> By reading you may visit all countries, converse with the wise, good, and great, who have lived in any age or country, imbibe their very feelings and sentiments and view every thing elegant in architecture, sculpture, and painting. By reading you may ascend to those remote regions where other spheres encircle other suns, where other stars illuminate a new expanse of skies, and enkindle the most sublime emotions that can animate the human soul.[14]

True, nineteenth-century black literary societies and newspapers drew their models mainly from the Western classics, if only because most African-American literature hadn't been written yet. But from the very start they promoted emerging black authors. *Freedom's Journal*, the first African-American periodical, celebrated Phillis Wheatley and Olaudah Equiano.[15] In his papers Frederick Douglass discussed slave narratives alongside Emerson, Hawthorne, Whittier, and Longfellow, sending the message that they were all partners in the construction of a distinctively American literature. He serialized *Bleak House* while reporting on the success of *Uncle Tom's Cabin*, and he ran two long and worshipful obituaries for Charlotte Brontë. Evidently some readers questioned why he put Charles Dickens and Harriet Beecher Stowe side by side, but it made perfect sense: *Bleak House, Uncle Tom's Cabin, Jane Eyre,* and *The Autobiography of Frederick Douglass* were all passionate denunciations of human bondage.[16]

And it was the most militant blacks who demanded the right to a classical education. While Booker T. Washington promoted vocational training, the Boston Literary and Historical Association directly opposed his accommodationist politics, warning that "the idea lying back of it is the relegating of a race to serfdom." In 1902 George W. Forbes, who had a degree from Amherst College and worked for the Boston Public Library, addressed the group about the great poets that every educated person had to read: Milton, Spenser, Homer, Aeschylus, Longfellow, Lowell, Emerson, Dryden, Pope, Browning, Pindar, Sappho. Today in some literature faculties you could be court-martialed for teaching that syllabus, which included no black authors. But someone in Forbes's audience said that he had kindled the "hope the great American epic of the joys and sorrows of our blood and kindred, of those who have gone before us, would one day be written." Black readers saw no conflict between classic literature and black literature, because they were confident that the first would fertilize the other. And of course they were right: Toni Morrison minored in Classics at Howard University.[17]

In the South most public libraries were segregated, separate and grossly unequal. (Elsewhere there usually was no formal segregation in libraries, but black neighborhoods were seriously under-served.) The black community in Tulsa organized its own library with little help from the city government and none from Carnegie, but it was destroyed (along with most of the black district) by a white pogrom in 1921.[18] In New Orleans in 1939 white libraries held 273,683 volumes, while blacks (more than a quarter of the population) were served by a single library with just 14,697 volumes. Only 42.73 percent of Southern whites had access to libraries, but that was twice the rate for blacks. In the rural South there was library service for just 5.48 percent of blacks—falling to absolute zero in Florida and Oklahoma.[19]

In turn-of-the-century Muncie, only fifteen library users (and 3.5 percent of the city's population) were black, compared with 2,585 borrowers who were identifiably white, but even this small sample offers an impressive glimpse into post-emancipation literary tastes. Much like white patrons, black readers borrowed mostly light fiction and children's books, but occasionally more serious literature. The library loaned out *Little Dorrit* to a barber's family, histories of prehistoric America and Europe since the fall of Rome to a farmer, *The Works of Daniel Webster* to a horticulturalist, *David Copperfield* to a janitor, George Eliot's essays and *The Mill on the Floss* to a teamster's daughter, Charles Darwin's *The Descent of Man* and Washington Irving's Hudson River stories to a day-laborer. A puddler at a rolling mill borrowed Israel Zangwill's *Dreamers of the Ghetto*: it was a collection of essays on eminent Jews, but perhaps the title resonated with him. Others took out *A Tale of Two Cities*, *Far from the Madding Crowd*, essays by T. H. Huxley, and (yes) *Uncle Tom's Cabin*. And a bootblack borrowed a hundred books in eight years, including *Jane Eyre*, *The Last of the Mohicans*, several works of ancient history, and (surprisingly, given his socioeconomic position) the social Darwinism of Herbert Spencer.[20]

As novelist Jessie Fauset confided to W. E. B. DuBois in 1907, the great books were her route to emancipation:

> Off in one of the little side-rooms stands my desk, covered with books that have caught my special fancy and awakened my thoughts. This is my *living*-room, where I pass my moods of bitterness and misunderstanding, and questioning and joy, too, I think. Often in the midst of a heap of books—the Rubaiyat and a Bible, Walter Pater's Essays, and "Robert Elsmere" and "Aurora Leigh," and books of belief, of insinuation, of open unbelief,—I bow my head on my desk in a passion of doubt and ignorance and longing, and ponder, ponder. Here on this desk is a book in which I jot down all the little, beautiful word-wonders whose truest meanings are so often unknown to me, but whose very mystery I love...High up on many of the shelves in the many rooms are books as yet unread by me, Schopenhauer and Tolstoi, Petrarch and Sappho, Goethe and Kant and Schilling [*sic*: it's not clear whether she meant Schiller or Schelling]...With such reading in store for me, is not my future rich?[21]

Like white clubwomen, black women in this period often organized Shakespeare clubs, though they usually had a broader curriculum than Shakespeare alone. Their mission was to build an educated class from the ground up, and therefore they promoted the study of classic literature in general as well as African-American authors. Not all black leaders endorsed this project of racial "uplift." Some dismissed the literary clubs as snobbish and pretentious. Booker T. Washington advised a student from an Alabama log cabin that she should forget her passion for Shakespeare and focus on learning "cooking and sewing and housekeeping and nursing and gardening." But the clubwomen were adamant: "Life without Literature is Death," was the credo of one club. As everyone remembered, under slavery they all had to live without literature. And there were men like the Galveston civil-rights leader Norris Wright Cuney, who studied ancient history, the classics, Byron, and especially Shakespeare. His daughter, musicologist Maud Cuney Hare, remembered that the family would perform selections from the plays, and a friend who walked with a limp would elicit from her father quotations of *Richard III*. Shakespeare was central to their lives, not something that had been borrowed from another culture.

Perhaps even more than the obvious Othello, black audiences identified with Shakespeare's other great black character, Macbeth. (Of course he was. Malcolm explicitly calls him "black Macbeth" (iv.iii.53)). It was a favorite role of Ira Aldridge, the first African-American stage star, and in the twenty-first century there have been a number of hip-hop productions, such as Ayodele Nzinga's *Mac, A Gangsta's Tale*. (Iambic pentameter translates easily into rap; arguably it *is* rap.) Orson Welles's celebrated 1935 "Voodoo Macbeth," reset in Haiti, was a huge hit in Harlem, but it was just one in a long history of similar productions, before and since. The Scottish play was habitually quoted by Frederick Douglass and anti-lynching activist Ida B. Wells-Barnett. And blacks offered a somewhat different reading of it than whites: for them, Macbeth was more combative and rebellious than manipulated, and Lady Macbeth admirably put steel into his spine. As a Chicago black paper editorialized, "God grant the race a few more Lady Macbeths like Ida Barnett to pump self-respect into our loud-mouthed Negro leaders."[22]

Oklahoma was only opened to non-Indian settlers in 1889, so while there was certainly racism and segregation, black and white settlers shared some common frontier values: self-reliance, assertiveness, adventurous entrepreneurialism, independent thinking, and a sense that culture was something that had to be built rather than inherited. In this milieu, young Ralph Ellison and his intellectual black friends embraced the ideal of the "Renaissance Man." "This, surely, would seem a most unlikely and even comic concept to introduce here," Ellison later recalled, and he couldn't explain where he had picked up the idea, but the answer should have been obvious. Though he was embarrassed by his middle name, Ralph Waldo Ellison clearly owed much to Ralph Waldo Emerson, who was very well known to black Oklahomans, was taught in the public schools, and was a favorite of black literary societies and magazines.[23] The *Woman's Era* recommended Emerson's rules for readers: "Never read any but famed books," and "Never read a book which is not a year old," which effectively limited the options to canonical literature.[24] Emerson's essay "The American Scholar" never used the term Renaissance Man, but it clearly defined him as a "whole man. Man is not a farmer, or a professor, or an engineer, but he is all. Man is priest, and scholar, and statesman, and producer, and soldier." He only becomes a "Man Thinking" when he breaks out of the prison of his particular vocation and embraces the entire human experience. He achieves that by studying classic literature, but not uncritically: reading past authors is a sterile exercise unless it inspires a new generation to create a new literature. "One must be an inventor to read well," Emerson asserts. "There is then creative reading as well as creative writing." These free readers are eternal nonconformists:

> For the ease and pleasure of treading the old road, accepting the fashions, the education, the religion of society, he takes the cross of making his own, and, of course, the self-accusation, the faint heart, the frequent uncertainty and loss of time, which are the nettles and tangling vines in the way of the self-relying and self-directed; and the state of virtual hostility in which he seems to stand to society, and especially to educated society.

And that individualism necessarily meant refusing narrow conceptions of identity:

Is it not the chief disgrace in the world, not to be an unit;—not to be reckoned one character;—not to yield that peculiar fruit which each man was created to bear, but to be reckoned in the gross, in the hundred, or the thousand, of the party, the section, to which we belong; and our opinion predicted geographically, as the north, or the south? Not so, brothers and friends,—please God, ours shall not be so. We will walk on our own feet; we will work with our own hands; we will speak our own minds.

That liberationist philosophy naturally appealed to the frontiersmen of Oklahoma—and black frontiersmen especially. It offered a "wide and unstructured latitude...which encourages the individual's imagination—up to the moment 'reality' closes in upon him—to range widely and, sometimes, even to soar." Among Ellison and his friends, it inspired "the voracious reading of which most of us were guilty and the vicarious identification and empathic adventuring which it encouraged." In his community there were already boys growing up without fathers (Ellison was only 3 when his father died), but they were effectively exempt from Oedipal conflict and free to seek surrogate parents anywhere, especially in literature:

We were seeking examples, patterns to live by, out of a freedom which for all its being ignored by the sociologists and subtle thinkers was implicit in the Negro situation. Father and mother substitutes also have a role to play in aiding the child to help create himself. Thus we fabricated our own heroes and ideals catch-as-catch can, and with an outrageous and irreverent sense of freedom. Yes, and in complete disregard for ideas of respectability or the surreal incongruity of some of our projections. Gamblers and scholars, jazz musicians and scientists, Negro cowboys and soldiers from the Spanish-American and First World Wars, movie stars and stunt men, figures from the Italian Renaissance and literature, both classical and popular, were combined with the special virtues of some local bootlegger, the eloquence of some Negro preacher, the strength and grace of some local athlete, the ruthlessness of some businessman-physician, the elegance in dress and manners of some headwaiter or hotel doorman.[25]

Ironically, this literary miscegenation was promoted by the racial obstacles in Oklahoma City, where segregation was real but less consistent than in the Deep South. A Carnegie-funded library opened in 1901, and for the next twenty years there was no trouble, until a black clergyman demanded to use it. No actual law barred him from entry, so the city fathers swiftly corrected that oversight by setting up a small black branch in what had been a pool-hall and stocking it with any books they could throw together. For Ralph and his friends, that very miscellaneous collection was a gold-mine, and they raced each other to read through it—first children's fiction, then westerns and crime novels, and in short order the classics. Fortunately, he did not yet realize they were classics, so he was able to read them with fresh eyes.

He also had access to Haldeman Julius Blue Books, published just across the state line in Kansas. Some black domestics brought home books and magazines discarded by their white employers, and Ralph's mother appropriated copies of *Vanity Fair* and *Literary Digest*, which (along with the pulps) he loved. His adoptive grandfather was the custodian of the law library at the Oklahoma state legislature, and it was marvelous to see him instruct white politicians on legal matters. The parents of a friend were schoolteachers who owned the Harvard Classics, in which he discovered Bernard Shaw and Guy de Maupassant. *Wuthering Heights* and *Jude the Obscure* "caused me an agony of unexpressible emotion": neither had any black characters, but it took no vast leap of imagination to identify with Heathcliff (the "dark-skinned" servant) and Jude Fawley (the stonemason barred from the great universities). And then there were the churches, schools, and barbershops—the (mainly oral) literary salons of the black community. "The drug store where I worked was such a place, where on days of bad weather the older men would sit with their pipes and tell tall tales, hunting yarns and homely versions of the classics." Confinement to segregated schools was a terrible injustice, but there at least African-American teachers could teach African-American literature, and one of them introduced him to Langston Hughes, Countee Cullen, Claude McKay, and James Weldon Johnson. Naturally he felt some pride, but his most compelling literary model was T. S. Eliot: he read *The Waste Land* at the Tuskegee Institute. "I was intrigued by its power to move me while eluding my understanding. Somehow its rhythms were often closer to those of jazz than were those of the Negro poets, and even though I could not understand then, its range of allusion was as mixed and as varied as that of Louis Armstrong." Any capable English teacher knows that you stretch students' minds by assigning them baffling books. Following up Eliot's footnotes, Ellison set to work decoding the poem, and his research led him to Ezra Pound, Ford Madox Ford, Sherwood Anderson, Gertrude Stein, Ernest Hemingway, F. Scott Fitzgerald, and eventually circled back to Melville and Twain. All of them were stocked in the Tuskegee Library and none of them was actually taught at the college—an ideal situation for Ellison, who could discover them on his own.[26]

His reading, then, was limitlessly promiscuous, a wonderful anarchy of print and orality, black and white, American and European, high and low and middlebrow. It meant drinking in "the diversity, fluidity and magical freedom of American life." "Diversity" was one of his favorite words, long before it became a fashionable cliché.[27]

True, this kind of self-education "violated all ideas of social hierarchy and order and all accepted conceptions of the hero handed down by cultural, religious and racist tradition." And a good thing too, for the result was the kind of inspirational cross-fertilization one finds in James Joyce and the Marx Brothers: "Our imaginations processed reality and dream, natural man and traditional hero, literature and folklore, like maniacal editors turned loose in some frantic film-cutting room." After all, "in our community, life was not so tightly structured as it would have been in the traditional South—or even in deceptively 'free' Harlem"—or, for that matter, in any college. After the leading universities began admitting substantial numbers of black students in the 1960s, they had to face the question of how much attention they would devote to black subjects, and inevitably there were struggles over resources and curricula. But there was no "culture war" in the black neighborhoods of 1920s Oklahoma City, where there were no course requirements, no budgets to fight over, and no deans' offices to occupy. If you wanted to do "black studies," it was all around you, and it in no way conflicted with the Western classics. In that unstructured symposium, jazzmen and Renaissance literature coexisted peacefully and creatively. As Ellison concluded, "it was no more incongruous, as seen from our own particular perspective in this land of incongruities, for young Negro Oklahomans to project themselves as Renaissance Men than for white Mississippians to see themselves as ancient Greeks

or noblemen out of Sir Walter Scott." At least the books read by
Ellison and his friends didn't impel them to start a civil war, but
neither were these young men "self-hating and defensive," as some
sociologists characterized black youth. No, their wide reading made
them divine egoists, as confident of their own genius as Oscar Wilde,
and with the same conviction that life must be lived as a work of art:

> We recognized and were proud of our group's own style wher-
> ever we discerned it—in jazzmen and prize fighters, ballplayers
> and tap dancers; in gesture, inflections, intonation, timbre and
> phrasing. Indeed, in all those nuances of expression and atti-
> tude which reveal a culture. We did not fully understand the
> cost of that style but we recognized within it an affirmation of
> life beyond question of our difficulty as Negroes.
>
> ... We felt, among ourselves at least, that we were supposed
> to be whoever we would and could be and do anything
> and everything which other boys did, and do it better. Not
> defensively ... but because we demanded it of ourselves. Because
> to measure up to our own standards was the only way of affirming
> our notion of manhood.[28]

In that autodidactic project, Ellison discovered "that nothing could go
unchallenged; especially that feverish industry dedicated to telling
Negroes who and what they are, and which can usually be counted
upon to deprive both humanity and culture of their complexity." He
found that white and black intellectuals alike fell into that reduction-
ism, not excluding "those of the so-called 'Negro Renaissance'." And
this meant that:

> the greatest difficulty for a Negro writer was the problem of
> revealing what he truly felt, rather than serving up what Negroes
> were supposed to feel, and were encouraged to feel. And linked
> to this was the difficulty, based on our long habit of deception
> and evasion, of depicting what really happened within our
> areas of American life, and putting down with honesty and
> without bowing to ideological expediencies the attitudes and
> values which give Negro American life its sense of wholeness
> and which render it bearable and human and, when measured
> by our own terms, desirable.

So how could you see the thing as it really is, and see it whole? By reading the great writers, and studying how they had achieved authenticity. True, most of them didn't address racial issues directly, and some of them were racists, but the reader could still selectively distill from them indispensable lessons. "Negro Americans have a highly developed ability to abstract desirable qualities from those around them, even from their enemies, and my sense of reality could reject bias while appreciating the truth revealed by achieved art." And without the sense of reality achieved by art, how will we deal with race or any other moral issue? Later, urged on by Richard Wright, he studied the technique of Dostoevsky, Henry James, Joseph Conrad, and James Joyce. He learned the literary uses of folklore from Eliot and Joyce. "No matter how strictly Negroes are segregated socially and politically, on the level of the imagination their ability to achieve freedom is limited only by their individual aspiration, insight, energy and will to do so." Though they were politically all over the map, and mostly ignored black people, "Marx, Freud, T. S. Eliot, Pound, Gertrude Stein and Hemingway...were to release me from whatever 'segregated' idea I might have had of my human possibilities. I was freed not by propagandists or by the example of [Richard] Wright—I did not know him at the time...—but by composers, novelists, and poets who spoke to me of more interesting and freer ways of life." He didn't reject the "protest novel" out of hand—Dickens, Dostoevsky, Twain, Malraux, and Kafka had all worked in that genre—but he was convinced that protest without art would be impotent.[29]

Of course, Ellison was an extraordinary reader, and we know quite a lot about him. What about our original subject, the black common reader, about whom we know very little? There were the aforementioned literary societies, but they appealed mainly to middle classes and focused mostly on classic literature. The Durham Colored Library in North Carolina had an impressive collection of black literature, but we don't know how often it was borrowed—and Durham had an exceptionally large and prosperous black middle class.[30] The black library users in Muncie offer us a glimpse, but can we find a larger and more representative sample?

The writers of the Harlem Renaissance were deeply committed to creating an African-American book reading public, without which they would be dependent on white fans and patrons. The question is, did such a public exist? In 1910 there were 288 black periodicals with a total circulation of 500,000, but they served a population of nearly 10 million. There were precious few bookstores in black communities, and white-owned bookshops often did not welcome black customers, who in any case had limited disposable income. "The average Negro has not yet learned the value of good books," was Amy Jacques Garvey's severe conclusion in 1927. "Take Chicago, New York, Philadelphia and Cleveland, cities where the average Negro lives at a fairly high standard, which is chiefly due to the credit system. His home or apartment has a parlor which is not completely furnished unless it has a player-piano, Victrola, banjo and ukulele, but never a bookcase, and rarely one finds a single book of readable worth. Occasionally a detective story, Snappy Stories, or *True Romance* magazine, but how can a young race thrive on such drivel?"[31]

However, for all her militancy, Amy Garvey may have been selling these readers short. There were some impressive efforts at literary self-help. Lulline Long, a leading black businesswoman in Birmingham, donated money and effort to promote education in her community and maintained a library (including books on black history) in her beauty parlor. (In the segregation era, beauty salons were one of the very few entrepreneurial fields open to black women, and they have always been reading spaces for women in general.)[32] Greensboro, North Carolina founded a "Carnegie Negro Library" in 1924—and unlike most segregated libraries, this one was organized by the black community rather than white-dominated local governments. Though it was cramped (one user called it a "dollhouse," with room for just twenty readers) and poorly funded, it became a heavily used cultural center. Somehow, in that tiny space, the library accommodated students from the local high school and Bennett College (a nearby black college), children's story hours and reading programs, film series for children and adults, discussion groups devoted to contemporary books and world affairs, lecture series, a Heritage Club (devoted to local history), a Teenagers Library Club, and a Great Books group co-sponsored with Bennett College. Surrounding rural areas were served by a bookmobile and often by the head librarian delivering books in her own car. The library served as a neutral meeting-ground for the entire community (unlike the churches, with their denominational differences) and a base for the Greensboro Art Center, which offered art education for black residents. And it provided an array of newspapers, including black papers, at a time when many of its users couldn't afford to subscribe.[33]

In 1943 a revealing study of the African-American common reader was conducted in Beecher Terrace, a Louisville public housing community. At this point "the projects" were new, clean, and well maintained, a vast improvement over the hovels they replaced, and not yet ridden by crime and drugs. The residents were nearly all domestic, service, and industrial workers, but only 11 percent of households were headed by single mothers, and the unemployment rate was just 4.4 percent. As for schooling, 44.2 percent had some elementary education, 44.8 percent had attended high school, and nearly 10 percent had some exposure to higher education. Beecher Terrace offered a range of social and recreational services and was located near a black business district and a segregated branch library. It was a stable and hopeful community, and although life wasn't easy, it was improving. The investigator, Juanita Offutt, visited 616 homes and interviewed the residents about the books they owned, read, and borrowed from the library. And when she asked about their leisure activities, the most popular answer, volunteered by nearly a third of all residents, was reading. A 1938 study of Cincinnati had found that 34 percent of black homes were bookless,[34] but the figure for Beecher Terrace was just 7.3 percent, though four times as many had only a Bible, and another 13.1 percent only a Bible and dictionary. Nearly half of the Beecher Terrace homes had more substantial libraries, averaging 3.7 novels, 2.3 religious books, and 1.5 works of non-fiction.

Offutt compiled a complete inventory of all the books she found in residents' homes, a total of roughly 1,800 volumes. Mostly they were standard romantic and detective fiction, Tarzan, westerns, children's books, religious tomes, Sherlock Holmes, Rudyard Kipling, Louisa May Alcott, and seven copies of *How to Win Friends and Influence People*. But there were also some classics: *The Arabian Nights*, *Pride and Prejudice*, *Wuthering Heights* (four copies), *Pilgrim's Progress* (four copies), James Fenimore Cooper (eight individual volumes plus his collected works), eleven volumes of Charles Dickens (including three of *Oliver Twist*), Lewis Carroll, *Silas Marner* (three copies), *Madame Bovary*, John Dryden's *Marriage à la Mode*, *The Vicar of Wakefield*, *Far from the Madding Crowd* and *The Return of the Native*, Nathaniel Hawthorne, *The Hunchback of Notre Dame, Moby Dick, Ivanhoe* (three copies), *Tristram Shandy, Gulliver's Travels, The Ballad of Reading Gaol,* Emerson's essays (four copies), *Brave New World, Das Kapital, Thus Spake Zarathustra,* and twelve individual Shakespeare plays plus two volumes of his collected works. Eighty-three households stocked some poetry, mainly Robert Browning, Burns, Byron, Chaucer, Coleridge, Virgil, Kipling, Longfellow, James Russell Lowell, Masefield, Milton, Thomas Moore, Dante Gabriel Rossetti, Tennyson, Whittier, Palgrave's *Golden Treasury,* and nothing really modern. There was some contemporary middlebrow fiction: Pearl S. Buck's *The Good Earth* (three copies), A. J. Cronin, Daphne du Maurier's *Rebecca* (four copies), John Galsworthy, James Hilton's *Lost Horizon, Main Street* and *Arrowsmith,* Somerset Maugham, O. Henry, *All Quiet on the Western Front, Treasure Island* (8 copies), *The Grapes of Wrath,* Booth Tarkington, H. G. Wells, and even P. G. Wodehouse. And Offutt found seventeen sex manuals, including Krafft-Ebing's *Psychopathia Sexualis,* but mostly common-sense guides for married couples, such as Harland W. Long's *Sane Sex Life and Sane Sex Living*— middlebrow erotics, if you will. As Offutt conceded, "Frequently the tenants admitted that the books were given to them and that many of them had not been read by any one in the family." But the sex guides clearly had been bought and thumbed through.

Very few households regularly subscribed to magazines, but some were bought and read at least occasionally: the most popular were *Life* (23.3 percent of homes), *True Stories* (21.9 percent), *Good Housekeeping* (13. 1 percent), and the *Ladies Home Journal* (8.2 percent), compared to just 3.1 percent for *Time* and 1 percent for the *Crisis,* the NAACP organ. Four out of five households read the *Louisville Defender,* the local black weekly, a comparable proportion read the white-owned Louisville dailies, and only 5.5 percent of households never took in a newspaper. (In 1943 total circulation for African-American newspapers was 1,613, 255, more than triple the figure for 1910, and rising rapidly.)[35]

Three blocks from Beecher Terrace was the Western Colored Branch Library, housing 16,545 volumes and circulating 51,553 loans annually. For the city as a whole, black residents borrowed just under two volumes per capita each year. In half of the Beecher Terrace homes someone had a library card, though nearly two-thirds of them were children, and females outnumbered males by about 60/40.

Offutt listed just eighty-seven volumes borrowed by adults over a two-year period, including ten by black authors, *The Well of Loneliness*, and *Mein Kampf*.[36]

But Offutt was taken aback to discover that these 616 households possessed between them just twenty-four nonfiction volumes on "Negro life," eleven of them by or about Booker T. Washington. There were two copies each of *Uncle Tom's Cabin* and Carl Van Vechten's *Nigger Heaven*, but hardly any black-authored fiction or poetry: a few volumes of Paul Lawrence Dunbar, W. E. B. Dubois's *Dark Princess*, Sutton Griggs's *The Hindered Hand*, and James Weldon Johnson's verse collection *God's Trombone*. At Beecher Terrace there were three copies of Richard Wright's *Native Son* but five of *Gone with the Wind*, which sent a very different message about race, and was also the most frequently borrowed book at the local public library: seven loans compared to just three for *Native Son*. Residents could have also borrowed Zora Neale Hurston's *Mules and Men*, but only one did over a two-year period.[37]

So the question before us is: Why was Margaret Mitchell more popular in this black community than Richard Wright? There's no denying that *Gone with the Wind* is a page-turner with some vivid black characters, and maybe Beecher Terrace read it on that level, accepting the racial prejudices as a given. Or perhaps it re-created a world and a war their grandparents had talked about. The pioneering black historian Carter Woodson may have put his finger on the problem when he protested (in 1933) that few localities mandated teaching African-American history and literature in black schools—and Louisville was not one of the exceptions. When black schoolchildren were taught about slavery and Reconstruction, the lessons usually followed the Ulrich B. Phillips school of historians:

> These rewriters of history fearlessly contended that slavery was a benevolent institution; the masters loved their slaves and treated them humanely; the abolitionists meddled with the institution which the masters eventually would have modified; the Civil War brought about by "fanatics" like William Lloyd Garrison and John Brown was unnecessary; it was a mistake to make the Negro a citizen, for he merely became worse off by incurring the displeasure of the master class that will never

tolerate him as an equal; and the Negro must live in this country
in a state of recognized inferiority.

This was exactly the version of history that *Gone with the Wind* novelized.
And what appalled Woodson was that so many black readers fell for
it. He remembered listening "to a conversation of Negro lawyers in
one of our Southern cities, in which they unanimously conceded
practically every contention set forth in this program of propaganda.
They denounced, therefore, all reconstructionists who advocated
equality and justice for all...These Negro critics were especially hard
on Negroes of our day who engage in agitation for actual democracy."[38]
Given that, it is all too plausible that the less-educated readers of
Beecher Terrace preferred Margaret Mitchell to Richard Wright.

Consider also that they were upwardly mobile. Probably they were
the children of sharecroppers and the grandchildren of slaves. Even a
decade earlier—in the depths of the Depression, before Beecher
Terrace had been built—they had been much worse off. Now they
had advanced to the ranks of the urban working class, steadily
employed and decently housed. This social stratum would be receptive to the uplifting can-do messages of Ralph Waldo Emerson,
Booker T. Washington, Dale Carnegie, and (fifty years later) Oprah
Winfrey. And that may explain why one black freight-handler with a
fourth-grade education was determined to read anything that would
"learn him something," and particularly liked *Robinson Crusoe*: "Crusoe
was like me, he made the best of everything."[39]

Neither middle class nor dirt poor, bordering the North and South,
equidistant from the ferment of Harlem and the isolation of rural
backwaters, you could call Beecher Terrace a black Middletown. And
Offutt's survey suggests that, in 1943, black and white reading tastes
were very similar and very middlebrow. Many Beecher Terrace residents were domestic workers, and no doubt some of the books in their
home libraries were cast-offs from their white employers—though
that wouldn't explain why they borrowed *Gone with the Wind* from the
public library. And more than a few whites had read *Native Son*, which
swiftly sold 215,000 copies after it had been adopted (and somewhat
expurgated) by the Book-of-the-Month Club.[40]

Whether readers choose to read books by members of their own
ethnic group should of course be entirely their decision. At the same
time, we should be neither surprised nor censorious if their reading

tastes are strikingly universal. In 1998, in response to demands that the San Francisco school board impose racial quotas on authors studied in high-school English classes, columnist Linda Chavez asked, "Whatever happened to the notion that reading is supposed to expand our universe, not contract it so that everything we encounter is familiar?" She recalled that, as Mexican-American girl who felt terribly dislocated in Denver, she identified closely with Johanna Spyri's *Heidi*, the story of blond Swiss girl exiled to Frankfurt. (The hair color was an irrelevant detail.)—

> My father, who had only a 9th-grade education, took me almost weekly to the library and introduced me to his favorite authors, including Fyodor Dostoyevsky, Leo Tolstoy, W. Somerset Maugham and John Steinbeck. When I was 13, he bought me a set of the *Great Books of the Western World*, where I encountered Aristotle and Aquinas, Shakespeare and Cervantes, Adam Smith and John Locke for the first time. It took him years to pay for those books out of the money he earned as a housepainter…It never occurred to my father or me that the Great Books were not a part of our intellectual heritage and tradition. We believed they belonged to us as much as to anyone.[41]

Her experience was far from exceptional. What stands out in Manuel Martín-Rodríguez's collection of Chicano autobiographies is the flourishing of a broad, diverse, and universal reading culture, which freely crossed ethnic lines as if they weren't there. These readers might or might not develop an interest in Chicano literature alongside world literature, but there was no sense of any conflict between the two. Poet Carlos Cumpián began his serious reading with Jack London's *White Fang* and *Call of the Wild* ("though I had never seen snow in real life"), and, after moving to Chicago, discovered Allen Ginsberg, Lawrence Ferlinghetti, Gregory Corso, and Khalil Gibran. In high school he hung out with "hybrid working-class biker hippies unafraid of the mockery that bull-neck jocks and gang-minded greasers" directed against poetry junkies. "Turned out, girls loved poetry." It was a rough neighborhood, where his girl and five other friends died while he was still in high school, so he turned for spiritual solace to the *Tao Te Ching*, the *Bhagavad Gita*, and *The Tibetan Book of the Dead*. Not until 1973, after he had been through all that, did he discover Chicano poetry.[42]

Novelist Eliud Martínez attended an Austin elementary school in the 1940s, where "some wonderful, *old-fashioned* (in a positive, superlative sense) teachers helped us when we were learning English, tactfully, helpfully and—CORRECTLY—to learn." His attitude toward books would have been very different if he had been punished for speaking Spanish, as happened at some other schools. But he went on to develop a "cosmopolitan" taste for English, French, Italian, and Spanish literatures, ranging across William James, Edgar Allan Poe, Eugene O'Neill, Ortega y Gasset, and (while studying in Mexico City) Mexican history and philosophy. Reading, he concluded, "can enable us to be citizens of the world without turning our backs on our cultural heritage."[43]

"It's my earliest memory of an intense, captivating literary experience," recalled Anthony Macías, "reading Edith Hamilton's *Mythology*"—all of it, before his ninth birthday. In high school he got hooked on science fiction (Wells's *The Island of Dr. Moreau*, Huxley's *Brave New World*, Philip K. Dick's *Do Androids Dream of Electric Sheep?*, Daniel Keyes's *Flowers for Algernon*) as well as *Death of a Salesman*, *The Old Man and the Sea*, *The Great Gatsby*, and Willa Cather's *My Ántonia*. At UC Berkeley he studied Latino and African-American literature (which by then had become hip), but also Homer, Herodotus, *Othello*, *Joseph Andrews*, Keats, Coleridge, T. S. Eliot, e. e. cummings, *Heart of Darkness*, and *Howl*. Macías alluded briefly to the "canon wars" then raging, but with the sense that it was all silly. Books aren't at war with each other. Professors might fight over syllabi, but these tempests in university teapots are irrelevant to general readers.[44]

Margarita Cota-Cárdenas grew up among the farmworkers of the San Joaquin Valley, and discovered literature when her father brought home from a second-hand store a set of books "by an American writer, some guy named Dickens…The owner told me it was a very famous writer, I don't know from where." That led her to *Don Quixote* (in English), Mark Twain, and Edna St Vincent Millay; and then (in college) to English, Spanish, American, French, and Italian literature; and ultimately (in graduate school) Latin American and Chicano authors. But it all began with "the complete works of Charles Dickens, a true *observador* of the human condition, in the 1950s."[45]

Maria Kelson remembered that "My first memory of a poem really taking the top of my head off, making my whole body answer 'yes,' was John Masefield's 'Sea Fever.'" ("I must go down to the sea again, to the lonely sea and the sky...."). She was in the fourth or fifth grade, she lived an hour-and-a-half from the Pacific shore, but she took this poem with her everywhere, because it opened a door "for experience, for freedom, for the breathing earth, itself."[46]

In a crime-ridden section of El Paso, María Teresa Márquez's father found an abandoned box of college textbooks on his way home from work at a lumber yard. It puzzled the family: they did not know anyone in their community who attended college. María discovered a volume of Thomas Hardy's poems and read it repeatedly, "pretending I understood what I was reading," but it "changed my life, opening new insights into literature," and inspiring her to aim at a college education.[47]

For Shannon Gutiérrez, "Reading saved me from the chaos." In school she struggled with learning delays and speech impairment, at home life could be rough ("Dad kicked the shit out of us at least once a day"), so she and her sister frankly found an escape in Tolkien's *The Hobbit*, C. S. Lewis's *The Chronicles of Narnia*, and Ray Bradbury's *The Illustrated Man*. Shannon read Laura Ingalls Wilder's *Little House on the Prairie* slowly but doggedly, checking unfamiliar words in the dictionary. Her formal education stopped at the eighth grade and she ended up a single mother, but she and her three children are all passionate readers.[48]

At her San Antonio Catholic high school, the nuns introduced Irma Flores-Manges to Arthurian tales, Shakespeare, Cervantes, Keats, Shelley, Dickens, Tolstoy, and Faulkner.[49] And for Beth Hernandez-Jason in Fresno, the liberating books were the Nancy Drew mysteries, which certainly challenged her vocabulary (*unscrupulous, exonerate, insoluble, titian*).[50] For my mother as well, growing up in the practically all-Jewish neighborhood of East New York in the Great Depression, Nancy Drew offered an alluring window into mainstream America— where, evidently, every girl drove her own roadster.

Yet in one crucial sense the experience of African-Americans was very different. Not that they were any less interested in pursuing the whole world of Western literature—to presume otherwise is an ethnic slur. But often whites imposed severe sanctions against that kind of literacy, sanctions which did not end with slavery. In 1945 Ralph Ellison explained that any kind of individual artistic expression might bring collective punishment on the entire community: "Lynchings have occurred because Negroes painted their homes." So as a matter of self-protection, the black community pre-emptively punished any individual attempts to expand intellectual horizons: "Within the ambit of the black family this takes the form of training the child away from curiosity and adventure, against reaching out for those activities lying beyond the borders of the black community. And when the child resists, the parent discourages him; first with the formula, 'That there's for white folks. Colored can't have it,' and finally with a beating." And unless the child breaks free of that, he learns "a masochistic submissiveness and a denial of the impulse toward Western culture when it stirred within him."[51] She probably didn't realize it, but Oprah Winfrey's mother had internalized that self-destructive attitude when she snatched books out of her daughter's hands. Not long ago President Obama alluded to the same problem, when he advised minority students on the importance of "knowing your culture—the traditional cultures out of which your families come, but also being part of the larger culture. Sometimes African Americans, in communities where I've worked, there's been the notion of 'acting white'— which sometimes is overstated, but there's an element of truth to it, where, okay, if boys are reading too much, then, well, why are you doing that?"[52]

The qualifier "overstated" is necessary here, because as we have seen, in the face of all obstacles there has also been a relentless and insatiable drive to literacy in black America from the very beginning to the present day. The attitudes Obama criticized may have been more common in his youth. More recent studies in sociology suggest that they have given way to increasingly positive attitudes toward intellectual achievement, spurred no doubt by famous examples of passionate black readers—Barack Obama and Oprah Winfrey, for instance.[53] Slavery and Jim Crow left a very long and damaging legacy, but fortunately it is not indelible.

Kurt Wootton taught English at a Providence high school, where the students were almost all black and half of them dropped out before graduation. He assigned them Richard Wright's *Black Boy* and jazz by John Coltrane, which they found hopelessly irrelevant. Then, in 1998, he organized what became the ArtsLiteracy Project, a summer program that brings students from Rhode Island's worst high schools to the Brown University campus to study and perform *Othello*, *The Taming of the Shrew*, Shaw's *Saint Joan*, Lorca's *Blood Wedding*, Sophocles's *Antigone*, and Ovid's *Metamorphoses*. "The real goal is to read the text and to use it to understand your own life," Wootton explained. "There's a sense of accomplishment these students feel to know *Othello*, to feel how it connects to them." When ESL teacher Richard Kinslow had his class prepare a production of *Macbeth*, one of his students was the type who got suspended about once a week (on average), but he would sneak into school for the daily rehearsals. "These kids had never been actively involved in any part of school except gym and art," explained Kinslow. "Doing Shakespeare honored them. If you want to talk about self-respect and pride, it made a big difference."[54]

Notes

1. Kathleen Rooney, *Reading with Oprah: The Book Club that Changed America* (Fayetteville, Ark.: University of Arkansas Press, 2005), 111.
2. Frederick Douglass, *Narrative of the Life of Frederick Douglass* (New York: Dover, 1995), 20–4, 38.
3. Leonard Black, *The Life and Sufferings of Leonard Black, a Fugitive from Slavery* (New Bedford, Mass.: Benjamin Lindsey, 1847), 18–19.
4. Ronald J. Zboray and Mary Saracino Zboray, *Everyday Ideas: Socioliterary Experience among Antebellum New Englanders* (Knoxville, Tenn.: University of Tennessee Press, 2006), 162.
5. Janet Duitsman Cornelius, *"When I Can Read My Title Clear": Literacy, Slavery, and Religion in the Antebellum South* (Columbia, SC: University of South Carolina Press, 1991), 7–9.
6. Ibid., ch. 3.
7. Ibid., ch. 5.
8. A. J. Raboteau, *Slave Religion: The "Invisible Institution" in the Antebellum South* (Oxford: Oxford University Press, 1980), 240–1.
9. Eugene Genovese, *Roll, Jordan, Roll: The World the Slaves Made* (New York: Vintage, 1976), 562–3.
10. Cornelius, *Read My Title Clear*, 142–50.
11. Cheryl Knott, *Not Free, Not for All: Public Libraries in the Age of Jim Crow* (Amherst and Boston: University of Massachusetts Press, 2015), ch. 1.
12. Elizabeth McHenry, *Forgotten Readers: Recovering the Lost History of African American Literary Societies* (Durham and London: Duke University Press, 2002), 50–7.
13. Ibid., 117.
14. Ibid., 104.
15. Ibid., 97–8.
16. Ibid., 115–18, 123–6.

17. Ibid., 165–74.

18. Knott, *Not Free*, 90–5.

19. Eliza Atkins Gleason, *The Southern Negro and the Public Library* (Chicago: University of Chicago Press, 1941), vii, 93, 95.

20. Frank Felsenstein and James J. Connolly, *What Middletown Read: Print Culture in an American Small City* (Amherst, Mass.: University of Massachusetts Press, 2015), 49–51, 81, 105–6, 110–31, 200–1.

21. Quoted in Jaime Harker, *America the Middlebrow: Women's Novels, Progressivism, and Middlebrow Authorship between the Wars* (Amherst and Boston: University of Massachusetts Press, 2007), 57–9.

22. See the various essays in Scott L. Newstok and Ayanna Thompson, eds., *Weyward Macbeth: Intersections of Race and Performance* (New York: Palgrave Macmillan, 2010).

23. Ralph Ellison, *Shadow and Act* (New York: Random House, 1964), xii–xiii, 151–3.

24. McHenry, *Forgotten Readers*, 232–3.

25. Ellison, *Shadow and Act*, xii–xv.

26. Knott, *Not Free*, 97–8. Ellison, *Shadow and Act*, 153–60.

27. Ellison, *Shadow and Act*, 109.

28. Ibid., xii–xxii.

29. Ibid., 15, 58, 116–17, 169.

30. Janice Radway, "The Library as Place, Collection, or Service: Promoting Book Circulation in Durham, North Carolina, and at the Book-of-the-Month Club, 1925–1945," in *Institutions of Reading: The Social Life of Libraries in the United States*, ed. Thomas Augst and Kenneth Carpenter (Amherst and Boston: University of Massachusetts Press, 2007), 258–63.

31. Shawn Anthony Christian, *The Harlem Renaissance and the Idea of a New Negro Reader* (Amherst and Boston: University of Massachusetts Press, 2016), ch. 1.

32. "Legends of Cosmetology: Lulline Long: Selling Care and Concern," *Shop Talk* (Spring 1985): 111.

33. Julia A. Hersberger, Lou Sua, and Adam L. Murray, "The Fruit and Root of the Community: The Greensboro Carnegie Negro Library, 1904–1964," in *The Library as Place: History, Community, and Culture*, ed. John E. Buschman and Gloria J. Leckie (Westport, Conn.: Libraries Unlimited, 2007), 79–99.

34. L. M. B. Wright, "A Survey of the Reading Materials in the Homes of Fourth, Fifth, and Sixth Grade Pupils of Jackson School," MA thesis, University of Cincinnati, 1938.

35. John H. Burma, "An Analysis of the Present Negro Press," *Social Forces* 26 (Oct. 1947): 172.

36. Juanita Harriett Offutt, "A Survey of Reading Materials Available to Negro Tenants in a Low-Rent Housing Project in Louisville, Kentucky," MA thesis, University of Cincinnati, esp. ch. 5.

37. Ibid., 110–42.

38. Carter Godwin Woodson, *The Mis-Education of the Negro* (Washington, DC: Associated Publishers, 1933), 83–7, 132–43.

39. William S. Gray and Bernice E. Leary, *What Makes a Book Readable* (Chicago: University of Chicago Press, 1935), 54.

40. Janice A. Radway, *A Feeling for Books: The Book-of-the-Month Club, Literary Taste, and Middle-Class Desire* (Chapel Hill: University of North Carolina Press, 1997), 186–7.

41. Linda Chavez, "With Respects to John Steinbeck,…" *Chicago Tribune* (18 Mar. 1998).

42. Manuel M. Martín-Rodríguez, ed., *With a Book in Their Hands: Chicano/a Readers and Readerships across the Centuries* (Albuquerque: University of New Mexico Press, 2014), 9–12.

43. Ibid., 17–27.

44. Ibid., 49–53.

45. Ibid., 59–62.

46. Ibid., 63–5.

47. Ibid., 67–8.

48. Ibid., 79–80.

49. Ibid., 42.

50. Ibid., 89–90.

51. Ellison, *Shadow and Act*, 89–93.

52. Nia-Malika Henderson, "What President Obama Gets Wrong about 'Acting White'," *Washington Post* (24 July 2014).

53. Erin McNamara Horvat and Kristine S. Lewis, "Reassessing the 'Burden of "Acting White"': The Importance of Peer Groups in Managing Academic Success," *Sociology of Education* 76 (Oct. 2003): 265–80.

54. Samuel G. Freedman, "On Education: To Fire Up Troubled Students, a Program Turns to the Classics," *New York Times* (18 Aug. 2004).

5

Shakespeare in Prison

There are any number of inspirational accounts of prison reading (such as Malcolm X), so let's begin with what doesn't work. Larry E. Sullivan, the leading scholar of this small but enthralling literary subfield, has concluded that probably the favorite author behind bars is Friedrich Nietzsche, and most frequently quoted sentence, "What does not kill me makes me stronger." Convicts also devour crime and escapist literature, but few read Plato, Boethius, Bunyan, or Dostoevsky. And the reason should be obvious. Typically, prison systems work relentlessly to crush the individuality of their inmates. Physical resistance only brings ever-more brutal punishment, so prisoners resort to the one form of rebellion they can get away with, which is to read the most extreme forms of antisocial philosophy: Schopenhauer, Herbert Spencer, Nietzsche. If you are caged like an animal, these ideologies offer some psychological compensation: you can imagine yourself radically free, infinitely superior to your jailers in terms of intelligence, courage, and authenticity. It all sounds romantically transgressive, but that's a very costly illusion, because it locks the prisoner into a battle with authority that he cannot win, and amplifies the behavior that got him incarcerated in the first place.[1]

Among black female inmates, the counterpart to Nietzsche is "urban fiction," a new genre where the *ubermenschen* are inner-city crime lords, as wealthy as they are sadistic. Their women are consistently beautiful, expensively dressed, and obscenely abused. The demand for these novels knows no limit, and they are smuggled in faster than wardens can confiscate them. Their fans want to know why these black-authored books are banned while the equally gruesome thrillers of James Patterson are allowed in, and they have a point. But whereas Patterson is clearly on the side of law and order, urban fiction glamorizes drugs and thugs—and all too many readers admit that they fall for it:

> "It excites me to read them. I look at all this money they're making. I can't wait to see the dollar signs...I like how they're hustlers. How they con someone. It gives me a feeling of oh man, is it that easy? I coulda tried that!"
>
> "The covers attracted me to the books. How the men looked, how the women were dressed—it was flashy. They represented money to me. Some type of hustle was transpiring and some money was being made."
>
> "I put myself in their shoes. With all the details about sex, I get those feelings. If they have money in their hands, if they're taking drugs, I feel it. I get that thing in my stomach to want to go flip the money or do heroin. My stomach starts bubbling...I want money and drugs to relieve my pain and so I can do whatever I want physically."

As one young woman rationalized, she enjoyed "rooting for the bad guy...the underdog or the guy that they think is a threat." But an older inmate recognized that these books only perpetuate "what brought [these women] to the penitentiary." Another reports that "Most of the ones who read urban books come back...They don't want to change mentally." And a former fan admitted that "I could relate to the joy of dealing and the pimping and playing," which "was exciting because what I was reading is what I was, and I wasn't ready to change that environment that I was in." She eventually realized that she could only change herself by changing her reading habits: "I owe myself that. I want to have a better life and a better relation with my family and my kids. I don't want to keep looking around over my shoulder worried about going back to prison."[2]

A prison sentence can be a period of enforced leisure with few distractions, and thus an opportunity to immerse oneself in books. Mohandas Gandhi publicly played down the importance of a literary education, but when he spent a total of more than four years in prison between 1908 and 1933, he used the opportunity to systematically work through a vast body of Western and Eastern literature: Leo Tolstoy (of course), Francis Bacon's essays, T. H. Huxley on education,

Thomas Carlyle on the French Revolution, Giuseppe Mazzini, Ralph Waldo Emerson, *Dr. Jekyll and Mr. Hyde*, *The Decline and Fall of the Roman Empire* (perhaps for its relevance to the British Empire), William James's *Varieties of Religious Experience*, the Koran, and Plato on Socrates (which he summarized for Gujarati readers).[3] In pre-Castro Cuba it was illegal for private citizens to own Communist books, but bookstores were permitted to sell them (on the principle of free enterprise), and prison libraries made them available for intensive study by political prisoners.[4]

South African anti-apartheid activist Neville Alexander conceded that, thanks to his incarceration on Robben Island, he read books that he would have never gotten around to otherwise: Shakespeare, Dickens, German literature, African history, and economics. "I had more banned books inside prison than I ever had outside," he recalled. The prison library was well stocked with official propaganda magazines, but as Archie Dick notes, "Political prisoners read them 'critically' by simply standing 'the news on its head', so that if an article in a government journal argued that Bantu Education was being accepted, they concluded that it was in fact being resisted." The works of Che Guevara were proscribed, but if activists wanted a handbook of guerrilla warfare, histories of Afrikaaner commandos during the Boer War were readily available. And you could learn much about organizing the poor from *The Grapes of Wrath*.[5] Communist books were banned in principle, but the white guards were often insufficiently literate to recognize them as such. Judging by its title, they assumed that *Capital* was about business and waved it on through. They were even persuaded that Isaac Deutscher's biography of Trotsky, *The Prophet Armed*, was a Christian tract.[6]

When Robben Island inmates were only allowed one non-religious book, Sonny Venkatrathnam smuggled in a complete edition of Shakespeare by pasting Diwali cards on the cover and persuading the guards that it was some kind of Hindu scriptures. It was circulated among and closely read by the political prisoners, thirty-three of whom marked and signed their favorite passages. Often it was something relevant to the anti-apartheid struggle. Shakespeare clearly did not intend *The Tempest* to be a critique of white supremacy, but what did that matter? Prospero's power lay in his books, and he taught Caliban only the elementary literacy he would need as a menial laborer: any black teacher got that message.[7] In fact, as the banned author Lewis Nkosi recognized, the world of Shakespeare was very much like apartheid South Africa:

> It was the cacophonous, swaggering world of Elizabethan England which gave us the closest parallel to our own mode of existence; the cloak and dagger stories of Shakespeare; the marvelously gay and dangerous time of change in Great Britain came close to reflecting our own condition. Thus it was possible for an African musician returning home at night to inspire awe in a group of thugs surrounding him by declaiming in an impossibly archaic English: "Unhand me, rogues!" Indeed, they did unhand him. The[se] same thugs...also delighted in the violent colour, the rolling rhetoric of Shakespearean theatre. Their favourite form of persecuting middle-class Africans was forcing them to stand at street corners, reciting some passage from Shakespeare, for which they would be showered with sincere applause.[8]

As the "coloured" (mixed race) activist Dennis Brutus explained, Shakespeare was required reading in South African high schools, and his limitless understanding of the human predicament "appealed to and touched on the many experiences the inmates had experienced." In a country profoundly divided by race, tribe, language, and ideology, the Shakespeare canon enabled communication among anti-apartheid activists by giving them a common scripture and frame of reference.[9]

Veterans of Robben Island remember it as a gulag that was also a university, where books were fervently read and debated. The prison library offered Dickens, Hardy, George Eliot, and Schiller in German. Nelson Mandela raced through *War and Peace* in three days, *Darkness at Noon* became a flashpoint between Communist and anti-Communist inmates, Thomas Mann's *The Magic Mountain* (set in an isolated sanatorium) and *The Diary of Anne Frank* spoke to everyone locked inside.[10] In spite of the daily brutalities and humiliations, those shared reading experiences elevated the morale of the inmates and left them free of the bitterness so common among ex-convicts. "The type of education that I got on Robben Island was unique—nowhere else in the world could I get a better education," Monde Colin Mkunqwana warmly recalled. "I can honestly say that in a psychological sense I hadn't been affected by my incarceration. In fact, I had become very proud of my Robben Island days."[11] "I can frankly say that today I do not bear any grudges against anybody," affirmed scientist Sedick Isaacs, though he had been subjected to torture, sleep deprivation, and solitary confinement. "I think I got a wonderfully balanced education together with this sharing that we could not have obtained in any other place or time in our lives."[12]

What these veterans sharply resented was the failure of post-Mandela South Africa to provide adequate public schools and school libraries for any but the most affluent pupils, an apartheid based on class rather than race. After 1976, Robben Island took in a younger generation of radicals who rejected the old study ethic and burned schools in Soweto, proclaiming that there could be "no education without liberation." Their elders warned them that there could be no real liberation without education, and one of those young activists, Stone Phumelele Sizani, later admitted that the old men were right. "In South Africa these days, people don't speak to each other, they don't communicate, they shout at each other. If they disagree with you they will howl you into silence, they will marginalize you, because nobody wants to listen to your point of view, they want to listen to those that are agreeing with them"—a problem certainly not limited to that country. "Intellectual discourse in South Africa is held back because there is no engagement, because very few people read these days, not in a manner in which you will read on Robben Island, read and engage."[13]

One might object that what works for political prisoners—who are well educated and intensely motivated by ideals, and who would be law-abiding in a more just society—will not work for your typical sociopathic criminal. In fact, the great books, and Shakespeare in particular, can have an exceptionally electrifying effect on ordinary convicts. The future boxing promoter Don King grew up poor in Cleveland, dropped out of Kent State University, found a career in the numbers racket, and served four years in prison for manslaughter:

> Jail was my school. I had one of the most delightful times under desperate conditions. I read Aristotle and Homer. I got into Sigmund Freud. When I dealt with William Shakespeare, I got to know him very well as a man. I love Bill Shakespeare. He was some bad dude. Intellectually, I went into jail with a peashooter and came out armed with a nuclear bomb.

In response to the party-game question of which great authors he would like to dine with, he mentioned Plato, Cicero, and Caesar alongside Frederick Douglass.[14]

We have records of prison performances of Shakespeare going back to the American Civil War, but using the Bard as a rehabilitative tool really took off in the 1980s. Numerous companies have sprung up in both the US and UK, such as the London Shakespeare Workout Prison Project, though they are all vulnerable to budget cuts and skeptical wardens.[15] Laura Bates created a marvelously successful program at supermax Wabash Valley Correctional Facility in Indiana, only to discover that the tenure committee of her university awarded more points for publishing in academic journals than transforming the lives of prisoners.[16]

Convicts are usually allowed only three arenas of freedom—the weight room, religion, and books. They can devote themselves single-mindedly to sculpting their bodies, souls, or minds. Academics are often astonished to meet convicts who have practically memorized the Shakespeare canon, but these readers are on a ten to fifteen-year sabbatical and can focus solely on the texts. Larry Norton, Laura Bates's most brilliant student, wrote a 60,000-word critique, as long as doctoral dissertation, with this difference: because he was in solitary and not allowed access to any scholarly literature other than the plays themselves, he had to be entirely original, rather than rehash and footnote what other academics had written.[17]

Convicts commonly report that they hated Shakespeare in high school English classes, and then, in jail, embraced the plays as a kind of bible. The participants in the Shakespeare Behind Bars program at the Luther Luckett Correctional Complex (LaGrange, Kentucky) fall into born-again language. "Shakespeare has changed my entire outlook on everything that is everything," says one, while another proclaims, "I can see redemption in the distance." As a third inmate puts it, "Shakespeare is like a god to a lot of the other guys here, because the majority of them don't believe in a god. They believe in sort of ... like ... revolution." While some convicts turn to evangelicalism or the Nation of Islam, others cannot find a home in any organized religion. "Shakespeare is *my* church. Shakespeare *is* my church. The chapel offerings here do not meet my personal needs. I'm not welcome in most of the services," explains a fourth prisoner, who admits that he killed his wife because he could not deal with his own homosexuality. Every Shakespeare play is a series of moral choices, where individuals think through alternatives. Sometimes they choose to kill, but their decisions always lead to either love, greatness, or destruction. Every inmate at Luther Luckett chose the last of these: Shakespeare reveals to them where and why they went wrong. "Big G," serving time for killing an undercover cop in a drug raid, believes that the crucial line in *Hamlet* is "to hold as 'twere a mirror up to nature":

> And that's what we try to do...And when you look in that mirror and you find it relates really strongly to your past or your crime, that truth, that pain just comes out. And it's almost like a mental breakdown, such an emotional release that it's just, whew, it's a trip to watch...It changes you. First of all, when you find that, some of the pain will go away. Your response that you have, your empathy that you have, all that will increase. And the truth, when you can touch it and you can let it out, it'll feel like a ton of bricks is off of you...I can't bring my victim back, and so what can I do about it? I can lay down and let my life be worth nothing, or I can make a decision to change my life and make my life mean something. That's what a lot of us are trying to do...And, as amazing as it seems, by experiencing Shakespeare and focusing on what Shakespeare wrote about 400 years ago and applying it in your life by either witnessing a character's mistakes and realizing why did he make those mistakes and if they mirrored your own life and what could you learn from them...or taking some of Shakespeare's more positive characters and seeing the traits that a positive character has and going, "Hey, I want those positive attributes in my life," you really can change. It's just an amazing transformation that you can undertake.[18]

If that implies personal responsibility, prisoners often respond to literature that affirms that principle, despite the fact (or perhaps because) they are behind bars. It gives them a sense of control over their destiny, and thus a kind of freedom. Amy Scott-Douglass was surprised when one inmate (serving a life sentence for kidnapping and homicide) told her that his favorite philosopher was René Descartes:

> Mainly I fell in love with him for... *Rules for the Direction of the Mind*, and that has always stuck with me because it's like basically

the limits and capabilities of any human being is only based upon the input that he puts into himself. And I agree with that. It's like, I always try to figure out why people do what they do. Why is it that we got eleven to twelve-hundred individuals on this prison yard and we all come from different backgrounds? It can't just be "Well, your environment leads you to prison" because if that was the case everybody here would come from a disadvantageous environment and vice versa. So it's got to be something more than that.[19]

As an American Indian prisoner explained it:

Every time we get together to do another play, it's not so much a matter of us picking a role as we read through a script and the role grabs us. So I guess you as an audience would see that we do live through Shakespeare, but that's only because we reflect ourselves. In that way it lends an authenticity to the characters because each of us are resolving issues through Shakespeare. Through the art of the theatre, Shakespeare helps us learn how to better cope with life on a day-to-day basis.[20]

In many ways, prison is an ideal classroom for studying Shakespeare. In an environment of extreme sensory deprivation, the beauty of the language becomes psychedelically vivid. That aesthetic rush is usually lost on sensory overloaded high-schoolers, who have a thousand other distractions. Even when prisoners are allowed to speak, they often stay silent for fear of being judged: Shakespeare gives them a language they can (and do) use with anyone, including professors. "Then you have the obstacle of understanding content," which is actually a plus in the mind of one white-collar Luther Luckett convict. For readers on the outside, obscurity and ambiguity may be confusing, but they give inmates a heady sense of interpretive liberty: "With Shakespeare you can extract from the text or you can read into it. It's like the text has a life of its own, and I have never experienced that with modern plays, with the Wilders or the Inges or the O'Neills or the Ionescos."[21] And Elizabethan London—with its crime, dirt, violence, music, swagger, rawness, over-crowding, poverty, and non-standard English—is much more familiar to convicts from the inner cities than it is to college students from manicured suburbs. "If you're up on intellect and game and if you come from the ghetto, there's a lot of that in these plays," shouted one prisoner in solitary to another. "Shakespeare is real shit, man."[22]

At Wabash Valley, Laura Bates assigned the doomed king's soliloquy from the final act of *Richard II*:

> I have been studying how I may compare
> This prison where I live unto the world:
> And for because the world is populous
> And here is not a creature but myself,
> I cannot do it; yet I'll hammer it out.
> My brain I'll prove the female to my soul,
> My soul the father; and these two beget
> A generation of still-breeding thoughts,
> And these same thoughts people this little world,
> In humours like the people of this world,
> For no thought is contented. The better sort,
> As thoughts of things divine, are intermix'd
> With scruples and do set the word itself
> Against the word...

This convinced some of the convicts in her class that Shakespeare must have done time. The response of Larry Newton, who had served ten years in solitary for murder and repeated escape attempts, is worth quoting at length:

His thoughts are his only companions, his method for populating this empty world so that it can be compared to the world outside of those walls. He had studied a way to compare the two—so it is clearly his attempt. I cannot tell if it is extremely complex or rather simple? It seems like you can spend time on just about each passage and come up with three different conclusions.

Like in the area dedicated to scripture. It appears as though he is a believer in the word as it is the "better sort" and having so much time to think, no thought is "contented" as he says, and the better thoughts are exposing flaws or contradictions. Making him doubt, or at least challenging him to doubt. If so, it must be a scary idea to lose the "better sort" of thought.

I struggle to bring out the comparisons, because to me it only speaks of his conduct in there... I can relate to much of it, if I am right in reading it, or maybe it is art left for interpretation?

"Not bad for a fifth-grade dropout," Bates commented. The essay continued:

> I can really relate to the thoughts of ambition plotting unlikely wonders! I can see him now pacing around and playing out these great fantasies and then the quick reality check and he feels silly...
>
> I guess as in art, I can overcomplicate the work, so I will just close it up. It seems to me that he has gone from king to prisoner, and in his thoughts goes back and forth, but seems to conclude with saying that until you have been at peace, or content, with nothing...you cannot be pleased with anything. Or that you cannot be truly happy until you have come to terms with being nothing.

"Wow," Bates sighed. "That was the most thoughtful response I had ever gotten to an initial Shakespeare assignment—in prison or on campus. And Newton didn't even know who Shakespeare was."[23] (Later in the course, he confirmed that Macbeth speaks exactly the panicked thoughts that typically race through a killer's mind.)[24]

Hamlet's dark phrase "Denmark's a prison" could be interpreted as a critique of all oppressive societies, and it certainly was read that way by dissidents in iron-curtain countries. Some of the inmates naturally saw it as a direct reference to Wabash Valley. But Larry Newton insisted that "this prison doesn't matter,...a lot of the guys here were in prison before they came here and they'll still be in prison when they leave here." He argued that Shakespeare was alluding to mind-forged manacles. Newton recognized that, in his pre-convict life, he had been imprisoned by hatred, self-hatred, and cowardice masquerading as belligerence. He freed himself only by:

> thinking for myself. Now, I feel more okay with myself. I'm feeling stronger in my abilities every day, and the world just opens up. You really can do anything, you can shape your life any way you want it to be. Because prison isn't the great prison. Prison is being entrapped by those self-destructive ways of thinking.[25]

In an all-important sense he was right. Any number of studies have confirmed that prison-education programs dramatically reduce recidivism. Laura Bates conducted her own survey of twenty inmates in her Shakespeare class, and found that between them they had committed in prison more than 600 Class A offenses (violence or weapons charges) before enrolling in the course—and none afterwards.[26] But one thing is essential to the success of such programs: the prisoners must be in control and free to discuss anything. As one convict lectured Amy Scott-Douglass:

> just remember, if you have a Shakespeare program for inmates, you gotta let it belong to the inmates as well as yourself. You gotta let it be a dialogue. They talk and then you respond. It's important that they're allowed to voice their own interpretations, and it's important that you give feedback and respond to them. Because I can tell you, I've been locked up in solitary confinement for years now, and there's nothing worse. People are social beings. They need to be able to participate in conversations. There's nothing worse than not being spoken to. It's worse than not being able to talk. Remember that, now.[27]

Freedom is everything. Let the students set the agenda. Earl Shorris and Allan Bloom were both products of the great-books curriculum at the University of Chicago, but where Bloom swung to the right in *The Closing of the American Mind*, Shorris grabbed the same ball and ran to the left. (That illustrates once again that canonical literature is ideologically ambidextrous, and can be used to advance a very broad range of political agendas.) Shorris created the Clemente Course in the Humanities, which brought classic literature and philosophy to poor students and prisoners (there was much overlap between these two audiences). He recalled in particular one brilliant student, Viniece Walker, who entered the maximum-security Bedford Hills Correctional Facility at age 19, "a high school dropout who read at the level of a college sophomore, a graduate of crack houses, the streets of Harlem, and a long alliance with a brutal man." He realized that it wouldn't make much sense to teach her the doctrine of regeneration through violence, as articulated by Jean-Paul Sartre and Franz Fanon. Where had violence gotten her? She told him that the only way out of prisons, literal and metaphorical, was to "learn the moral life of downtown"—that is, acquire the same intellectual wealth that the affluent classes enjoyed. They both knew all too well that prison is "a place in which spies and informers rob people of their very thoughts, putting them, as Tacitus said, into a life worse than slavery." Without independent minds, the poor would never be able to lift themselves out of poverty: no top-down solutions would work.[28] And these students had to be encouraged to craft essays in their personal voices, certainly not academic jargon, which Shorris considered "the literary equivalent of bringing smallpox-laden blankets to indigenous peoples...Academic writing has no relation to autonomy, while literary writing encourages the measured expression of the self. Academic writing has all the characteristics of tribalized work, while literary writing liberates the self-governing aspect of the person."[29] Though Shorris was a leftist who made some effort to incorporate non-Western cultures into his teaching, he unfashionably affirmed that:

> The humanities, contrary to the views of some critics of what they refer to as "the canon" or the works of "dead white European males," generally comprise the works of troublemakers, artistic and intellectual dissidents, those who were both critics and builders. When the study of the humanities leads students to understand that the world, including the world they recognize as "the establishment," is as protean as gifts of mind can make it, they suffer new and unexpected terror. I believe it is the terror of the newly free.[30]

When Shorris proposed to teach a course on American history to a class of black and Latino residents of the Bronx, their white social worker vetoed the idea, insisting that he teach African history—like a Victorian missionary dictating what the natives should and should not read. But you can understand Shorris's rationale: if you find yourself trapped in an American slum or an American prison, and you want to understand how you ended up there, reading American history would be a logical starting point.[31] In many ways Shorris was behind the times. He was less concerned with equality of cultures than equality of individuals. He addressed his students as Mr and Miss, an important mark of respect for people on the bottom rung.[32] He taught Boethius, who had obvious relevance for maximum-security prisoners. For anyone debating whether to deal drugs, Kant's categorical imperative and

Bentham's greatest-good principle were clearly useful.[33] (Shorris also noted that "They learn from Kant that each of them has dignity and that they are, rich or poor, no matter where they have been or what they have done before, an end in themselves").[34] The irreconcilable struggle between our obligations to the state and our families, dramatized in *Antigone*, brought tears to the eyes of one mother, who had reported her daughter to the FBI.[35] When one student asked, "If the [Founding] Fathers loved the humanities so much, how come they treated the natives so badly?" another could answer, "That's what Aristotle means by incontinence, when you know what's morally right, but you don't do it, because you're overcome by your passions."[36] And Viniece insisted that Plato's *Republic* was absolutely essential reading: "How can you teach philosophy to poor people without the Allegory of the Cave? The ghetto is the cave. Education is the light. Poor people can understand that."[37]

Among Shorris's ex-con alumni, recidivism was practically zero, and psychological testing found improved self-esteem, more benevolence, more spirituality, a decrease in verbal aggression, and greatly sharpened problem definition.[38] Britain's Prison Reading Groups program (founded 2000) is less like a great-books seminar and more like reading groups on the outside (devoted mainly to contemporary quality fiction and the occasional standard classic), but Jenny Hartley and Sarah Turvey report similar positive results achieved by respecting the autonomy of the prisoner.[39] Books are chosen democratically, and the moderator intervenes only to ensure that everyone has a chance to speak. One group asserted its aesthetic independence by pointedly choosing not the bestseller *Fifty Shades of Grey*, but its tonier antecedent *The Story of O*. Of course, dystopian fiction (*The Hunger Games*, *Animal Farm*) is also popular. "I enjoy the way the book club is run without any lock and key stuff. I feel confident enough to express my opinions without the fear of repercussions," said one prisoner. "It was a non-judgemental space to enjoy reading," reported another. Group members do exercise critical judgment, but that includes the capacity for respectful dissent. "Oh, so it's OK to disagree about a book is it, not like school?" said one surprised prisoner. As another acknowledged, it was a very novel experience to "hear others' opinions, often polar opposites, pitted intelligently against one another," and it inspired him to enroll in a creative-writing module with the Open University. Another observed:

> For one hour a month the walls of my confinement crumble to dust and I feel respected. Not just by fellow inmates, but by citizens from the wider community, members of the society into which I'll one day be released—by the two women who run the group, and by the visitors they invite. For one hour a month my opinion is valid, I am listened to and others care what I say. In the book group, everyone is given a voice, all have an equal say. For one hour a month I am allowed to be the individual I used to be and not defined by my crime.

Prisoner rehabilitative and therapeutic programs tend to be highly structured and scripted, where prisoners cynically suss out and feed back the right answers. ("I know what I'm supposed to think," says one.) But as Hartley and Turvey note:

> The virtue of the reading group—as extolled by many groups in our surveys—is that you don't always know what you are supposed to think, and you cannot always guess what others are thinking. Unpredictability is the big feature, the big gift to and from the imagination. It is when you do not know what you are supposed to think, that the work starts happening, with the critical engagement with the text.

At the same time, book groups promote empathy, which is essential to rehabilitation, given that most crimes involve a serious empathy deficit. A male prisoner, discussing Penelope Lively's *Making It Up* in a session attended by the author, admitted that though he had never much liked novels, "fiction has made me realise that there's someone else in the room, and what's going on in their head you have no idea, and fiction makes you think what's going on in that other head." (The author was most impressed.)

Book-group members were more likely to do volunteer work. Rehabilitation involves learning "desistance"—recognizing moral crossroads and choosing the right paths, something literary characters either do or tragically fail to do.

There is a scientific explanation for the ethical effects of reading. Performing a series of controlled experiments with books and readers, psychologists David Comer Kidd and Emanuele Castano found that literary fiction "increases self-reported empathy," enhances "our knowledge of others' lives," and "forces us to engage in mind-reading and character construction." If criminals lack empathy, literature can fill that void, because it compels readers to confront moral quandaries, understand characters different from themselves, contend with multiple perspectives and voices, and deal with the complexities of life. All that involves the active exercise of intellectual freedom, which only happens when we deal with works of real art. Popular romances, thrillers, and "urban fiction" don't have the same effect, because they are formulaic and meant to be read passively, relying on predictable characters and situations. We can empathize with a Shakespeare hero, or even perhaps a villain, but not with a stereotype.[40]

As Hartley and Turvey appreciate, Adam Smith arrived at essentially the same conclusion in *The Theory of Moral Sentiments*: "By the imagination we place ourselves in his situation, we conceive ourselves enduring all the same torments, we enter as it were into his body, and become in some measure the same person with him, and thence form some idea of his sensations, and even feel something, which, though weaker in degree, is not altogether unlike them." It's relevant here to note that Smith taught the world's first university-level courses in English literature, at Edinburgh and Glasgow. Though he was confident that the invisible hand would work for the long-run benefit of all, he realized that capitalism might degenerate into organized thievery in a society without moral foundations. Those foundations could be supplied by literature: that is why, as a moral philosopher, Smith insisted on teaching the subject to the sons of Scotland's emerging entrepreneurial class.[41] And surely, what works for capitalists will work for criminals.

Notes

1. Larry E. Sullivan, "Reading in American Prisons: Structures and Strictures," *Libraries & Culture* 33 (Winter 1998): 113–19.
2. Megan Sweeney, "Books as Bombs: Incendiary Reading Practices in Women's Prisons," *PMLA* 123 (May 2008): 666–73.
3. Ian Desai, "Books Behind Bars: Gandhi's Community of Captive Readers," in *The History of Reading*, Volume 1: *International Perspectives, c.1500–1990*, ed. Shafquat Towheed and W. R. Owens (Basingstoke: Palgrave Macmillan, 2011), 178–81.

4. Patricia Maria Smorkaloff, *Readers and Writers in Cuba: A Social History of Print Culture, 1830s–1990* (New York and London: Garland, 1997), 45–6.

5. Archie L. Dick, "Remembering Reading: Memory, Books and Reading in South Africa's Apartheid Prisons, 1956–90," in *History of Reading*, ed. Towheed and Owens, 203–4.

6. Ashwin Desai, *Reading Revolution: Shakespeare on Robben Island* (Pretoria: Unisa Press, 2012), 58–9, 89.

7. Ibid., 34.

8. Ibid., 12–30.

9. Ibid., 58.

10. Ibid., ix, 43–4, 105.

11. Jan K. Coetzee and Asta Rau, "Narrating Trauma and Suffering: Towards Understanding Intersubjectively Constituted Memory," *Forum Qualitative Sozialforschung/ Forum: Qualitative Social Research*, 10(2) (2009), Art. 14 <http://nbn-resolving.de/urn:nbn:de:0114-fqs0902144>.

12. Desai, *Reading Revolution*, 90.

13. Ibid., 10, 93–4, 100, 117–18.

14. Thomas Hauser, "The Quotable Mr. King and the Quotable Mr. Hopkins," *Secondsout.com*.

15. Amy Scott-Douglass, *Shakespeare Inside: The Bard Behind Bars* (New York and London: Continuum, 2007), 4–5. See also Jean Trounstine, *Shakespeare Behind Bars: The Power of Drama in a Women's Prison* (New York: St Martin's Press, 2001).

16. Laura Bates, *Shakespeare Saved My Life: Ten Years in Solitary with the Bard* (Naperville, Ill.: Sourcebooks, 2013), 146.

17. Ibid., 251–5.

18. Scott-Douglass, *Shakespeare Inside*, ch. 1.

19. Ibid., 44–5.

20. Ibid., 12.

21. Ibid., 15.

22. Ibid., 113.

23. Bates, *Shakespeare Saved My Life*, 18–20.

24. Ibid., 77–8, 95–9.

25. Ibid., 139–40.

26. Ibid., 179–80.

27. Scott-Douglass, *Shakespeare Inside*, 114.

28. Earl Shorris, *Riches for the Poor: The Clemente Course in the Humanities* (New York and London: W. W. Norton, 2000), 96–100.

29. Ibid., 176.

30. Ibid., 225.

31. Ibid., 125.

32. Ibid., 161.

33. Earl Shorris, *The Art of Freedom: Teaching Humanities to the Poor* (New York and London: W. W. Norton, 2013), 26–7.

34. Shorris, *Riches for the Poor*, 183.

35. Ibid., 141.

36. Ibid., 149–50.
37. Ibid., 136.
38. Ibid., 152–3.
39. Jenny Hartley and Sarah Turvey, *Prison Reading Groups: What Books Can Do Behind Bars* (Roehampton: University of Roehampton, 2013).
40. David Comer Kidd and Emanuele Castano, "Reading Literary Fiction Improves Theory of Mind," *Science* 342 (18 Oct. 2013): 377–80.
41. Franklin E. Court, *Institutionalizing English Literature: The Culture and Politics of Literary Study, 1750–1900* (Stanford: Stanford University Press, 1992), 17–30.

6

On Not Believing What You Read

Every student should, before graduating, see the 2006 teen-comedy movie *Accepted*. It's a broad satire built around some high-school misfits whom no college admissions officer in his right mind would accept, not even in this economy. So they commandeer an abandoned mental asylum and construct their own college based on Marxism (Groucho), and they do to higher education what *A Night at the Opera* did to *Il Trovatore*. To a flabbergasted visitor, the teenage president of the college recommends the school newspaper, *The Rag*. "There's a great op-ed piece in there about not believing everything you read," he explains.

Like all absurdist comedy, *Accepted* poses that subversive question, "Who's absurd here?" It stands upside-down all the pretenses of university life, including its most fundamental pretense, that if we spend years here reading, we will get closer to the truth. Is there, though, any necessary relation between reality and what we find on the printed page? It's a question that has become particularly acute today, when it seems that every man is his own deconstructionist. When Paul Ricoeur coined the phrase "hermeneutic of suspicion," he was only recommending this reading strategy to literary theorists, but his students took it quite seriously and in 1968 turned the University of Nanterre into, well, something like the campus in *Accepted*. And today that skepticism is thoroughly mainstream. According to the Gallup Poll, only 32 percent of Americans in 2016 have confidence in the media, down from a high of 72 percent in 1976, post-Woodward and Bernstein.[1] Among millennials (18-to-29-year-olds), just 11 percent trust the media.[2] In Britain, back in 1975, only about a third of tabloid readers and just 3 percent of readers of "quality" broadsheets felt that their paper "often gets its facts wrong."[3] But by 2012 no British daily was trusted by a majority of the public "to report fairly and accurately." In something of a contradiction, the *Sun* enjoyed both the largest circulation and the lowest level of trust (just 9 percent). But even the quality papers, with much smaller readerships, did not enjoy much public confidence, ranging from 37 percent for *The Times* to 48 percent for the *Financial Times*.[4] Overall, in 2014, just 22 percent of the British public trusted journalists to tell the truth, ranking them lower than bankers (31 percent).[5]

According to the 2017 Edelman Trust Barometer, this suspicion is global in scope and to some extent class-based—that is, those who have college degrees and upper-bracket incomes tend to place more trust in established institutions (including the media) than the rest of the world's population. Worldwide, just 43 percent of people trust the media, down from 48 percent a year earlier. In the United States just 47 percent of those questioned have confidence in the media, compared to a dismal 32 percent in Murdoch-dominated Australia and Britain. Search engines are trusted much more than editors, 59 to 41 percent. What is remarkable is that there is no positive correlation between democracy and public confidence in the media, which is often greatest in authoritarian societies like China (65 percent) and Singapore (54 percent).[6]

The disappearance of independent, family-owned newspapers, and the increasing concentration of surviving media outlets in the hands of a few very large conglomerates only feeds this skepticism. Growing numbers of readers, especially younger readers, simply see no point in reading newspapers and magazines at all. In 1970, 73 percent of 18-to-24-year-olds and 77 percent of 25-to-34-year-olds regularly read newspapers; by 2007 both figures had collapsed to 34 percent.[7]

You might blame it all on the Internet, and the cacophony of voices it pipes into your home. But skeptical reading has a much longer history, which can help us understand its ebbs and flows and roots and causes. Certainly it has been a huge asset for one politician: a December 2015 Rasmussen poll found that 47 percent of likely American voters thought the media was biased against Donald Trump, and another 22 percent were unsure, whereas just 23 percent thought the media was slanted against Hillary Clinton, and 59 percent disagreed. Fully 71 percent said that reporters abandon objectivity to help candidates they personally favor.[8] So it didn't matter what the papers said about Trump, because readers no longer trusted them. In Woody Allen's *Deconstructing Harry*, a darkly sardonic author faces the accusation: "You have no values! With you it's all nihilism, cynicism, sarcasm, and orgasm!'" "Hey," he shoots back, "in France I could run for office with that slogan, and win!" In the United States, Donald Trump ran for President on a platform of a hermeneutic of suspicion, and won.

That skepticism is probably as old as writing. In an oral culture you can literally interrogate the author, face to face, to assess his reliability. There is far more uncertainty in script—you're not sure who wrote it, you can't ask him for clarification, he isn't looking you in the face, he's not addressing his remarks to you exclusively, you don't know what his agenda is, and it's very hard to determine whether he can be trusted. That sums up Socrates's complaint in *Phaedrus*.

In *The Invention of News*, Andrew Pettegree shows that readers have always treated verbal reports as more credible than written reports, and written reports as more credible than printed reports. Two monasteries in eleventh-century Wales shared news not by exchanging letters but by exchanging two monks, who visited for a week and related all the latest events.[9] But newspapers, invented 500 years later, were a business, and therefore less trustworthy than personal acquaintances. A newspaper would tell you anything that boosted profits. William Shakespeare did not live to see the first English newspapers, but he realized that news was a commodity that could be marketed:

> CELIA: Here comes Monsieur Le Beau.
> ROSALIND: With his mouth full of news.
> CELIA: Which he will put on us, as pigeons feed their young.
> ROSALIND: Then shall we be news-crammed.
> CELIA: All the better; we shall be the more marketable.
>
> (*As You Like It*, I.ii.82–7)

Or as the seventeenth-century wit Samuel Butler put it:

> A news-monger is a retailer of rumor, that takes upon trust, and sells as cheap as he buys. He deals in a perishable commodity, that will not keep: for if it be not fresh it lies upon his hands and will yield nothing. True or false is all one to him; for novelty being the grace of both, a truth grows stale as soon as a lie; and as a slight suit will last as well as a better while the fashion holds, a lie serves as well as truth till new ones come up.[10]

The first true newspaper—that is, a printed serial reporting current events, published at regular intervals under a running title—appeared in Strasbourg in 1605. The Thirty Years War broke out in 1618, and even if England wasn't involved, English readers were keenly interested in reading about the continental struggles between Protestants and Catholics. That demand called into existence the first English newspapers, and printer Nathaniel Butter was involved in launching two of them: the *Corante* (1621) and the *Weekly News* (1622). Butter's print shop, in St Paul's churchyard, became the first news agency, which collected information, put it into print, and sold it to eager customers.

John Pory, a well-connected political figure, supplied Butter with news by exchanging letters with movers and shakers (hence the term "correspondent"), and in that sense could be called one of the first "access journalists." (Remember that concept: it will cause serious problems later on.) He also studied as many other news publications as he could obtain, though knew that they were hardly reliable sources:

> A man that reads these toys every week as they come forth is like one that stands in a field of Archers, where though he sees not the mark, but observing how the arrows fall, some short, some gone, some on the right and some on the left hand, he hath a near guess where about the mark is; so that he that reads those babble for a year or however will be able very handsomely to conjecture at the general state of Christendom.[11]

Three hundred years before Ben Hecht and Charles MacArthur's *The Front Page*, Ben Jonson wrote the first dramatic satire of journalism, *A Staple of News* (1625). Like any Marxist media critic, Jonson exposed the commoditization of journalism: a "staple" could be anything that customers bought and consumed on a regular basis, like coffee or butter. Jonson had wicked fun punning on Nicholas Butter's name, and in fact taverns and coffee-houses drew in customers by making newsletters available for perusal: one Oxfordshire alehouse served up news stories for a halfpenny each.[12] Jonson was a master of scam-artist comedies, like *Volpone* and *The Alchemist*, and likewise he lampooned the news business as a racket. But—and this makes *The Staple of News* a truly remarkable document—Jonson also anticipated developments in journalism that would not be fully realized until the nineteenth, twentieth, and twenty-first centuries. And he feared and loathed what was coming. Jonson had seen the future, and it lied.

Jonson's journalists breathlessly describe a revolutionary new venture, like today's social-media entrepreneurs pitching to investors. It will be "a staple of news!...a brave young office set up. To enter all the news, sir, o' the time. And vent it as occasion serves! A place of huge commerce it will be!" There will be an office with desks and tables and shelves, "Where all the news of all sorts shall be brought, and there be examined, and then registered, and so be issued under the seal of the office, as staple news; no other news be current." Jonson imagined the newsrooms of any modern newspaper or television network, a highly futuristic vision of a business in the very earliest stage of development. A "master of the office" would manage and dispatch "emissaries"—that is, "Men employed outward, that are sent abroad to fetch in the commodity. From all regions where the best news are made. Or vented forth. By way of exchange or trade" (I.ii.23–8, 33–6, 48–53). The words "editor" and "reporter" had not yet been invented, but Jonson fully grasped the concept. He imagined "jeerers" (professional iconoclasts like H. L. Mencken and Jon Stewart), and even anticipated tools of information management, where news is sorted and classified by source, subject, and credibility. His seventeenth-century editor sounds uncannily like a twenty-first century editor bragging about the organization of his personal computer (I.v.5–8):

> And here I have my several rolls and files
> Of news by the alphabet, and all put up
> Under their heads.

It all sounded so persuasive that evidently some theatergoers thought Jonson was celebrating this new form of journalism. He had to insert a warning between the second and third acts that this was satire. His intent was to show that the news was simply "a weekly cheat to draw money...wherein the age may see her own folly, or hunger and thirst after published pamphlets of news, set out every Saturday, but made all at home, and no syllable of truth in them" (To the Readers, ll. 8–13).

A Staple of News is accompanied by a Greek chorus of four women, who make clear that the readers want gossip about celebrities: "Who wears the new suit today: whose clothes are best penned, whatever the part be: which actor has the best leg and foot: what king plays without cuffs, and his queen without gloves: who rides post in stockings, and

dances in boots …, and which amorous prince makes love in drink, or
does overact prodigiously in beaten satin" (Induction, ll. 35–41). What
these Jacobean ladies demanded was essentially *People* magazine,
reporting who was wearing what and having affairs with whom and
which bodies were hot. In fact early newspapers did supply celebrity
gossip, but as the seventeenth-century journalist Gregorio Leti observed,
that kind of pabulum can destroy credibility even among readers who
enjoy it as a guilty pleasure:

> What difference does it make to the people of France to know
> that the emperor held a dance for the dames? Why do the
> Germans have to know that the Most Christian King was or
> was not at the hunt? What effect will it make on the Roman
> people, to know that the king of Spain went to see a bullfight?
> What profit may the English people gain from hearing that the
> Pope went to Sant'Andrea della Valle?

Obviously, Leti concluded, it's all dope for the masses, and the masses
are wise to it: "Such bagatelles…serve for nothing but for making
everyone laugh who reads them." We see the same law of journalism at
work today, when gossip magazines are booming, news magazines are
going out of business, and nobody believes any of it.[13]

Given that early newspapers published fantastic stories about pigs
born with three heads or blood raining from the sky or an impossibly
long-necked African creature supposedly called a "giraffe," readers
grew understandably skeptical when the same news sources told them
of great military victories, especially when other sources reported that
these battles had been fiascos or never really happened. Early newspapers were actually quite scrupulous about attribution, prefacing
stories with qualifying phrases like, "it has been heard," "it is reported
that," "according to letters from Antwerp or newspapers in Milan,"
signaling to readers that these reports were mediated and might not
be entirely reliable. And, especially when reporting complicated civil
wars, where battle-lines were not clearly drawn, news writers often
honestly confessed that they did not know what the hell was going on:
"The affairs of the [English] kingdom have never been as confused…as
they are at present;" "The news we have concerning the affairs of Turin
is so rare and uncertain that one might almost with more frankness
talk about the affairs of Japan;" "The news of Naples is very exciting,
and it is contradictory in many things."[14]

In the English Civil War, Royalists and Roundheads both sponsored their own newspapers, and one historian gave newsmen on both sides credit for pioneering "such nineteenth- and twentieth-century journalistic practices as carefully planted rumors, trial balloons, supposedly authentic gossip, destructive innuendos, and blatantly political atrocity stories."[15] When John Rushworth wrote one of the first histories of the war, he found that the pamphlets he relied on as sources were wholly unreliable: "Men's fancies were more busy than their hands...printing declarations, which were never passed; relating battles which were never fought, and victories which were never obtained; dispensing letters, which were never writ by the authors."[16] The marginal jottings made by seventeenth-century readers suggests that they were often skeptical, frequently scribbling "false" or "a better Poet than Historien," or "Nothing but fooleries & rascallitiy" or "Newes and I must still be at odds."[17]

And yet practically every literate person read the news, from the artisan classes up to Prince Charles (in exile). Even illiterate soldiers, in both armies, had newspapers read aloud to them by their officers. John Bunyan confessed that, as a young man, he preferred them to the "dead letter" of Scripture: those who walked with the Lord had to follow reports of the theological struggles that were convulsing England. The husband of one Puritan woman recalled that, "When any Diurnalls, weekly, were brought to the house, she would say, let me hear so far as concerns the Church, and cause of God; for other things, I let them passe." Extensive comments scribbled in the margins of newsbooks, along with lengthy summaries copied into diaries, provide evidence that these publications were read intensively and critically. Readers recognized propaganda everywhere, and did not necessarily believe that their own papers had a monopoly on truth. Though he was a Roundhead officer and MP, Sir Samuel Luke closely followed the Royalist paper *Mercurius Aulicus*, mining it for useful intelligence, and he did not entirely trust his own parliamentarian news sources: "I fear the Cavaliers have had good success which makes [our] Diurnalls so silent at London." Then as now, readers were sensitive to media bias and often exaggerated it: newsbooks were commonly accused of propagandizing for the radical Independents, though in fact they mostly reflected the views of the moderate Presbyterians. But whatever your political sympathies, you had to read and compare as many papers as you could get your hands on to get a full sense of the revolutionary turmoil of the times. And useful clues could be gleaned even from unreliable sources, much as Soviet readers 300 years later decoded *Pravda* for evidence of power-struggles in the Kremlin. When newsbooks in 1649 reported that Oliver Cromwell was using the royal "we" in proclamations, some readers took that as sign that he was about to declare himself king. (He never did, though as "Lord Protector" he enjoyed more arbitrary power than any monarch.)[18]

"Grub Street" was an actual slum in London, fetid and disease-ridden, named after the "grub" (refuse ditch) that bordered it. During the English Civil War it acquired a reputation as a home to scurrilous writers and printers, who became known as "hacks," a term previously applied to horses for hire and prostitutes.[19] The end of pre-publication censorship in England in 1695, combined with the rise of a two-party system, ensured that there would be a raucous ongoing debate between Whig and Tory papers. But if each exposed the errors and lies of the other in a fiercely partisan spirit, that damaged the credibility of the press as a whole. It didn't help matters that some papers presumed to be above it all, and told their readers that surely they were too sophisticated to believe what they read in print. "The newspapers of this island", pronounced the *Tatler*, "are as pernicious to weak heads in England as ever books of chivalry to Spain." Journalists in eighteenth-century Britain enjoyed a poisonous reputation, for the most part well deserved. Newspapers in this period were usually either bought-and-paid-for government mouthpieces, or they were scandal sheets that published damaging gossip about the high and mighty—unless the high and mighty paid them not to publish. A parliamentary committee found that the first prime minister, Robert Walpole, spent £10,000 a year of taxpayers' money bribing newspapers. The difficulty was that any newspaper perceived as whoring for the political establishment lost credibility, lost circulation, and (hence) lost money. The owner of one opposition newspaper actually did the spreadsheet and concluded that, if he sold out to the authorities, his annual profits would fall from £960 to £124. By the end of the century, British newspapers would secure financial independence from a huge increase in advertising income (from £1,023 in 1715 to £54,890 by 1790), and then government bribes were no longer worth accepting.[20]

We know the indispensable role of printers in fomenting the American Revolution, but we should be more aware of the fact that there were deep ideological divisions in the press of that era. In 1768, as the controversy over the Townshend Acts exploded, Jane Franklin, writing to her brother Benjamin from Boston, advised him that "the newspapers will not infallibly inform you for the truth. Every thing that every design-ing person has a mind to propagate is stuffed into them, & it is difficult to know whether either party are in the right."[21] Covering the Battle of Breed's Hill, the *Pennsylvania Packet* reported that 1,500 continental troops had fought 2,000 redcoats to a standstill, and pulled back only when given an erroneous order; while the *New York Gazette and Weekly Mercury* claimed that 5,000 British regulars were held off by 2,000 Americans until the latter ran out of ammunition; whereas the *New York Gazetteer* hailed "the bravery of the king's troops, who under every disadvantage, gained a complete victory over three times their number, strongly posted, and covered by breastworks." It wasn't a matter of ideological bias: all three papers were Loyalist.[22] No wonder Jane and Ben were bewildered.

One solution to this problem was to establish a royal news monopoly, as Louis XIV did with his official *Gazette*. As long as the *Gazette* had glorious military victories to report, its credibility was quite high, buoyed by a spirit of French patriotism. But when the War of the Spanish Succession went badly for Louis, the *Gazette* fell suspiciously silent. For real news, readers turned to manuscript newsletters, which were remarkably well informed, thoroughly illegal, and impossible for the government to control. This episode taught the French literate classes that official media could not be trusted, ushered in the episteme of Enlightenment skepticism, and created a market for the clandestine subversive publications of the Société Typographique de Neuchâtel, whose role in fomenting revolutionary sentiment has been chronicled by Robert Darnton.

But here's a problem that Darnton bumps up against in his studies of scurrilous literature and the French Revolution. We can be reasonably sure that the official gazettes before 1789 didn't have much credibility, but does it necessarily follow that readers believed the *libelles*, particularly those that spun fantastic conspiracy theories and sex scandals in high places? The end of censorship in 1789 led to the creation of a vast range of newspapers, from reactionary monarchist to radical republican, but as in the case of the recently concluded American Revolution, it was difficult to know whom or what to believe, as these papers reported on fast-moving events, breathlessly and with extreme bias.

Where Addison and Steele established their credibility by writing like gentlemen, revolutionary French journalists did exactly the opposite, appropriating the language of the street. Jacques Hébert adopted the persona of *Père Duchesne*, a pipe-smoking folk character whose language was earthy, vulgar, and violent. To be denounced by *Père Duchesne* was often enough to get you guillotined, which suggests that it did enjoy a high level of credibility in revolutionary circles. And why not? Clearly, here was a true man of the people who told it like it is. Under the title of his paper Hébert ran the subtitle *Je suis le véritable Père Duchesne, foutre!*, which is sometimes rendered in English as: "I am the real Père Duchesne, fuck you!" There were, in fact, other periodicals that appropriated the title *Père Duchesne*, so it may be that Hébert was simply asserting his right to exclusive use of this trademark, but I don't think that translation captures the nuance of *foutre*. Obscenity is often used (for example, by drill sergeants) as a verbal signal that we have switched off the internal censor we normally use in polite conversation, thus underscoring the truthfulness of the statement to which it is attached. So perhaps Hébert was saying, in effect: *Yes, there are a variety of journals reporting diverse versions of current events, but Père Duchesne is telling you the fucking truth!* If Hébert had edited out obscenity, each issue would have been less credible and about a page shorter.

However, in revolutionary France there was one subject where it was easy to verify the claims of journalists: what they wrote about other journalists. And they published quite a lot on that topic, most of it denunciatory. For a few sous one could patronize a *cabinet de lecture* which carried current issues of all the Paris papers, so if two journalists vilified each other, you could easily check if one was caricaturing the other's views, just as today bloggers embed links to other blogs that they're debating. The difficulty was that, when you read what the other side was printing, it was increasingly scary. Not long after the storming of the Bastille, journalistic rhetoric escalated out of control. Valerae Hurley has counted the frequency of the word "vengeance" in papers on the left and the right: it was hardly used at all in 1789, but soon thereafter her Geiger-counter goes beserk.[23] "Citizens of every age and every station!" thundered Jean-Paul Marat in his *L'Ami du peuple* (26 July 1790): "The cutting off of five or six hundred heads would have guaranteed your peace, liberty and happiness. A mistaken humanity has crippled your arms and held back your blows; it will cost the lives of millions of your brothers...Your enemies need only to triumph for a moment, and blood will flow in torrents." The same kind of superheated prose appeared in monarchist papers, and journalists left and right were pointing to each other and writing: *You see what they're saying about us, they are not disguising their bloodthirsty plans, it's either them or us!* And any reader could see that they accurately presented each other's views. The press—and on this issue at least it was a highly credible press—led straight to the Terror, in which one out of six revolutionary-era journalists were executed or assassinated, including both Marat and Hébert.

It led John Adams to question the radical optimism of his youth: "The empire of the press, over the passions, in the hands of Marat and others was more tyrannical than the government of Cesar Borgia...There has been more error propagated from the press in the last ten years than in an hundred years before."[24] His Alien and Sedition Acts were considerably more oppressive than the Stamp Act had ever been. Denounced by Thomas Jefferson, they provoked a public backlash against censorship and in the long run strengthened press freedoms, but by 1807 Jefferson himself was growing disillusioned. "Nothing can now be believed which is seen in a newspaper," he protested:

> Truth itself becomes suspicious by being put into that polluted vehicle. The real extent of this state of misinformation is known only to those who are in a situation to confront facts within their knowledge to the lies of the day...Defamation is becoming a necessary of life...Even those who do not believe these abominations still read them with complacence to their auditors; and...betray a secret pleasure that some may believe them, though they do not themselves.[25]

As editor of *The Times* of London from 1817 to 1841, Thomas Barnes made that paper a leader in terms of circulation, influence, breadth of coverage, and credibility. The paper's unsparing report on and denunciation of the 1819 Peterloo Massacre, when eleven peaceful demonstrators for parliamentary reform were killed by the local militia, established the paper's reputation as an honest voice for change. In 1834 Barnes announced that *The Times* would no longer take advantage of what would later be called "access journalism"—that is, accepting inside tips from official sources, with the understanding that the paper would publish the official version of events. That, Barnes proclaimed, would compromise "the pride and independence of our journal." In an age of reform this was a great step forward, perhaps as significant as Catholic Emancipation and the extension of the franchise. During the Crimean War, *The Times* would exercise that independence by ruthlessly exposing blundering generals and horrific conditions at military hospitals. One historian concludes that those reports "had a similar impact on the British public in the 1850s as the televising of the Vietnam War had on the American public in the 1960s." But that editorial independence, as we will see, was never universal or permanent: it could be rolled back, and often would be.[26]

In the American Civil War, soldiers knew all too well the unreliability of newspapers, as when they reported the capture of Atlanta some time before the Union army arrived there. Sherman's troops burned not only much of Georgia, but also the New York newspapers that criticized their commander. In response to a stinging editorial in the *New York Tribune*, a sergeant suggested that editors should be drafted into a new unit called the Horace Greeley Guards, but then decided that they would be utterly useless in combat.[27] David Curtis started to assemble a scrapbook of war news, "fired with boyish enthusiasm," but he was soon disabused of "the idea newspapers were published for the purpose of telling the truth," and abandoned the project well before Appomattox. Scrapbookers sometimes pasted differing accounts of the same battle from various newspapers, in the apparent hope that they might piece together the truth from all of them. And scrapbooks could preserve reports, predictions, and rumors that were thoroughly discredited by later events. One Confederate POW collected clippings from Northern newspapers with a view toward exposing all their contradictions.[28]

The Progressive Era was the heyday of muckraking and "Yellow Journalism," even if it was sometimes difficult to tell them apart. But two compelling pieces of evidence suggest great and growing public confidence in print publications. The first was their surging circulation. W. T. Stead's 1885 exposé of child prostitution in London, "The Maiden Tribute of Modern Babylon," boosted the circulation of the *Pall Mall Gazette* ten times over. And as *McClure's* discovered when they published Ida Tarbell on Standard Oil, nothing sold papers like an exposé of the rich and powerful, who were deeply resented by the middle classes, industrial workers, farmers, and immigrants. Moreover, every important political reform of that era (such as the foundation of the Food and Drug Administration) was inspired by investigative reporting: journalism was believed and translated into action.

In the 1920s American newspapers squandered much of that hard-won credibility, as investigative journalism retreated in the face of tabloid scandalmongering. In New York City, the *Daily News*, *Daily Mirror*, and *Daily Graphic* swiftly raced to the bottom. The *Graphic* was the louche creation of pulp-magazine publisher Bernarr Macfadden, and he brought to daily journalism the literary techniques of lowbrow fiction. The *Graphic* specialized in obviously faked photographs (Rudolph Valentino entering heaven, for instance), but that was only the most blatant example of what was, at the time, a very common practice. The invention of photomechanical reproduction did not necessarily make newspapers more believable. And though we can be nostalgic for a time when everyone (it seemed) read and believed in the *Saturday Evening Post*, in Muncie high-school students were evenly split between those who had confidence in the magazine and the small-town Menckens who thought it was so much malarkey.[29]

The *Daily Graphic* was bankrupted by the Great Depression and libel suits, and in the 1930s public trust in newspapers hit new lows. Not only had they failed to anticipate the 1929 crash, they had fed the frenzy by publishing dubious stock tips. Before the Senate Banking Committee, Congressman Fiorello LaGuardia produced a trunkful of clippings and cancelled checks proving that financial reporters commonly accepted bribes from financial promoters to puff dodgy stocks.[30] With Franklin Roosevelt in the White House, the majority of newspapers were hostile to the New Deal, and most of them were owned by huge press combines. That there was no necessary connection between the truth and what newspapers printed was the working assumption behind Hollywood films of the era: *The Front Page*, *Libeled Lady*, *Nothing Sacred*, *Citizen Kane*. Charles Foster Kane begins his journalistic career by busting trusts and exposing sleazy politicians (and yes, starting a war in Cuba), but he ends it complacently predicting that there will be no war in Europe, as William Randolph Hearst and Lord Beaverbrook actually did in their papers.

In Britain the press lost the public trust in part because it failed to report the two most sensational scandals of all. By gentlemen's agreement, it blacked out the romance of King Edward and Mrs Simpson as long as possible. American papers had no such inhibitions, but they were removed from UK news-stands, and incriminating pages were torn from *Time* magazine.[31] Generally pro-appeasement, British newspapers also pulled their punches in reporting on Nazi Germany, and tried to give Winston Churchill as little coverage as possible. Neville Chamberlain and his Cabinet colleagues were masters of spin, quietly influencing publishers and editors, and rewarding cooperative journalists with private briefings at 10 Downing Street—yet another disgraceful episode of access journalism. Many readers turned to a kind of alternative press—mimeographed newsletters that promised to report the real deal about European diplomacy, most famously Claud Cockburn's *The Week*. And when American journalist John Gunther published his book *Inside Europe*, British readers made it a bestseller, because it offered what they could not find in their own newspapers: tough reporting about the Fascist threat.[32]

In his 1939 autobiography *Days of Our Years*, Pierre van Paassen, a foreign correspondent for American and Canadian papers between the wars, revealed that he had to censor himself when covering European dictatorships:

> Since I could not afford to be excluded from a single European country with so general an assignment, it was in my interest to remain on the good side of all the nascent censorships in Europe. Hence many things I investigated or saw remained unreported. For example, in 1928... [about] the methods of the reactionary governments of Rumania and Bulgaria in suppressing popular movements—twelve thousand peasants and workers had been slain in Bulgaria alone that year—I could not send out a word. The police dogged our every footstep... The managing editor, Mr. John H. Tennant, warned me more than once that I had not been sent over on a crusading mission. He added, moreover, that there was no confirmation from any reliable source on that horrible business in Bulgaria. The local agency correspondents had not sent a word. So I, too, remained silent. It was the only policy. Correspondents like George Seldes, Samuel Spivak, David Darrah Gedye, and myself discovered only too soon that if we did speak out, we did not last very long, either in the countries in which we were stationed or in our jobs.[33]

The revelations in *Days of Our Years* made it a Book-of-the-Month Club selection and the number-one bestselling non-fiction book of 1939.

That was the message of Alfred Hitchcock's 1940 thriller *Foreign Correspondent*. Set in August 1939, with the world on the verge of war, an American newspaper editor loses patience with his lazy European reporters, who only send him anodyne press releases issued by diplomats. He dispatches across the Atlantic intrepid newsman Joel McCrae, who has absolutely no knowledge of European affairs, but who brings to the job the same hard-hitting investigative skills that made him New York's top crime reporter. And he scoops the world with an exposé of yet another criminal conspiracy, revealing that a so-called "peace organization" is in fact a nest of Nazi spies. The final scene of the movie flashes forward one year, to the Blitz on London. Joel McCrae has somehow moved from print to broadcast journalism, but even as the bombs fall around him he heroically stands by his microphone, warning Americans to prepare for the coming Nazi onslaught. Of course, it's an allusion to Edward R. Murrow and his riveting reports from London under fire. In fact, at the time, American audiences found live radio far more real and credible than what they read in the papers. Just as Socrates had predicted, you could believe Murrow, because he was speaking directly to you, and you could hear the bombs exploding.

Hitchcock may also have had in mind George Seldes, a fiercely independent muckraker whose main target, throughout the 1930s and 1940s, was the media itself. His weekly newsletter *In Fact* was subtitled "An Antidote for Falsehood in the Daily Press." Seldes said he published stories the newspapers wouldn't touch for fear of offending advertisers: he was among the first to reveal that tobacco caused cancer. For a while he attracted a large following, including Ralph Nader, Daniel Ellsberg, I. F. Stone, and Nat Hentoff.

By 1940 public suspicion of advertisers was so great that one daily newspaper tried to banish ads. *PM* was an experimental leftish New York tabloid that survived by charging a staggeringly high news-stand price of 5 cents. But its finances were precarious, and it learned painfully that advertising is itself news: readers wanted to know about the latest sales at Macy's, Gimbel's, and Bloomingdale's. So *PM* was ultimately forced to print summaries of department store ads from other papers, giving large capitalist enterprises free publicity.

In Britain the only major advertising-free news medium was the BBC, which enjoyed an unrivaled reputation for objectivity during the war. The newspaper press had been sullied by its pro-appeasement stance before the 1939, its tub-thumbing patriotism thereafter, suspicions of government censorship, and its slanted reporting. A 1942 Mass Observation survey reported that: "There is a common tendency to divide any news in the paper by half," and that "reading between the lines of a newspaper is becoming a national pastime."[34] One reader took refuge in the *New Statesman*, "in the hopes of gleaning a few facts which newspapers and radio studiously avoid," another read the sedate *Christian Science Monitor*, because "it doesn't mix its news and views up together, like Beaverbrook's dirty rags do," and still others relied on books rather than newspapers for serious reporting on politics.[35]

But nothing enhances journalistic credibility more than reporting on a victorious war—or a mostly victorious Cold War. By 1950, *In Fact* and *PM* were out of business. For the next generation there was whole new sense of confidence in the American press. Yes, there were a few glitches, like that notorious "Dewey Defeats Truman" headline, but the *Chicago Tribune* was actually the only paper that called the 1948 election wrong. True, when a young Robert Darnton briefly worked as a cub reporter for the *Newark Star-Ledger*, he had to learn that missing debutantes were big news, black-on-black homicides weren't worth reporting, and every story had to follow a stereotyped narrative formula, but no one else in the newsroom seemed to have a problem with that.[36] And granted, PR genius Edward Bernays lobbied Arthur Hays Sulzberger (a relative by marriage) to slant *New York Times* coverage of the Arbenz regime in Guatemala and prepare public opinion for the invasion of that country in 1954. But Bernays was proud of his work, bragged about it, and obviously thought Arbenz had it coming.[37] Anyway, it all conformed to the national consensus of Cold War liberalism.

Two journalistic challenges to that consensus would be launched in 1955, just a few days apart. William F. Buckley's *National Review* almost from the start charged the liberal media with bias. It would zero in especially on Herbert Matthew's sympathetic coverage of the Cuban Revolution in the *New York Times*. Back then the *Times* promoted its own job ads section in subway placards, which always featured a smiling white-collar worker in an attractive office, under the running caption: "I got my job through the *New York Times.*" *National Review* ran the same slogan over a picture of Fidel Castro.

Meanwhile, the *Village Voice* attacked the *Times* from the left, with Jack Newfield and Alexander Cockburn (son of Claud Cockburn) reporting what (they charged) the establishment media was not reporting. Later, on the West Coast, there was the glossy New Left monthly *Ramparts*, which carried on the muckraking tradition by denouncing the use of napalm and the collusion of American universities in the Vietnam War effort.

And they had a prime target: James Reston, *New York Times* editor, the most distinguished journalist of his day, two-time winner of the Pulitzer Prize, the very model of an establishment insider. He enjoyed privileged access to everyone in Washington, including Lyndon Johnson, Henry Kissinger, and Edward Kennedy. His tragic flaw was that he habitually believed what these powerful men told him, and he uncritically presented their versions of the truth in the *Times*. On at least one occasion he spiked a story that reflected badly on Kissinger, and promised him that he would persuade fellow *Times* columnist Anthony Lewis to tone down his criticisms of the Secretary.

By the late 1960s not just the *Times*, but the mainstream press as a whole was under attack from the counter-culture. It seemed that every city of any size had its own alternative weekly, and every college and high school had an underground newspaper, publishing what heavily censored student papers could not. Even newspapers had underground newspapers, such as the *Chicago Journalism Review*, where working journalists criticized the very papers they worked for. The *Village Voice*, ensconced in the relatively bourgeois West Village, was itself denounced as dismally establishmentarian by a more radical paper, the *East Village Other*, which was in turn challenged by the still grottier *Rat: Subterranean News*. And then the editors of *Rat* resorted to a routine circulation-booster used by any number of similar papers: they put a naked woman on the front page. And what do you know, they found themselves assailed by an even newer and more radical movement called women's lib. Who saw that coming? But you see the pattern here: a succession of increasingly radical papers, each one denouncing its predecessors as sellouts, each one asserting that it alone told it like it is, until the feminists commandeered *Rat* and rechristened it *Women's LibeRATion. Je suis la veritable Mère Duchesne, foutre!*

The underground newspapers actually did not have much of an impact. They usually lasted only a few years and their readership was fairly small: most Americans were repelled by their editorial mix of sex, drugs, rock-and-roll, and ultra-left politics. Whatever the *East Village Other* might say, the mainstream media wasn't all bland and conformist: if Sixties readers wanted edginess, they could find it in glossy mass-circulation magazines like *Esquire*. Hugh Hefner was outraged that New Frontier officials had manipulated the news during the Cuban Missile Crisis, and warned his readers "that such censorship is more apt to be used to cover up Government mistakes than for any strategic advantage in the Cold War."[38] A few years later Playmates were patriotically delivering copies of *Playboy* to our boys in Vietnam, but soon the magazine turned sharply critical of the war. Willie Morris took over the venerable *Harper's* and proceeded to publish Norman Mailer on the tumultuous 1968 presidential conventions, Gay Talese on the *New York Times*, and Seymour Hersh on the My Lai massacre. After four years of this the bottom-line boys had had enough ("Who are you editing the magazine for—a bunch of hippies?"), but rather cave in to corporate pressure, Morris quit on principle, along with most of his writers. Even the middlebrow *Saturday Evening Post* ran a cover story on Barney Rosset and the "dirty books" he was profitably publishing at Evergreen Press in its 25 January 1969 issue. (It was a last desperate attempt at cool, and two weeks later the magazine expired under the strain.) At first the press followed the official line on Vietnam, but as the reading public soured on the war, so did mainstream journalists. At the *New York Times*, James Reston might have believed Lyndon Johnson, but Harrison Salisbury reported that his bombers were killing civilians in Hanoi.

And then there was Woodward and Bernstein. They were by no means solely responsible for digging up the Watergate story, but the affair did much to restore public confidence in newspapers, which rose from 39 percent in May 1973 to 51 percent in April 1979.[39] After all the terrible disillusionments of the 1960s, they proved that the system could work. A mainstream newspaper had done what newspapers were supposed to do: it revealed wrongdoing in the highest places and made the chief perpetrator pay a price. This was a story that the underground press had missed: *Ramparts* dismissed it all as a shootout between two rival establishmentarian gangs, not worth the attention of true radicals. Nixon resigned in 1974, and in 1975 *Ramparts* closed down.

The final quarter of the twentieth century would be the second golden age of American investigative reporting. Most American cities had by this point become one-newspaper towns. With the demise of the *Herald Tribune* in 1966 and the *Washington Star* in 1981, the *New York Times* and the *Washington Post* no longer had any effective competition. But the surviving papers now enjoyed secure monopoly profits, which they were happy to invest in investigative journalism. Everyone hoped to emulate the triumph of Woodward and Bernstein and snag a Pulitzer Prize.

That should have enhanced their credibility among their readers, who, as members of the Sixties Generation, expected and demanded hard-hitting journalism. But the polls clearly indicate that, after hitting a high-water mark in the late 1970s, public trust of the media began a slow but very steady decline. If the press was indeed telling it like it is, why did that happen? Several converging factors were at work.

First, journalists and their audience were drifting apart politically. Jim Kuypers counted the ideological slants of American newspaper editorials between 1958 and 1973, and found a dramatic shift from right to left. But their readers, if anything, went in the opposite direction, turning sharply against the Democrats in 1968. Running against George McGovern in 1972, Richard Nixon saw that "the Eastern Establishment media finally has a candidate who almost totally shares their views," opening up a huge credibility gap: now Americans would "find out whether what the media has been standing for during these last five years really represents majority thinking." Nixon won by a landslide, and every Republican administration since has gained traction alleging "liberal media bias." And in reality, since then journalists have been far more liberal and likely to vote Democratic than the American public as a whole. The Kennedy assassination also opened a big divide between the mainstream press (which generally supported the conclusions of the Warren Commission) and their readership (where belief in conspiracy theories was widespread).[40]

Second, there was the problem of the revolving door, where journalists became operatives for powerful politicians and operatives went to work in newsrooms. News professionals found themselves employed by John F. Kennedy (Pierre Salinger), Lyndon Johnson (Tom Johnson,

Jack Rosenthal, Leslie Gelb), Jimmy Carter (Gelb again, Chris Matthews, Brian Williams, Rick Inderfurth), Bill Clinton (David Shipley, Sidney Blumenthal, Strobe Tablott, Tara Sonenshine, George Stephanopoulos), or other Democratic politicians (Tim Russert, Jeff Greenfield, Ken Bode, Elizabeth Brackett, Jane Pauley, Ken Aluetta, Walter Pincus, Carolyn Curiel), or they were the children of Democratic politicians (Cokie Roberts, Eleanor Mondale, Chris Cuomo).[41] It all looked increasingly incestuous.

Third, a succession of prominent journalists were publicly exposed for extensively fabricating material: Janet Cooke of the *Washington Post* (1980), Patricia Smith of the *Boston Globe* (1998), Stephen Glass of the *New Republic* (1998), and most recently a report in *Rolling Stone* of a gruesome campus rape that never happened. Most devastating of all was Jayson Blair of the *New York Times*, who invented reports about the Beltway Sniper. That ended the career of his editor, Howell Raines, and forced the *Times* to police itself by creating a "Public Editor" who would (it was hoped) criticize the paper that was paying his or her salary. But it was a humiliating reminder to readers that the *Times* was not infallible—at least until the position was axed in June 2017.[42]

A fourth factor is counter-intuitive. We assume that Woodward and Bernstein inspired a whole cadre of young idealists to enroll in journalism school and become investigative reporters, but some in that age cohort learned a very different lesson. There was at least prominent member of the Sixties Generation who, by 1977, was warning that: "One of our problems is trying to control a press that is far out of line because of Watergate." It was Hillary Clinton.[43] Bill had begun his long march to the White House, and she correctly foresaw that pesky reporters could create difficulties for both of them. Never before (or since) had a newspaper brought down a president, a fact that struck terror into the heart of anyone with high political ambitions. Veterans of the Washington press corps generally recall that presidents tolerated reporters as a fact of life up through George Bush I, but that changed abruptly when the first member of the post-Watergate generation entered the White House. There had always been a passageway leading from the press room to the West Wing, and immediately after Bill's inaugural, Hillary had it closed. That set the pattern for the First Couple, who stumbled from one scandal to the next, frantically covering their tracks, with an exasperated press corps in hot pursuit. Soon

Hillary gave up reading newspapers in disgust—which only further impaired her ability to anticipate train-wrecks. When she later lashed out at the "vast right-wing conspiracy," her anger was in fact directed generally at the Washington press corps, most of which was left of center. The White House worked out on paper an elaborate blueprint for this "Communication Conspiracy," according to which stories damaging to the Clintons would originate in journals on the right, or British tabloids (looking for another Profumo scandal), or in one case the *Economist* magazine, and then were picked up by the *New York Times*, *Washington Post*, *Los Angeles Times*, *USA Today*, AP, UPI, and Reuters. In the Clintons' conspiracy theory, they were all in on it, as either instigators or enablers.[44]

We also have to consider (fifth) the rise of a new type of political organization devoted solely to monitoring and denouncing perceived media bias. It began on the right with the foundation of Reed Irvine's Accuracy in Media in 1969, later identified by the Clintons as a key player in the "Communication Conspiracy." It wasn't until 1986 that the left responded with its own Fairness and Accuracy in Reporting, and in 2004 Media Matters for America. There are also single-issue watchdogs: The Media Bullpen is specifically devoted to defending charter schools, and assigns "batting averages" to media outlets according to whether their coverage is favorable or unfavorable. Of course, these organizations all have their own pronounced biases and agendas and obviously seek to slant news coverage as far as possible in their own direction. They can become, in effect, bodyguards for prominent politicians: Hillary Clinton was an early supporter of Media Matters for America, which was devoted largely to rebutting stories about Hillary Clinton.[45] You could call it anti-investigative journalism, protecting the powerful against nosy reporters, and its method involves attacks on the reporters themselves. Sharyl Attkisson, formerly of CBS News, summarizes the strategy concisely:

> The PR officials wait until the story is published to find out how much the reporter really knows. Then they launch a propaganda campaign with surrogates and sympathizers in the media to divert from the damaging facts. The officials controversialize the reporter and any whistleblowers or critics to try to turn the focus on personalities instead of the evidence.[46]

Thus the reported scandal is no longer the issue—the media is the issue, with functionaries loyal to those in power attacking journalists who are trying to discover what the hell is going on. The reader may well conclude, like Jane Franklin, that she doesn't know who to believe—but in that case, the exposé is neutralized, and those in power have won, while public trust in the media is eroded still further.

Attkisson goes on to describe how government officials and corporate advertisers badger editors to rein in their most dogged reporters, with increasing success. When she exposed the "Fast and Furious" scandal (a bungled drug-enforcement operation that dumped thousands of guns into the hands of Mexican drug cartels), Department of Justice publicist Tracy Schmaler emailed that she was "calling Sharyl's editor and reaching out to [CBS news anchor Bob] Schieffer. She's out of control." Evidently Schmaler assumed that it was right and natural for government officials to control reporters. She was clearly much more comfortable with access journalism, where a Justice official might do "a pen and pad w. select reporters to talk about vision going forward."[47]

Attkisson's pessimistic outlook is representative of American journalists as a whole. A 2013 survey conducted by the Indiana University School of Journalism found that 59.7 percent of working journalists felt their profession was headed in the wrong direction, with just 23.1 percent who said the right direction. One clear problem was a lack of fresh blood: the median age of journalists was just 32 in 1982, but rose to 47 by 2013, mainly because media outlets are hollowing out rather than hiring. For some time there have been more Democratic than Republican journalists, but the big story here is the huge increase in Independents: nearly two out of three journalists do not identify with either of the two main parties. That suggests a growing lack of confidence in mainstream politics, and may explain why even liberal journalists aggressively investigated the Clinton and Obama administrations (or at least tried to); see Table 6.1.

Journalists left the Republican Party in droves following Watergate and the Second Iraq War. They deserted the Democratic Party in large numbers following the Clinton administration, and the hemorrhaging continued into Obama's first term. Still more striking, job satisfaction among journalists has plunged from 49.0 percent in 1971 to 23.3 percent in 2013. Confirming what Sharyl Attkisson observed,

Table 6.1. Political affiliations of US journalists, 1971–2013 (%)

	1971	1982	1992	2002	2013
Democrat	35.5	38.5	44.1	35.9	28.1
Republican	25.7	18.8	16.4	18.0	7.1
Independent	32.5	39.1	34.4	32.5	50.2
Other	6.3	3.6	5.1	13.6	14.6

there has been a marked and fairly recent loss of professional autonomy. In 1971 and 1982, 60 percent of journalists felt they enjoyed
"almost complete freedom" to pursue any stories they wished, falling to
just 33.6 percent by 2013. In that year an all-time high of 78.2 percent
emphasized the importance of "investigating government claims,"
but that may reflect the rueful realization that journalists are no longer
so free to do that. Likewise, 68.8 percent said "analyzing complex
problems" should be a high priority, well up from 50.9 percent in
2002, but that again may be a reaction against the rising tide of short
and superficial reports in print and web news platforms. And whereas
66.8 percent of journalists thought "getting information to the public
quickly" was a top priority in 1992, that figure had fallen to 46.5 percent
by 2012, when the web had imposed relentless pressure to rush stories
out, whether or not they were complete or accurate. Though 39.0
percent of journalists wanted to reach "the widest possible audience"
in 1971, that figure had fallen to an all-time low of 12.1 percent by
2013. That probably reflected the fragmentation of the national
media into an array of niche publications and partisan outlets, but
also the hopelessness of trying to write for a truly national audience.
At the same time, there is an increasing reluctance to use some of the
tried and true techniques of enterprising investigative journalism. In
1992, 62.9 percent of journalists saw nothing wrong with "getting
employed to gain inside information," plummeting to 25.2 percent by
2013. In the same period, support for publishing "confidential business
or government documents without authorization" (the Pentagon Papers
comes to mind) fell from 81.8 to 57.7 percent.[48] Is it any wonder, then,
that readers have lost confidence in the media? *Journalists* have lost
confidence in the media.

Investigative reporting is an expensive and labor-intensive operation, and it was one of the first things to be cut in the twenty-first century, when traditional news outlets lost both advertising and readers to the web. Hard-hitting scoops were a prime weapon in circulation wars, which raged everywhere in 1910, when 689 American towns had competitive daily newspapers, but that number fell to just twenty-six by 1989. As exposés give way to soft news, readers increasingly suspect that the media is catering to its remaining advertisers and spiking anything too controversial. They were not reassured when the *New York Times* in 2013 dissolved its environmental bureau and reassigned its reporters to other departments. According to Dean Starkman's *The Watchdog that Didn't Bark*, that explains why the financial press, with a few exceptions, failed to report the warning signs leading up to the 2008 financial meltdown. Like James Reston in the 1960s and the pro-appeasement British journalists in the 1930s, they had abandoned investigative journalism for access journalism, relying on insider tips rather doing the kind of legwork which could turn up real scandals, but might also antagonize their sources.

Just four years after the Crash, the *New York Times* launched DealBook, a section devoted to mergers and acquisitions. At the invitation-only inaugural party, Margaret Sullivan, the *Times* Public Editor, noticed that journalists and Wall Street giants were once again schmoozing on very cordial terms. She couldn't help but be troubled by "the overall friendly questioning of prominent newsmakers,... the incessant rubbing of journalistic and corporate elbows—the word 'adversarial' did not come to mind. Nor did the word 'watchdog.'" No doubt DealBook generated desperately needed revenue for the *Times*, but was it all "too chummy, too clubby"?[49]

Barack Obama began his presidency with a pledge "to creating an unprecedented level of openness in government." "Instead," wrote Margaret Sullivan in 2013, "it's turning out to be the administration of unprecedented secrecy and unprecedented attacks on a free press." David E. Sanger, the *Times*'s top Washington correspondent, called it "the most closed, control freak administration I've ever covered." Another *Times* journalist, James Risen, called the Obama White House "the greatest enemy of press freedom that we have encountered in a generation." Its aim is to "create a path for accepted reporting," especially on national-security issues, and any reporter who strays from that narrow road "will be punished." For a 2013 report for the Committee to Protect Journalists, former *Washington Post* editor Leonard Downie Jr. interviewed thirty experienced Washington reporters: they agreed that efforts to obstruct and manipulate news coverage had grown progressively worse under Clinton, Bush, and Obama. Downie concluded that, "The [Obama] administration's war on leaks and other efforts to control information are the most aggressive I've seen" since Nixon and Watergate (which he had been involved in covering). The ostensible purpose was to protect national security, but a McClatchy newspapers investigation found government documents that reveal "how some agencies are using that latitude to pursue unauthorized disclosures of any information, not just classified material. They also show how millions of federal employees and contractors must watch for 'high-risk persons or behaviors' among co-workers and could face penalties, including criminal charges, for failing to report them. Leaks to the media are equated with espionage."[50] Ellen Weiss, Washington bureau chief for the Scripps newspapers, reported that "the Obama administration is far worse than the Bush administration" in stonewalling, and pointed to the Environmental Protection Agency, which "just wouldn't talk to us" about environmental review bodies "filled by people with ties to target companies." Journalists were stunned to learn in May 2013 that the Justice Department had secretly subpoenaed and seized the telephone records of more than a hundred Associated Press journalists, apparently as part of an effort to identify leakers. "These records potentially reveal communications with confidential sources across all of the newsgathering activities undertaken by the AP during a two-month period, provide a road map to AP's newsgathering operations and disclose information about AP's activities and operation that the government has no conceivable right to know," protested AP chief Gary Pruitt. "The message being sent is: If you talk to the press, we're going after you." All the major American news organizations (more than fifty all) published a collective protest. And a new low point was reached a few days after, when it was learned that the Justice Department had raised the specter of prosecuting Fox News reporter James Rosen under the Espionage Act, for his investigation of American surveillance of North Korea's nuclear program. Tony Mauro, reporter for the *National Law Journal*, said it clearly violated "the free press guarantee of the First Amendment. This subpoena puts an arctic chill on the invaluable information reporters glean from confidential sources every day, thwarting the public's right to know what its government is doing."[51]

Reporters Without Borders publishes an annual World Press Freedom Index, ranking all nations, and under President Obama the United States fell from twentieth place in 2009 to number forty-nine in 2015, mainly the result of "the government's war on whistleblowers." (There was a similar decline during the Bush administration.) The United States recovered a bit to forty-one in 2016, compared to thirty-eight for the United Kingdom, but both were well behind Ghana (twenty-six) and Namibia (seventeen).[52]

As I write, the Trump administration and the media are fighting the opening battles of what promises to be a grinding war of attrition. This is only the latest escalation of a very long conflict (as the preceding discussion should make clear), and it is much too early to predict the outcome. But shortly after the first shots were fired, two *New York Times* reporters warned Donald Trump that neither he nor any other President "can master an entrenched political press corps with far deeper connections to the permanent government of federal law enforcement and executive department officials than he has...The iron triangle of the Washington press corps, West Wing staff and federal bureaucracy is simply too powerful to bully."[53] In effect, they admitted that the media would hold the elected President accountable (as well they should), but would closely collaborate with and echo unelected officials, who are (after all) valuable sources. Access journalism strikes again. And while putting the final touches on this manuscript, I read that CNN.com has retracted a website story alleging that the Senate was investigating the Russian ties of Trump associate Anthony Scaramucci, and has accepted the resignations of three experienced journalists, one of them a Pulitzer Prize winner. This is not a promising start.

Ever-increasing distrust of the media, the government, and all other authorities, has led readers to the Internet, a world where newspapers seem an anachronism. Lampooning mainstream journalism was the stock in trade of Jon Stewart's *The Daily Show*, and the key to its popularity among younger viewers. In 2010 a *Daily Show* correspondent dropped in on the *New York Times* and incredulously described the newsroom as something out of "Colonial Williamsburg": reporters were still using landlines and producing a newspaper printed in ink on paper. In fact, by then the *Times* had a continually updated news website, but the paper's response made it appear even more hopelessly stuck in the twentieth century. It was a portentous account of the daily 4:00 p.m. editorial meeting that determined which stories would go on the Front Page (of the print edition, of course): "Eighteen editors had gathered at a table to discuss tomorrow's news. The table was formidable: oval and elegant, with curves of gleaming wood. The editors no less so: 11 men and 7 women with the power to decide what was important in the world." Well, this was bound to impress hip media-savvy readers. Clearly, if these eighteen people were sitting around such a tastefully designed table, they were entitled to decide for the rest of us what should and should not be reported. But the article conveyed the impression that the editors had not quite come to terms with the fact that rival news-sites with very different priorities were springing up all over the world. Even within the offices of the *New York Times*, power had already shifted from the print edition to the online edition, where one or two editors decided what would go on the home page. It resembled a proclamation by a late Byzantine emperor, asserting powers that were rapidly melting away.[54]

Editors have great difficulty dealing with this new reality: the Internet enables readers to decide what is important. But on the web, how can one distinguish information from a morass of disinformation? Not long ago the magazine *New Scientist* warned that "The Internet is stuffed with garbage," but they assured us that "Google has devised a fix—rank websites according to their truth." But what is Truth? Not to worry, Mr Pilate, Google is developing a software for that. "The software works by tapping into the Knowledge Vault, the vast store of facts that Google has pulled off the Internet. Facts the web unanimously agrees on are considered a reasonable proxy for truth. Web pages that contain contradictory information are bumped down the rankings." So this Knowledge Vault draws in "facts" from the web, which (we've just been told) is stuffed with garbage. These are ostensibly "facts the Web unanimously agrees on," but is the web unanimous about anything? Certainly not Barack Obama's place of birth. And if the web is unanimous, how can some web pages contain contradictory information? Moreover, as of August 2014, the Knowledge Vault had vacuumed in 1.6 billion "facts," of which about 17 percent were "confident facts," meaning they had a better-than 90 percent chance of being true. So five out of six "facts" in the Knowledge Vault are dubious, and even the other one in six aren't absolutely certain. And the beauty of it, *New Scientist* breathlessly reported, is that it's all done "without any human help," totally automatic, using algorithms to pull stuff off of the web.[55] Thanks to Big Data, we can answer Pontius Pilate's question without contextualization, nuance, or interpretation, without considering whether these "facts" are selective or biased or even really factual; indeed, without thinking at all. More recently there have been a number of attempts to flag "fake news," which is certainly proliferating on the web, but all these efforts run aground on the same epistemological shoals. Can a machine be relied on to check facts? And if we rely on human beings, don't they bring their own biases and blind-spots to the process? Who checks the checkers? Recently the *Guardian* published a report on an interview with Julian Assange which, as Glenn Greenwald noted:

> recklessly attributed to Assange comments that he did not make … Those false claims—fabrications, really—were spread all over the internet by journalists, causing hundreds of thousands of people (if not millions) to consume false news … Those who most flamboyantly denounce Fake News, and want Facebook and other tech giants to suppress content in the name of combating it, are often the most aggressive and self-serving perpetrators of it.[56]

Having exhausted every other alternative, today's readers simply have to find the truth themselves. In sixteenth-century Cologne a burger named Herman Weinsberg, who had nothing much to do other than live off his rents, spent his time investigating the news and recording it in a revealing diary. He spoke with friends, bought pamphlets, and when possible questioned eyewitnesses, but often these sources were irreconcilably conflicted: "Each person cannot truly say and know more than what he had seen at the place where he was at that hour. But if he heard about it from others, the story may be faulty; he cannot truly know it." Five hundred years later, we find ourselves in the same fog. I recently questioned a class of honors students at my university, and found that none of them regularly reads a paper-and-ink newspaper. Instead, they surf the web, they collate and compare accounts from various sources, and thus they try to figure out what the hell is going on. As economists Matthew Gentzkow and Jesse Shapiro have found, web users do not exclusively read sites they agree with, they usually consult diverse news sources representing a range of views.[57] So we now inhabit something resembling Robert Darnton's *Ancien régime*, where no one trusts the official media, and the Internet is our Société Typographique de Neuchâtel—scurrilous, pornographic, scandalmongering, sometimes paranoid, but often highly enlightening, and in any case irresistible reading.

Notes

1. <http://www.gallup.com/poll/195542/americans-trust-mass-media-sinks-new-low.aspx>.
2. Hunter Walker, "Harvard Poll Shows Millennials Have 'Historically Low' Levels of Trust in Government," *Business Insider* (29 Apr. 2014).
3. Royal Commission on the Press, *Attitudes to the Press* (London: HMSO, 1977), 62.
4. Andrew Pugh, "Poll Suggests *The Sun* is Least Trusted Newspaper," *Press Gazette* (12 Sept. 2012).
5. IPSOS Mori poll, 5–19 Dec. 2014.
6. <http://www.edelman.com/trust2017/>, slides 10, 12, 33.
7. Rachel Davis Mersey, *Can Journalism Be Saved? Rediscovering America's Appetite for News* (Santa Barbara, Calif.: Praeger, 2010), 42.
8. "Voters See Media Biased Against Trump but Not Clinton," <www.rasmussenreports.com>, 9 Dec. 2015.
9. Andrew Pettegree, *The Invention of News: How the World Came to Know about Itself* (New Haven and London: Yale University Press, 2014), 2.
10. Samuel Butler, *Character and Passages from Note-Books*, ed. A. R. Waller (Cambridge: Cambridge University Press, 1908), 126–7.
11. Ian Atherton, "The Itch Grown a Disease: Manuscript Transmission of News in the Seventeenth Century," in Joad Raymond, ed. *News, Newspapers, and Society in Early Modern Britain* (London: Routledge, 1999), 45.
12. Ibid., 44. *The Staple of News* is quoted from G. A. Wilkes, ed. *The Complete Plays of Ben Jonson* (Oxford: Clarendon Press, 1982), vol. 4.
13. Leti is quoted in Brendan Dooley, *The Social History of Skepticism: Experience and Doubt in Early Modern Culture* (Baltimore and London: Johns Hopkins University Press, 1999), 85.
14. Ibid., 76–7.
15. Joseph Frank, *Cromwell's Press Agent: A Critical Biography of Marchmont Needham, 1620–1678* (Lanham, Md.: University Press of America, 1980), 29.
16. John Rushworth, *Historical Collections of Private Passages of State*: Volume 1, *1618–29* (London: D. Browne, 1721), preface.
17. Joad Raymond, "Irrational, Impractical and Unprofitable: Reading the News in Seventeenth-Century Britain," in Kevin Sharpe and Steven N. Zwicker, eds.

Writing Readers in Early Modern England (Cambridge: Cambridge University Press, 2003), 185–212.

18. Joad Raymond, *The Invention of the Newspaper: English Newsbooks 1641–1649* (Oxford: Clarendon Press, 1996), 244–68.

19. Bob Clarke, *From Grub Street to Fleet Street: An Illustrated History of English Newspapers to 1899* (Aldershot: Ashgate, 2004), ch. 1.

20. Ibid., 58–9, 97–103.

21. Jill Lepore, *Book of Ages: The Life and Opinions of Jane Franklin* (New York: Vintage, 2013), 151, 176, 192–4.

22. Philip Davidson, *Propaganda and the American Revolution 1763–1783* (Chapel Hill, NC: University of North Carolina Press, 1941), 237–8.

23. Valerae M. Hurley, "The Discourse of Vengeance in the French Revolution: A Study of Rhetoric in the Extremist Press, 1789-1794", PhD diss., Drew University (2003).

24. Elizabeth Eisenstein, *Divine Art, Infernal Machine: The Reception of Printing in the West from First Impressions to the Sense of an Ending* (Philadelphia: University of Pennsylvania Press, 2011), 151.

25. *Niles' Register* (30 Sept. 1826): 76–7.

26. Clarke, *Grub Street to Fleet Street*, 227–32.

27. David Kaser, *Books and Libraries in Camp and Battle: The Civil War Experience* (Westport and London: Greenwood Press, 1984), 30–2.

28. Ellen Gruber Garvey, *Writing with Scissors: American Scrapbooks from the Civil War to the Harlem Renaissance* (Oxford: Oxford University Press, 2013), 3: 28.

29. Robert S. Lynd and Helen Merrell Lynd, *Middletown: A Study in American Culture* (New York: Harcourt Brace Jovanovich, 1957), 477.

30. Dean Starkman, *The Watchdog that Didn't Bark: The Financial Crisis and the Disappearance of Investigative Journalism* (New York: Columbia University Press, 2014), 58–64.

31. Jason Rodrigues, "1936: British Press Finally Break Silence on Wallis Simpson Affair," *Guardian* (9 Dec. 2011).

32. Richard Cockett, *Twilight of Truth: Chamberlain, Appeasement and the Manipulation of the Press* (New York: St Martin's Press, 1989).

33. Pierre van Paassen, *Days of Our Years* (New York: Hillman-Curl, 1939), 162–3.

34. Adrian Bingham, "'Putting Literature out of Reach'? Reading Popular Newspapers in Mid-Twentieth-Century Britain," in *The History of Reading*, Volume 2: *Evidence from the British Isles, c. 1750–1950* (Basingstoke: Palgrave Macmillan, 2011), 150.

35. Katie Halsey, "'Something Light to Take My Mind off the War': Reading on the Home Front during the Second World War," in *The History of Reading*, Volume 2: *Evidence from the British Isles, c. 1750–1950* (Basingstoke: Palgrave Macmillan, 2011), 95–6.

36. Robert Darnton, "Journalism: All the News That Fits We Print," in *The Kiss of Lamourette: Reflections in Cultural History* (New York and London: W. W. Norton, 1990), 60–93.

37. Larry Tye, *The Father of Spin: Edward L. Bernays and the Birth of Public Relations* (New York: Crown, 1998), 165–9.

38. Hugh Hefner, "The Playboy Philosophy," *Playboy* (May 1963): 71–2.

39. <http://www.gallup.com/poll/1597/confidence-institutions.aspx>.

40. Jim A. Kuypers, *Partisan Journalism: A History of Media Bias in the United States* (Lanham, Md.: Rowman & Littlefield, 2014), 61–4, 72–3, 88–9, 92, 179–83.

41. Ibid., 220–1.

42. Ibid., 192–4, 246–7.

43. Carl Bernstein, *A Woman in Charge: The Life of Hillary Rodham Clinton* (London: Hutchinson, 2007), 199.

44. Rhonda Young, "Communication Conspiracy," Clinton Presidential Records, Counsel's Office, Jane Sherburne, Clinton Library, OA/Box Number: CF 426.

45. Jeff Gerth and Don Van Natta Jr., *Hillary Clinton: Her Way. The Biography* (London: John Murray, 2007), 268–70.

46. Sharyl Attkisson, *Stonewalled* (New York: Harper, 2014), 65. See also her more recent *The Smear: How Shady Political Operatives and Fake News Control What You See, What You Think, and How You Vote* (New York: Harper, 2017).

47. Tracy Schmaler, two emails to Eric Schultz (4 Oct. 2011, 7:46 and 8:43 a.m.), <http://www.judicialwatch.org/wp-content/uploads/2014/11/She-is-out-of-Control.pdf>.

48. Lars Willnat and David H. Weaver, *The American Journalist in the Digital Age: Key Findings* (Bloomington, Ind.: School of Journalism, Indiana University, 2014), 3, 5, 11–19.

49. Margaret Sullivan, "DealBook Conference Was Impressive, Lucrative and Chummy," *New York Times* (13 Dec. 2012).

50. Marisa Taylor and Jonathan S. Landay, "Obama's Crackdown Views Leaks as Aiding Enemies of U.S.," *McClatchyDC* (20 June 2013).

51. Leonard Downey Jr., "The Obama Administration and the Press," Committee to Protect Journalists, 10 Oct. 2013; Andrew Beaujon, "Risen: Obama Administration is this Generation's 'Greatest Enemy of Press Freedom'," *Poynter* (24 Mar. 2014).

52. <https://rsf.org/en/ranking>.

53. Glenn Thrush and Michael M. Gyrnbaum, "Trump Ruled the Tabloid Media: Washington is a Different Story," *New York Times* (25 Feb. 2017).

54. Nikki Usher, *Making News at 'The New York Times'* (Ann Arbor, Mich.: University of Michigan Press, 2014), ch. 3.

55. Hal Hodson, "Google's Fact-Checking Bots Build Vast Knowledge Bank," New Scientist (20 August 2014); Hal Hodson, "Google Wants to Rank Websites Based on Facts not Links," *New Scientist* (25 February 2015).

56. Glenn Greenwald, "The Guardian's Summary of Julian Assange's Interview Went Viral and Was Completely False," *Intercept* (29 Dec. 2016).

57. Matthew Gentzkow and Jesse M. Shapiro, "Ideological Segregation Online and Offline," *Quarterly Journal of Economics* (2011) 126, 1799–839.

7

Fayned News

When my students ask me, "What will be the next big thing in historical studies?," I tell them to watch out for the history of public relations. The University of Bournemouth in the UK has a fairly new center devoted to the subject, Baruch College in Manhattan has just set up a Museum of Public Relations, and I think that's just the beginning. Yes, plenty of work has been done on the history of advertising and propaganda, but PR is different: Dan Draper and Joseph Goebbels were perfectly upfront about what they were doing, but PR is a medium that commonly and deliberately disguises its own authorship. Let me state at the outset that everyone today uses publicists, and much of their work is entirely ethical. For publishers, they write up promotional material, send out review copies, arrange author interviews, and extract blurbs from reviews of their books—this one, for instance. But the main focus of this chapter is the kind of PR that surreptitiously plants stories in various media. It works only insofar as readers don't recognize it, and therefore distrust of the media is in large measure a function of reader recognition of PR.

The standard narrative holds that public relations was invented by Ivy Lee and Edward Bernays in the early twentieth century, but the basic concept of publicity can be traced back as far as Socrates's *Phaedrus*, who observed that "an orator does not need to know what is really just, but what would seem just to the multitude who are to pass judgment, and not what is really good or noble, but what will seem to be so; for they say that persuasion comes from what seems to be true, not from the truth" (260a). One of the most brilliant PR agents of the pre-newspaper era was working before Shakespeare staged his first play. As Meaghan Brown explains, in summer 1588 Catholic publicists barraged England with pamphlets announcing that the vast and powerful Spanish Armada was on the way. Lord Burghley (top advisor to Elizabeth I) wrote to Francis Walsingham (the Queen's intelligence chief) that he wanted "some expert learned man, would fayne an answer as from a number of Catholics that...profess their obedience and service with their lives and power against all strange foreigners offering to land in the realm." Burghley envisioned a pamphlet that would create a misleading impression of grassroots support for Elizabeth among English Catholics, what would now be called "Astroturf." The pamphlet would appear to be written by an English Catholic, but would in fact be authored by a PR "expert"—ultimately, Burghley himself. And note the ambiguous word "fayne," which might mean to fashion or to make, but could also mean "to fake." The intent would be to conceal the real author and deceive the reader.

The tract Burghley produced, *Copie of a Letter Sent Out of England to Don Bernardin Mendoza*, was ingenious. It purported to reproduce a letter written by one Richard Leigh, an English Catholic priest, to Mendoza, a notorious Spanish diplomat and propagandist. The pamphlet claimed that the letter had been intercepted in a raid on Leigh's chambers, and that he had subsequently been executed for high treason. It all seemed plausible, given that letters were regarded as more credible than print, and Leigh had in fact been put to death after a highly publicized trial, though that meant he wasn't around to point out that the letter was a fake.

In that letter, the fictional Leigh presents himself as a loyal agent of Mendoza, but one who is forthrightly warning his chief about a disastrous PR failure. He argued that no one in England believed Spanish propaganda, because Mendoza had claimed in print a victory for the Armada. Mendoza had indeed done that: it's difficult to live down a "Dewey Defeats Truman" headline. What's more, the *faux* Leigh claimed that nearly all English Catholics were steadfastly loyal to their Queen, in part because they had grown deeply skeptical of anything published out of Spain. Catholic propagandists quickly recognized that Burghley was the real author of the pamphlet, and one of them swiftly responded with a rebuttal that employed all the same deceptive techniques, including false authorship and fake letters. Printing in England was only a century old, but from this English readers of all faiths learned that they couldn't trust everything in print.

Burghley also perfected the PR technique of custom-tailoring his message to suit different audiences. The editions aimed at Protestants

in England, the Netherlands, and France splashed Leigh's execution
all over the front page, but the Italian version played that down, to
avoid offending Catholic readers, and instead stated that this translation
had been prepared "at the insistence and desire" of honest Italians
who wanted to know the truth about lying Spanish propaganda
(more Astroturf).[1]

In the early seventeenth century, Paolo Sarpi, a publicist for the city
of Venice, developed a sophisticated theory of public relations. The
growing public demand for news, he argued, seemed to suggest that
Venice should manufacture and disseminate its own version of events.
The problem was, once you supplied a reader with information, however selective it might be, he would come to expect information on a
regular basis, and would become suspicious if it wasn't forthcoming.
"He gradually begins to judge the prince's actions," Sarpi warned.
"He becomes so accustomed to this communication that he believes it
is due him, and when it is not given, he sees a false significance or else
perceives an affront and conceives hatred." Ultimately, Sarpi concluded that "the true way of ruling the subject is to keep him ignorant
of and reverent towards public affairs." On the other hand, Evangelista
Sartonio, based in Bologna, warned against censorship or official
silence, not out of a Miltonian commitment to freedom of expression,
but solely on pragmatic grounds. "One must never, in any city or
place, prohibit people from reasoning, especially about things that one
does not want them to know, for surely those things will only be all
the more diffused because of that very privation, which is the fertile
mother of curiosity and appetite." He cited the example of the Roman
Emperor Vitellius, who imposed a news blackout during his war with
Vespasian: the resulting rumors were more damaging than the reality.[2]
The censorship machinery of early modern European states was full
of holes, so much so that writers often courted proscription in order to
score a *succès de scandale*. If neither suppression nor stonewalling
worked, the only alternative was publicity, and seventeenth-century
Italian princes became quite adept at planting stories in both manuscript newsletters and printed newspapers.

In the English Civil War, Lucy Hutchinson, the wife of Colonel
John Hutchinson, was well aware that his fellow parliamentary army
officer, General Sir John Gell, was indulging in PR puffery. Gell, she
recorded, "kept the diurnall makers in pension, so that whatever was

done in any of the neighbouring counties was ascribed to him; and he hath indirectly purchased himself a name in story which he never merited." But PR overexposure, she added, undermines its credibility: "That which made his courage the more doubted was the care he took, and expense he was at, to get it weekly mentioned in the diurnals, so that when they had nothing else to renown him for, they once put in that the troops of that valiant commander, Sir John Gell, took a dragoon with a plush doublet." (When her husband reprimanded the flack, he apologized and tried to make it up by offering the Colonel his services.)[3]

Public relations came close to changing the outcome of the American Civil War, given that the Confederacy mounted a nearly successful effort to persuade Britain to enter the conflict. Henry Hotze ran a publicity machine that planted pro-Confederate articles in *The Times*, the *Morning Post*, the *Morning Herald*, and the *Saturday Review*. Reports of anti-Irish prejudice in the North were strategically placed in Irish newspapers. He created Astroturf, such as the Society for Promoting the Cessation of Hostilities in America, which pretended to be a peace group but in fact worked for British intervention on the side of the South.[4] His propaganda weekly the *Index* was widely read among British elites, politicians, capitalists, and Anglican clergymen. There was a rival pro-Union paper, the *London American*, but a subscriber list reveals that it was read mainly by nonconformist ministers, radical abolitionists, and American expats—that is, nobodies. No MPs or aristocrats subscribed, and the journal folded in March 1863. Just days later the Confederacy floated a £3 million loan offering a lavish 7 percent return: the objective was to give Europeans a vested interest in a Southern victory. The investors included editors of *The Times* and the owner of the *Morning Post*, two reliably pro-Confederate papers.[5]

By the late nineteenth century the patent-medicine industry had become one of the largest buyers of newspaper advertising, and they wielded that power with ruthless ingenuity. In November 1905 muckraker Mark Sullivan, writing in *Collier's*, noted that the Massachusetts legislature had recently debated a bill to require content labels on patent medicines—worthless and addictive concoctions of alcohol and opiates. But in the press this debate was almost totally blacked out, and Sullivan had discovered why. The industry had total annual revenues of $100 million, of which $40 million was ploughed back into newspaper advertising. And nearly every paper in the country (more than 15,000 of them) had signed a standard industry advertising contract stating that the agreement would be voided if (1) the newspaper published anything critical of patent medicines, or (2) any legislation restricting these nostrums was enacted. The second clause bought more than silence: it compelled editorialists to denounce loudly any attempt by state legislatures to regulate snake oil. One exception was North Dakota, where a truth-in-labeling bill was enacted with the support of the press. The difference, Sullivan explained, was that this rural state had no big-city dailies, only ornery one-man small-town weeklies, which (like blogs today) were more difficult to control than large profit-oriented newspaper chains.[6]

William Kittle's "The Making of Public Opinion," published in the July 1909 *Arena*, was another early exposé of public relations, a term so new that Kittle never actually used it. But he did show that privately-owned utilities, insurance companies, and Standard Oil had, in a new departure:

> organized news bureaus to furnish to the newspapers adroitly prepared articles, interviews, letters and news items. These appear in the public press without a suggestion of their real source. They are not accompanied by any of the marks of advertising matter. Very often, especially in the case of city utility companies, the "interests" deal directly with the newspapers by liberal purchase of advertising space and thus secure control of the news columns and of the editorial page itself. During the last four years, a large number of these news bureaus have been actively engaged in the work of forming public opinion in all parts of the country.

In 1905, when President Theodore Roosevelt and members of Congress demanded more railroad regulation, the railroads set up a network of PR offices in Washington, New York, Chicago, St Louis, and Topeka, which developed publicity into a sophisticated social science. The Chicago office alone had forty-three employees, including some experienced journalists. It maintained a card file, called "The Barometer," which kept track of newspaper editors throughout the American north-west. "Each editor was accurately characterized on a card as to politics, financial condition and peculiarities. If an editor was too active against the railroads, a traveling agent went to his town and organized some of the local shippers against him." And their methods were quite effective: in "the week ending June 5th., 1905, before the bureau began its work, 412 columns of matter opposed to the railroads had appeared in the Nebraska papers, but...three months later, after the bureau had been in operation, 202 columns favorable and only 4 against the railroads were published in that state in one week."

But there were ways of running the media blockade, Kittle noted. Four muckraking monthlies—the *Arena*, *McClure's*, *Everybody's*, and the *American Magazine*—had a combined circulation of 1.3 million. Book publishers were not subject to advertising pressure, so they were able to bring out muckraking novels that scaled the bestseller lists: *The Pit* by Frank Norris, *The Jungle* by Upton Sinclair, and *Coniston* by Winston Churchill (an American progressive novelist, not the British politician).

Public exposure of public relations continued with Stuart Chase, writing in the *New Republic* in the 1920s. Chase would have a huge influence on F. R. Leavis, I. A. Richards, and their associates, who were developing "Practical Criticism" at Cambridge University. Drawing on Chase's denunciations, they built a highly influential school of criticism: it would teach students to distinguish between true literary art and PR. Trained to be close and careful readers, they would not only appreciate the great tradition of English literature, they would learn to recognize when newspapers were manipulating them with clichés, stereotypes, and sloganeering.[7]

By the 1950s public relations had acquired a vile reputation on both sides of the Atlantic. It received a devastating film-noir treatment in *Sweet Smell of Success* (1957). John F. Kennedy disparaged PR phoniness in *Profiles in Courage*, which celebrated politicians who supposedly cared nothing for public image.[8] (Of course, Kennedy would make extensive use of image-makers, and came off as far more glamorous than his frumpy rivals, Adlai Stevenson and Richard Nixon.) It didn't help matters that PR agents were dismayingly upfront about their tactics. In his 1959 guide to the profession, *The Image Merchants*, Irwin Ross applauded the firm Hill & Knowlton for taking down those pesky anti-tobacco activists. Ross granted that bribing a journalist to plant a story was crossing an ethical boundary, but surely there was nothing wrong in paying his "research expenses."[9]

J. Edgar Hoover built up a legendary PR operation that (at least until everything fell apart in the 1960s) burnished the image of the FBI. Of course, Hoover never called it PR, and assured Congress that the Bureau didn't stoop to that sort of thing. But the Crime Records Division performed the classic PR service of writing up stories that reporters could easily adapt—"Interesting Cases" expertly cracked by heroic G-Men. They edited news copy, broadcasts, and movie scripts before they reached the public. They closely monitored everything published about the Bureau. Shrewdly, Hoover cultivated a friendship with Morris L. Ernst, general counsel of the American Civil Liberties Union, and it paid off handsomely. In 1950, at the height of the McCarthyite scare, when some liberals were warning that the FBI had become an American secret police, the Bureau persuaded the *Reader's Digest* to publish Ernst's apologia, "Why I No Longer Fear the FBI." (The Bureau checked out the article beforehand.) Surely, if the head of the ACLU said that the FBI "has a magnificent record of respect for individual freedom," there was nothing to be anxious about. (Today much the same technique is used in "greenwashing," where corporations coopt environmental groups to say yes, these companies polluted in the past, but now they've cleaned up their act.)

In 1959 Hoover ordered the division to investigate "subversive" journalists who were "discrediting our American way of life," and they researched files on 100 newsmen, ultimately concluding that at least forty of them were troublemakers. For instance, Joseph Alsop of the *New York Herald Tribune* was a homosexual, and Murray Kempton and James Wechsler of the *New York Post* had been in the Young Communist League long, long ago. All this dirt was distilled into blind memoranda that were distributed to friendly journalists, who were free to use them to attack the FBI's critics, so long as they did not reveal the Bureau as a source. *The FBI Story* (1956), a bestselling history by Pulitzer Prize winner Don Whitehead, convinced most readers that it was objective journalism: in fact he wrote it in an FBI office, relying on material provided by FBI PR men, and had the manuscript vetted by FBI agents.[10]

But the FBI publicity machine was neither innovative nor exceptional. Every federal department had (or would soon have) a similar operation. The New Deal was promoted by a vast publicity effort, which included pioneering the development of scientific polling. By

1936 the Roosevelt administration had 146 full-time and 124 part-time publicists distributing 7 million copies of 48,000 press releases.[11] In the 1920s Secretary of Commerce Herbert Hoover had a PR office so effective that it boosted him into the White House, and as President he built a government publicity machine in advance of Roosevelt.[12]

In 1962 Rachel Carson proved that it was still possible to prevail against a hostile and well-funded PR campaign, though it was a damned close-run thing.[13] *Silent Spring* challenged head-on the chemical industry, agribusiness, the US Department of Agriculture, and the dominant scientific consensus. She only prevailed against all of those powerful interests because she had several exceptionally strong cards in her hand. She was a competent scientist and the author of two bestselling nature books, *The Sea Around Us* (1951) and *The Edge of the Sea* (1955). The royalties allowed her to quit government work and devote all her energies to writing, without fear of professional retaliation. And she was well-connected: her friends included Interior Secretary Stewart Udall, Supreme Court Justice William O. Douglas, and the wife of Eugene Meyer, publisher of the *Washington Post*. She endorsed John F. Kennedy in the 1960 election and got to schmooze with Jackie Kennedy. Her literary agent, Marie Rodell, was herself a superb publicist who made sure that advance copies of *Silent Spring* were distributed to the nation's movers and shakers.

Carson's publisher, Houghton Mifflin, was a respected independent Boston firm with a long record of publishing nature writers, going back to Henry David Thoreau. Its editor-in-chief, Paul Brooks, was a dedicated conservationist, a prominent member of the Audubon Society, the Nature Conservancy, and the Sierra Club. Brooks believed that publishers should be "concerned more with good books than with quick and easy profits," though he added that "excellence can indeed be profitable," and proved it with *Silent Spring*. For Brooks, "book publishing was as much a profession as a business, with the personal relationship between writer and editor at its core." He spent years advising Carson on her manuscript, helping to make it scientifically credible as well as accessible to lay readers.

But most Americans became aware of the contents of *Silent Spring* without actually reading the book. Carson realized that she had to reach a larger public through the mass media. Earlier, she had attempted to publish warnings against pesticides in several popular magazines, but they had been repeatedly rejected by editors who did not want to lose advertisers. The *New Yorker*, however, agreed to serialize *Silent Spring* in June 1962, three months before it appeared in book form. More than any other major periodical, the *New Yorker* strictly prohibited its advertising department from influencing editorial decisions. In any case, its demographic of urban sophisticates was so attractive that some of its issues sold out all their ad space. It was the most profitable magazine in America, and therefore impervious to corporate pressure. Three chemical companies (DuPont, Cyanamid, and Esso/Humble) advertised regularly in the *New Yorker*, but none of them pulled their ads when *Silent Spring* was serialized: those ads were essential to projecting a positive corporate image to the magazine's influential readership. DuPont needed the *New Yorker* more than the *New Yorker* needed DuPont.

Both the *New Yorker* and Houghton Mifflin were pressured by a chemical-industry lawyer to drop or tone down the story. "Everything in those articles has been checked and is true," the *New Yorker*'s lawyer shot back. "Go ahead and sue." Thanks to a rigorous fact-checking policy, the magazine enjoyed an unequalled reputation for reliability. And their readers responded to *Silent Spring* with a record outpouring of letters to the editor, nearly all of them positive.

One of those readers was President Kennedy. At a 29 August press conference a reporter raised the issue of the dangers of pesticides: "Have you considered asking the Department of Agriculture or the Public Health Service to take a closer look at this?" "Yes," Kennedy responded, "and I know that they already are. I think particularly, of course, since Miss Carson's book..."

Of course, the Department of Agriculture was outraged by Miss Carson's book, but they held their fire for PR reasons. As one official shrewdly noted in an internal memorandum, a "typical bureaucratic response which never quite joins the issue" would only provoke "a strong adverse public reaction." Congressmen were already receiving angry letters from constituents, passing them on to the USDA, and demanding explanations. And no federal bureaucrat was eager to contradict the President of the United States. Ultimately, the Kennedy administration laid down the line that more research into pesticide safety was needed, a policy that bureaucrats and scientists could live with, since it meant more government funding for themselves.

Kennedy ordered the President's Science Advisory Committee to investigate the issue, and their report the following May mostly substantiated Carson's warnings.

The chemical industry and agribusiness exercised no such restraint. "This was, for us, an opportunity to wield our public relations power," one Monsanto executive said. The National Agricultural Chemicals Association ponied up $250,000 to fund a campaign against *Silent Spring*. The Manufacturing Chemists Association commissioned Glick & Lorwin, a New York public relations firm, to launch a counter-attack. Scientists could be mobilized to assert that the book was unscientific. William Darby, a nutritionist at Vanderbilt University, charged that Carson used "literary devices to present her thesis and make it appear to be a widely held scientific one. She 'name-drops' by quoting or referring to renowned scientists out of context." (What Darby called "name-drops," Carson preferred to call "footnotes"). *The Desolate Year*, a pamphlet widely distributed by Monsanto, warned (in ghoulish language) that without their products human civilization would be overrun by hordes of pests and deadly epidemics. Dr Robert White-Stevens, an American Cyanamid biochemist, aggressively defended pesticides in a national speaking tour. "If man were to follow the teachings of Miss Carson," he warned, "we would return to the Dark Ages, and the insects and diseases and vermin would once again inherit the earth."

But others in the industry worried that attacking Rachel Carson would only give more publicity to *Silent Spring*, and suggested a more indirect tactic. "It has generally been decided to ignore Miss Carson herself and accentuate the positive side of agricultural chemicals," an advertising trade journal reported. "Producers of the pesticides wisely decided to let the popular authoress alone and step up educational and informational programs instead." Starting in the summer of 1962, US newspapers and magazines ran numerous articles touting the benefits of pesticides, without mentioning *Silent Spring*. They appeared objective, but they repeated the same talking points. It is impossible to prove that these articles were placed by the chemical industry's PR agents—but the first principle of good PR is to ensure that readers do not recognize it as PR.

None of these strategies worked. If the chemical industry criticized *Silent Spring*, they called attention to the book. If they ignored it, then

Rachel Carson's allegations went unanswered. When the *New Yorker* and President Kennedy endorsed the book, they ignited a media firestorm that was impossible to put out. Along with John Glenn's flight into space, the Cuban Missile Crisis, and civil-rights struggles, Rachel Carson was one of the biggest news stories of 1962. *Silent Spring* became a Book-of-the-Month Club selection, and by the end of the year it had sold a half-million copies. As one PR magazine asked, "How Do You Fight a Best-Seller?"

The public controversy climaxed the following April, when the prestigious news program *CBS Reports* broadcast "The Silent Spring of Rachel Carson," moderated by Eric Sevareid. Some advertisers, including two agribusiness corporations (Standard Brands and Ralston Purina) and a chemical product (Lysol disinfectant) pulled their commercials, but the program went ahead anyway. Equal time was allotted to Carson and her critics, including Dr Robert White-Stevens. There is no question who won the debate. Carson became an American icon, while White-Stevens is remembered today only as a blustering corporate shill.

Silent Spring thus slipped through a narrow historical window of opportunity, which had opened only recently and soon closed down. For a moment in time, American readers were receptive to serious works of social criticism by the likes of Vance Packard, Jane Jacobs, Michael Harrington, Betty Friedan, and Rachel Carson. But corporations were now on the alert, and they took care not to allow another *Silent Spring* to slip past their guns. In 1968 the book-publishing subsidiary of *Reader's Digest* got as far as distributing advance copies of an exposé of the advertising industry, but advertisers applied pressure to the magazine and forced the withdrawal of the book. Six years later Time Inc.'s Fortune Book Club withdrew a book critical of DuPont when the chemical corporation warned that it would pull ads from magazines published by Time. Women's magazines are notorious for allowing advertisers to dictate content, so much so that *Ms.* ultimately could only preserve its independence by refusing all advertising.[14] And the kind of independent family publishers that would take a chance on a controversial book like *Silent Spring* have been absorbed by a few vast media conglomerates: Houghton Mifflin was swallowed up by Vivendi Universal in 2001.

In a 1978 survey of editors of popular magazines, 49 percent claimed to enjoy full independence from the business office—or to put it another way, 51 percent felt at least somewhat constrained. Moreover, 55 percent admitted that they would consult with the business office before running a story that might alienate an advertiser, and another 24 percent said they would accept the story but alert the business office—suggesting that some of those 49 percent were kidding themselves. A survey published in the *New England Journal of Medicine* found that the more a magazine earned from tobacco ads, the less likely it was to publish articles linking cigarettes to cancer. More than 80 percent of real-estate editors and 62 percent of agricultural editors reported threats to withdraw advertising in response to unfavorable coverage, and 48 percent of the agricultural editors said that these threats were carried out. And then there are admissions of guilt: a *New Republic* editor conceded that the magazine had spiked an article criticizing the tobacco industry "because of the relative size of the [advertising] account." Even a few incidents of withdrawn advertising can be a powerful deterrent to a news organization, encouraging an instinctive self-censorship where journalists don't feel the tug of the leash because they have accepted and internalized the rules of the game. As advertising executive C. Terence Clyne testified in 1959, "There have been very few cases where it has been necessary to exercise a veto, because…the writers involved are normally pretty well aware of what might not be acceptable."[15] And in 1987 Marvin Olasky warned that corporate PR was creating a new economic order of crony capitalism, "designed to minimize competition through creation of a government–business partnership supposedly in the public interest."[16]

By 1980, the number of public-relations agents in the United States had surpassed the number of working journalists. Today the ratio is four to one, and growing rapidly worse. As newspapers lay off reporters, they commonly go over to the dark side, where their writing skills and connections can be very useful. The surviving staff at newspapers are stretched thin, so they're inclined to accept press releases composed by their former colleagues and publish them with little alteration. And as they are deserted by advertisers, the media is ever more reluctant to offend those who remain. (Over drinks, investigative journalists admit that they can't touch pharmaceuticals, hospital corporations, and car dealerships.[17] They continue to advertise in paper-and-ink newspapers, which are still read by their target demographic: the elderly.) "Happy news" is so much more pleasant to read than exposés of politicians and corporations, and anyway, you might be working for them someday. An inside source told Sharyl Attkisson that more than 1,200 federal employees were doing PR for the US Department of Agriculture alone.[18] In fact the Obama administration employed, in its upper strata, unprecedented numbers of former journalists as well as spouses of working journalists.[19] The title sequence of the TV series *Mad Men* has it backwards: the publicists have vaulted to the commanding heights of the American media, while the real journalists are in freefall.

Though she is sometimes labeled a journalist of the right, Sharyl Attkisson finds herself agreeing with Edward Herman and Noam Chomsky on the far left. "Commercial news organizations disseminate propaganda on behalf of dominant private interests and the government," she concurs. On social issues there may be liberal media bias, but "there's also a competing conservative, corporate bias that favors specific companies, industries, and paid interests."[20]

The success of PR depends on public confidence in the very media it seeks to manipulate, but excessive and obvious PR debases the currency of journalism. "Every time that a newspaper offers an advertorial section that offers free puff pieces to advertisers ... media organizations cheapen the value of their product," warned *Public Relations Quarterly* in 1994. "When a news medium covered a story in the past, the ... client, product or cause gained salience, stature and legitimacy." But we are rapidly approaching the point where readers assume that all news is PR, and then, "A loss of public reliance upon and confidence in the mass media could be devastating."[21] And sure enough, a 2013 Pew Research Center Survey found that nearly a third of American adults had recently given up following a news outlet, usually citing a decline in the quality of coverage.[22]

In response, some may say, well, that's the way the world works, you can't abolish PR, so get used to it. But that's precisely the point: the reading public has become so used to PR that they habitually disbelieve everything that journalists, politicians, and "opinion leaders" write. That skepticism is fueling the populist revolt now in progress throughout the Western world. In 2000, 70 percent of Danish parliamentarians and nearly all of the Danish media, as well as the business community and labor unions, favored joining the Euro, but the popular vote went against them.[23] In 1996—well before the Second Iraq War and the 2008 market crash—Lawrence Susskind and Patrick Field warned movers and shakers that they had to deal with an "angry public," and that the old PR tactic of attempting "to blunt or undercut the public's concerns by dredging up countervailing 'facts' or rebuttals from pseudo-independent experts" was no longer working:

> The public has seen business and government respond to their concerns in the past with slick advertising campaigns, denials of risk, misleading information, and false fronts…It is no wonder, given the history of many public-relations efforts, that the public is not easily appeased. Too many mistakes have been made, and too many situations have been mishandled for the public to trust the opinions and reports of high-level executives and government officials. With good reason. From the beginning of a crisis, the public assumes they are not getting the basic facts, let alone the full story.[24]

It may be that the real message of *Mad Men* is not that Dan Draper and his fellow suits were master manipulators, but that their methods were laughably primitive compared to today's propaganda weapons. In one early episode an exec with a cigarette account is reduced to asking his bartender what would persuade him to switch brands. The Obama campaigns in 2008 and 2012 and the Clinton campaign in 2016 were light-years ahead of that. They used Orwellian data-mining (a perfectly legal form of espionage) to accumulate anything they wanted to know about pretty much all American voters: what they had purchased, how they had voted in previous elections, their online posts and Internet searches. "We knew who these people were going to vote for before they decided," bragged one of their Mad Men, and certainly their operation was more sophisticated than anything the Republicans had. Then they crafted an array of tailored and not entirely consistent messages to send to different categories of voters, pushing their respective buttons. "In one case, the campaign sent seven different customized email invitations to one fundraising dinner in New York," reported the *Wall Street Journal*. You could argue that this strategy worked for Obama (twice), but eventually newspaper readers will come to see all conventional politicians as two-faced (or rather, seven-faced).[25]

Changing public attitudes toward the press are reflected in two versions of a classic journalism joke, eighty years apart. The first is a memorable scene in the 1931 film *The Front Page*. A fast-breaking story at City Hall propels a half-dozen reporters to a half-dozen telephones, and they call in a half-dozen versions of the story, no two of which bear much resemblance to each other. But today late-night television comedians run rapid-fire series of clips of TV anchors reporting the same event, all of them following exactly the same script, using the same clichés and buzzwords, because they're obviously reading from the same press releases. A 2006 survey of Britain's "quality" papers found that more than half the news in the *Guardian* and about two-thirds of *The Times* and *Daily Telegraph* exactly or mostly reproduced pre-packaged stories from PR agents or news agencies (and the latter are highly dependent on the former).[26] That's why younger audiences today call reporters "stenographers."

Nine years before the 2008 Wall Street meltdown, Anthony Hilton, city editor of the *Evening Standard*, warned that under a "constant barrage" of PR financial journalists "seem to be losing their independence of judgement... The press has moved away from being an observer of the business scene to a participant in it." Bankers, brokers, and hedge-fund managers supply cooperative journalists with inside tips about the wonderful prospects for deals they themselves are promoting, and don't return the calls of journalists who ask rude questions. Thus, "media manipulation has become a legitimate way for increasing shareholder value."[27]

Practically the only mainstream financial journalist who saw the meltdown coming was Gillian Tett of the *Financial Times*. Because she was trained as an anthropologist, she was able to stand back and see dangerous behavior patterns in the financial community that financiers were oblivious to. She noted that the investment world was fracturing into "silos"—that is, small, self-contained cliques that had their own private languages which were unintelligible to outsiders. They invented jargon like "collateralized debt obligations" and "structured investment vehicle," but before August 2007 the meaning of the first term was hardly ever explained in the mainstream press, and the second was never mentioned at all. Journalists had no clear sense of what these instruments were, and ignored them. Even within a single firm, other departments had no idea what these silos were up to. Essentially, it was a problem of reading: the texts produced by each silo could not be read by anyone else. Chris Hedges compares it to the opacity of literary theory,[28] but there is a difference. Lacanian critics merely took up space in academia, and otherwise did no real harm. But because no one could decipher the silos, no one could connect the dots and realize they were steering the financial world to disaster.[29]

Conceivably, a newspaper might have assigned reporters to master the jargon, explore the larger picture, expose the risks, and produce a story as big as Woodward/Bernstein. But that would have required an expensive investment in investigative journalism, and faced with plummeting advertising revenues, newspapers were drastically shrinking staff: a quarter of all journalist jobs were eliminated between 2000 and 2009, and the survivors were expected to churn out more stories. Dean Starkman describes the hollowing out at the *Wall Street Journal*:

> the atmosphere at the office darkened, and the gap between the managers on the ninth floor and reporters on the tenth became a yawning chasm. The culture shifted from one of confidence, swagger, muckraking, and storytelling to keeping one's head down and career survival. In some indefinable way, the power of reporters—not unlike that of rank-and-file employees in other industries—diminished, while that of managers increased. Dissent from reporters all but disappeared. Office politics became byzantine, and productivity demands on the newsroom grew ever more pronounced. Time-consuming investigations were undertaken at the reporter's own risk: If a lead didn't pan out—no matter the reason—your productivity numbers took a hit, putting your career in peril. This wasn't subtle.[30]

This was before Rupert Murdoch took over the paper in 2007. "Stop having people write articles to win Pulitzer Prizes," he promptly ordered. "Give people what they want to read"—though polls and letters to the editors consistently showed that readers wanted to read stories that held the rich and powerful accountable.[31]

Under these pressures, investigative journalism was sacrificed to access journalism. And no doubt, in the heady investment climate of the early twenty-first century, insider tips could supply reporters with great stories and save them a lot of legwork. But it allowed firms to plant stories that puffed their offerings, essentially unpaid advertising

("Washington Mutual is Using a Creative Retail Approach to Turn the Banking World Upside Down"). By 2007 there were some reports warning that the bubble was close to bursting, but they were too little and too late.[32]

One of the most successful PR campaigns in recent years has been carried out by the immensely wealthy Gates Foundation, and this troubles sociologist Linsey McGoey: "While positive news stories appear almost daily, only a small handful of media and academic articles have suggested there may be a downside to the foundation's activities." One obvious reason is that Bill Gates has contributed to media organizations that are supposed to be covering his activities. (Jeff Bezos hasn't been so charitable, and perhaps for that reason we hear more about brutal working conditions at Amazon.) In 2013 the Gates Foundation paid Ogilvy, a PR firm, $100,000 to promote the message: "Aid is Working: Tell the World." Representatives of the *New York Times*, the *Guardian*, NPR, NBC, and the *Seattle Times* were summoned to the Gates headquarters to confer about emphasizing "success stories" in covering global aid initiatives, such as those sponsored by the Gates Foundation—rather than failures, corruption, and programs that profit Western corporations without helping people in poor countries. The Gates people called these journalists "strategic media partners," a fairly explicit signal that they were no longer independent watchdogs, but collaborators in a planned campaign to burnish the image of Bill and Melinda Gates. And in 2012 the Gates Foundation doled out more than $25 million in media grants, subsidizing NPR's Global Health Beat and the *Guardian*'s Global Development page. But the history of global aid is littered with failures, and we can't develop successful policies unless we know what doesn't work. If a Gates project goes horribly wrong, will these "strategic media partners" report it? Here's a possible answer to that question: some years back Microsoft developed its own blacklist of unsympathetic journalists, and succeeded in getting John Dvorak fired as a columnist for *PC Magazine Italy*.[33]

At the turn of the last century corporations (including Standard Oil and Armour) often paid newspapers (even the *New York Times*) to publish articles touting their products—in effect, advertisements disguised as objective news. That was outlawed by the Newspaper Publicity Act of 1912, a Progressive reform supported by much of the press, because they realized it would enhance their credibility in the eyes of readers.

But now we have the rise of what is called "native advertising." No one knows who invented the term, but it is a stroke of PR genius, evoking in the mind of the reader something earthy and indigenous, suggesting artisanal ads hand-crafted by Navaho Mad Men. In fact, as the *New York Times* characterizes its own native advertising, it's "advertising that more closely resembles editorial matter." That is, it skirts as closely as possible to the Newspaper Publicity Act without crossing the line. (If native advertising does not succeed in getting the *Times* out of the red, perhaps they can try printing native money—not counterfeit money, mind you, but fake money that more closely resembles real money.) In 2015 Condé Nast created a department where editors worked directly with marketers to create ads that resembled legitimate articles. Condé Nast owns the *New Yorker*, which used to pride itself on the absolute separation of its advertising and editorial departments, but journalism professor Jay Rosen warned that this new policy "seems to suggest that actually the editors can be bought."[34] Whatever its practitioners say, clearly the intent of native advertising is to fool at least some of the readers some of the time: otherwise advertisers would not pay a premium for it. University of San Francisco law professor David J. Franklyn surveyed 10,000 readers and found "deep confusion about the difference between paid and unpaid content." As a journalist who covers the media, Bob Garfield realized that native advertising was undermining the foundation of journalism: trust. In 2013 he correctly predicted that: "Those deals [with advertisers] will not save the media industry. They will, in a matter of years, destroy the media industry, one boatload of shit at a time."[35]

We also have to consider a historic contradiction in PR: publicists must first of all publicize themselves. To drum up customers, they advertise their services and trumpet their successes. But in so doing, they inevitably violate the first rule of PR: don't let on that it's PR. Edward Bernays had to convince businessmen that his brand-new profession could be useful to them, so he showcased his proudest achievement—in 1928, on behalf of the American Tobacco Company, he organized a smoke-in that broke the taboo on women lighting up cigarettes in public. He publicized that episode in his 1947 essay "The Engineering of Consent," the title of which was itself a PR blunder: that phrase, with all its manipulative connotations, would be thrown back in his teeth by every critic of PR.

Today, this kind of hubris is vastly more blatant. Often, when covering politicians or business, the media focuses more on the images they project rather than substantial issues, continually reinforcing the impression that the media itself is all about illusions and manipulation. In 2010, when Toyota faced allegations that its cars accelerated out of control, the *Huffington Post* treated it as a PR crisis: whether the reports were true or not (they weren't) was at best secondary. Blogs commonly and brazenly advise publicists on the art of placing stories in blogs, with headlines like "How to Pitch a Blogger" or "The Do's and Don'ts of Online Publicity." "From a reader's perspective this is all rather strange," notes publicist Ryan Holiday. "Why is the blog revealing how it can be manipulated? In turn, why do we not head for the hills when it is clear that blogs pass this manipulation on to us?"[36]

In April 2011 *Business Insider* streamlined the process: it openly invited publicists to write up stories promoting their clients, which *Business Insider* would publish as news. "In short, please stop sending us e-mails with story ideas and *just contribute directly to Business Insider.* You'll get a lot more ink for yourself and your clients and you'll save yourself a lot of wasted work."[37] For any publisher aiming to hollow out reportorial staff, this makes perfect sense. But the result, concludes Holiday, is "unreality":

> A netherworld between the fake and the real where each builds on the other and they cannot be told apart. This is what happens when the dominant cultural medium—the medium that feeds our other mediums—is so easily corrupted by people like me.
>
> When the news is decided not by what is important but by what readers are clicking; when the cycle is so fast that the news cannot be anything else but consistently and irregularly incomplete; when dubious scandals pressure politicians to resign and scuttle election bids or knock millions from the market caps of publicly traded companies; when the news frequently covers itself in stories about "how the story unfolded"—unreality is the only word for it.[38]

Ryan Holiday's official title was marketing director of American Apparel, but he describes himself as, to put it bluntly, a media manipulator—I'm paid to deceive. My job is to lie to the media so they can lie to you...I have funneled millions of dollars to blogs through advertising. I've given breaking news to blogs instead of *Good Morning America* and, when that didn't work, hired their family members. I have flown bloggers across the country, boosted their revenue by buying traffic, written their stories for them, fabricated elaborate ruses to capture their attention, and courted them with expensive meals and scoops. I've probably sent enough gift cards and T-shirts to fashion bloggers to clothe a small country...I used blogs to control the news.[39]

He mainly focuses on big blogs—*Gawker, BuzzFeed, Huffington Post, Politico, Business Insider*—because what they publish is picked up and (often uncritically) disseminated by mainstream journalists as well as millions of ordinary readers. "Blogs need traffic, being first drives traffic, and so entire stories are created out of the whole cloth to make that happen." As press secretary for a US Congressman, Kurt Bardella found that Washington journalists were happy to let him do their job: "There are times when I pitch a story and they do it word for word. That's just embarrassing."[40] Or conversely, journalists cite "experts" who often have no real expertise but who, for the sake of publicity, are willing to provide a quotation validating whatever point the journalist wants to make. There is even a widely used service, Help a Reporter Out, which links reporters with self-described "experts." Holiday admits, "I've used it myself to con reporters from ABC News to Reuters to the *Today Show*, and yes, even the vaunted *New York Times*."[41] And in stark contrast to those lengthy in-depth *New Yorker* articles and *Playboy* interviews from the 1960s, blogs today assume that their readers suffer from Attention Deficit Disorder. Nick Denton of *Gawker* said that posts should be about 100 words long, 200 at most. Even when blogs deal with cancer, a dense and complicated subject, the average post is just 335 words.[42] Holiday frankly concludes that the media today is a "racket":

There is no other definition for the modern media system. Its very business model rests on exploiting the difference between perception and reality—pretending that it produces the "quality" news we once classified as journalism without adhering to any of the standards or practices that define it. Online, blogs have to publish so much so quickly and at such razor-thin margins that no media outlet can afford to do good work. But of course, no one can admit any of this without the whole system collapsing.

Publicly the media denounced or ignored his revelations, but privately media people usually told him, "Ryan, it's *even* worse than you imagine." And his book *Trust Me, I'm Lying* got Holiday "more requests from potential new clients than I knew what to do with"—evidently his ability to game the system impressed them.[43] No one has actually added up all the people now working in PR, advertising, marketing, politics, and the law, but it's clear that we now have a vast professional class devoted to manipulating customers, voters, juries, and readers. For them, the concept of truth is an irrelevant annoyance, but they are keenly interested in new and more effective methods of spin.

And that raises some troubling existential questions for today's journalists and editors. If they solicit native advertising, have they any right to complain about "fake news"? If they rely on press releases, do they wonder why they have lost credibility in the eyes of the public? Have they any awareness that they may be a big part of the problem?

Notes

1. Meaghan J. Brown, "'The hearts of all sorts of people were enflamed': Manipulating Readers of Spanish Armada News," *Book History* 17 (2014): 94–116.
2. Brendan Dooley, *The Social History of Skepticism: Experience and Doubt in Early Modern Culture* (Baltimore and London: Johns Hopkins University Press, 1999), 33–5.
3. Lucy Hutchinson, *Memoirs of the Life of Colonel Hutchinson*, ed. N. H. Keeble (London, 1995), 92–3.
4. Thomas E. Sebrell II, *Persuading John Bull: Union and Confederate Propaganda in Britain, 1860–1865* (Lanham, Md.: Lexington Books, 2014), 85, 163, 181–4.
5. Ibid., chs. 6–7.
6. Mark Sullivan, "The Patent Medicine Conspiracy against the Press," in *The Muckrakers*, ed. Arthur and Lila Weinberg (New York: Simon & Schuster, 1961), 179–94.
7. Christopher Hilliard, *English as a Vocation: The Scrutiny Movement* (Oxford: Oxford University Press, 2012), ch. 2.
8. John F. Kennedy, *Profiles in Courage* (New York: Harper & Brothers, 1956), 18.
9. Irwin Shaw, *The Image Merchants: The Fabulous World of Public Relations* (Garden City, NY: Doubleday, 1959), 106–7, 235–9.

10. Matthew Cecil, *Hoover's FBI and the Fourth Estate: The Campaign to Control the Press and the Bureau's Image* (Lawrence, Kan.: University of Kansas Press, 2014), 13–14, 27–30, 36–41, 117–18, 142.

11. Kevin Moloney, *Rethinking Public Relations*, 2nd edn. (London and New York: Routledge, 2006), 43.

12. Craig Lloyd, *Aggressive Introvert: A Study of Herbert Hoover and Public Relations Management, 1912–1932* (Columbus, Ohio: Ohio State University Press, 1973); Mordecai Lee, "Government Public Relations during Herbert Hoover's Presidency," *Public Relations Review* 36 (Mar. 2010): 56–8.

13. This account is drawn from Priscilla Coit Murphy, *What a Book Can Do: The Publication and Reception of 'Silent Spring'* (Amherst and Boston: University of Massachusetts Press, 2005).

14. C. Edwin Baker, *Advertising and a Democratic Press* (Princeton: Princeton University Press, 1994), ch. 2.

15. Ibid., 45–9.

16. Marvin J. Olasky, *Corporate Public Relations: A New Historical Perspective* (Hillsdale, NJ: Lawrence Erlbaum, 1987), preface.

17. Sharyl Attkisson, *Stonewalled* (New York: Harper, 2014), 29–32.

18. Ibid., 45.

19. Paul Farhi, "Media, Administration Deal with Conflicts," *Washington Post* (12 June 2013); Elspeth Reeve, "Rick Stengel Is at Least the 24th Journalist to Work for the Obama Administration," *Atlantic* (12 Sept. 2013).

20. Attkisson, *Stonewalled*, 46–7.

21. K. Hallahan, "Public Relations and the Circumvention of the Press," *Public Relations Quarterly* 4, (1994): 18–32.

22. <http://www.stateofthemedia.org/2013/special-reports-landing-page/citing-reduced-quality-many-americans-abandon-news-outlets/>.

23. Molony, *Rethinking Public Relations*, 67.

24. Lawrence Susskind and Patrick Field, *Dealing with an Angry Public* (New York: Free Press, 1996), 1–9.

25. L. Gordon Crovitz, "Trump's Big Data Gamble," *Wall Street Journal* (24 July 2016).

26. Justin Lewis, Andrew Williams, and Bob Franklin, "A Compromised Fourth Estate? UK News Journalism, Public Relations and News Sources," *Journalism Studies* 9, (2008): 1–20.

27. Quoted in Molony, *Rethinking Public Relations*, 158–9.

28. Chris Hedges, *Empire of Illusion: The End of Literacy and the Triumph of Spectacle* (New York: Nation Books, 2009), 97–8.

29. Gillian Tett, "Silos and Silences: Why So Few People Spotted the Problems in Complex Credit and What That Implies for the Future," *Financial Stability Review*, 14 (July 2010): 121–9.

30. Dean Starkman, *The Watchdog that Didn't Bark: The Financial Crisis and the Disappearance of Investigative Journalism* (New York: Columbia University Press, 2014), 242–5.

31. Ibid., 295–7.

32. Ibid., ch. 9.

33. Linsey McGoey, *No Such Thing as a Free Gift: The Gates Foundation and the Price of Philanthropy* (London and New York: Verso, 2015).

34. Steven Perlberg, "Write Ads? Condé Nast Staff is Wary that Allowing Editors to Work with Marketers Would Break Down a Boundary," *Wall Street Journal* (27 Jan. 2015).

35. Tracie Powell, "Native Ads Aren't as Clear as Outlets Think," *Columbia Journalism Review* (5 Dec. 2013).

36. Ryan Holiday, *Trust Me, I'm Lying: Confessions of a Media Manipulator*, rev. edn. (New York: Portfolio/Penguin, 2013), 188–93.

37. Ibid., 219.

38. Ibid., 216–17.

39. Ibid., 1.

40. Ibid., 13–17.

41. Ibid., 55.

42. Ibid., 108–9; S. Kim, "Content Analysis of Cancer Blog Posts," *Journal of the Medical Library Association* 97 (Oct. 2009): 260–6.

43. Holiday, *Trust Me*, xiii–xvii.

8

Death to Gradgrind

There has always been a "reading crisis," at least for the last two hundred years. Up to the end of the nineteenth century critics fretted over the spread of mass literacy, which (they anticipated) would degrade the quality of literature. And then, at various points over the twentieth century, critics warned that the Book-of-the-Month Club, or middlebrow literature, or paperbacks, or the *Great Books of the Western World*, or Oprah Winfrey would mean the end of serious reading.[1] As documented here, none of these irrational fears had any basis in reality. But even if others frequently cried wolf in the past, there are real and present threats to reading, and often (ironically) they come from the very quarters that warn that reading is in a crisis that must be addressed.

Perhaps the most deeply troubling development on the reading instruction front is Common Core, a set of educational standards that promises "career and college readiness." It has been adopted by most of the fifty states in the US, though several are having second thoughts and pulling back. The Gates Foundation has heavily promoted Common Core, donating a total of $150 million to teachers' unions, universities, foundations, state departments of education, and think tanks that support the program.[2] What Bill Gates prefers to call "philanthropy" was in this case more like an investment, given that the Common Core would require much greater use of computers in classrooms. Likewise, publishing giant Pearson stood ready to corral a huge and largely captive market for textbooks oriented to Common Core. (Historians of textbooks know that, because they are usually sold to a government monopsony, opportunities for corruption are enormous.) Championed as well by Education Secretary Arne Duncan and many state governors, Common Core thus involves the takeover of school reading instruction not by capitalism, but by crony capitalism, cutting out both teachers and parents in shaping educational policy. Pearson was awarded contracts that effectively ensured that the company would be the only qualified bidder.[3]

In a 28 February 2014 meeting, Pearson CEO John Fallon and CFO Robin Freestone discussed the company's long-term profitability with eight market analysts. Fallon conceded that 2013 had not been a very good year, but Pearson would return to "sustained earnings growth" once the nation's schools had effected "a major curriculum change brought about by Common Core," and that was happening "slowly as budgets and policy align state by state." (This somewhat contradicts what proponents of Common Core said publicly: they promised that it would not dictate curricula and would not be imposed on the states by the federal government.) Once that curriculum change was complete, Fallon continued, Pearson would "successfully embed ourselves with our customers...shift[ing] us much more quickly and much more irreversibly to where our biggest sources of future demand are... [and reducing] our exposure to the corresponding risks." The words "embed" and "irreversibly" suggest that, with the adoption of Pearson's standardized tests, schools will be compelled to buy Pearson textbooks to prepare for those tests. They will never be able to break that addiction, reducing the risk that they will drop Pearson and offer their business to a competitor. And as with any captive market, the seller can reap monopoly profits with no incentives for quality control: Pearson already has a long and dismal record of misgrading tests.[4]

Whatever the faults of Common Core, we should not imagine that there was a lost golden age of American textbooks. A 1960–1 survey of high-school literature anthologies found that teachers almost unanimously disliked them. There were complaints about too much abridgement, too much middlebrow literature mixed in with classics, too much apparatus and illustration crowding out text.[5] But the current Pearson twelfth-grade anthology of British literature greatly magnifies every one of these shortcomings.[6] It is a doorstop running to more than 1,500 pages, crammed with Technicolor illustrations. A bewildering assortment of texts is accompanied by meticulous instructions for reading and analyzing them, fencing in any temptation to indulge the imagination. *Beowulf* is heavily abridged, and discussion of the epic is interrupted by the Wikipedia page for Davy Crockett. If you ask what it is doing there, the stated intention is to teach research skills, but it might also serve to illustrate the vocabulary word *fragmentary*, which is also the word that immediately springs to your lips when you plough through this textbook. Except for *Macbeth* and some short poems, the volume consists almost entirely of snippets. There are just six pages of *Hard Times*, where Gradgrind propounds a fact-based educational philosophy very similar to Common Core, which may explain why the textbook asks students to consider whether there might be "a positive side to this viewpoint that Dickens neglected or deliberately ignored?" Speaking of utilitarianism, the section on Wordsworth is accompanied by a government report on traffic management in the Lake District. And though Gulliver never visited Georgia, ten pages of *Gulliver's Travels* are prefaced with an Atlanta rapid-transit map. There is a section on *Frankenstein*, a book which would be an ideal candidate for reprinting in full—provocative, notorious, short, perfect for instigating discussion of scientific ethics. But in fact nothing of the original novel is included, though there is a *Saturday Night Live* lampoon of it. None of this will prepare students for college, unless they commute to Georgia Tech by subway. "Frankly," one critic concluded, "you wonder at first if these tomes have been compiled by people who hate books and want you to hate them, too."[7]

Well before Common Core, standardized testing was already forcing teachers to assign less reading (in some cases abandoning novels altogether) to allow more classroom time for test preparation. Schools in poor neighborhoods were much more likely to fail those tests, in which case the usual remedies were to cut their school budgets or require more standardized tests, both of which only aggravated the problem.[8] And when schools cut back on other subjects to focus on reading, that made matters still worse, because (as E. D. Hirsch recognized) reading cannot be taught in isolation: unless students know something about history, science, art, music, and a range of other subjects, they won't comprehend what is on the page.[9] And whereas reading literary fiction enhances empathy, high-stakes testing has exactly the opposite moral effect, encouraging an epidemic of cheating on the part of students, teachers, and school administrators.[10]

There were no experimental trials of Common Core before it was adopted by the states, and the standards were written by committees working under strict secrecy. The guidelines that emerged were themselves unreadable, "more like the U. S. Tax Code than a treatise on teaching literature," according to educator Terrence Moore. And in the spirit of Gradgrind, Common Core assigns arbitrary quotas for the amount of imaginative literature (versus utilitarian "informational texts") that can be assigned: 50/50 in grade 4, declining to 30/70 in grade 12. "Your children love to read books, especially stories," Moore protested. "You have read them hundreds of stories since they were toddlers." But then why does Common Core aim "to *take away stories* rather than teaching better stories or, equally important, doing a better job of teaching stories"?

Visiting a Common Core classroom, Moore noticed that the teachers spoke "in a sing-song voice and in single syllables as though the students, even in the fifth grade, are toddlers." In fact there wasn't much teaching at all: students either read quietly, filled out worksheets, or spent time (a lot of it) on computers. And teachers read aloud books that were dumbed down to a 3- or 4-year-old level, books "wholly devoid of a gripping story."

Middle-school English classes offered close readings of "informational texts," such as the *Virginia Department of Historic Resources Form*, or the gripping *California Invasive Plant Inventory*. There was also some real literature, "Yet the students never spend more than a single class period on them. The teachers will ask a few, predictable questions. The students, when they are even interested, offer a few predictable answers, and then the class moves on to another book (or portion of a book) the next day." What is the point of this "one-day-Twain-next-day-Alcott" pedagogy? Maybe it supplies ready fill-in-the-bubble answers to standardized tests. Or perhaps Common Core is a Potemkin Village of literary studies, allowing principals to assure parents that they teach a long list of great books, when in fact pupils are only exposed to snippets. And sometimes not even that: in one class students read an essay explaining (vaguely) that the Declaration of Independence "means different things to different people," but never read the Declaration itself.[11] Of course, if the students had read it, they might have taken seriously all that business about equality and inalienable rights. For exactly that reason, segregated schools a century ago often did not teach the Declaration to black students, but today Common Core does not discriminate.[12]

All this, Moore concludes, aims "to remove the *humanity* out of … the humanities." The Common Core slogan, "career and college ready," looks like the old adman's trick of promising exactly what the product doesn't deliver. The curriculum prepares students for only the most robotic jobs, and for no college-level literature courses whatsoever. Likewise, Common Core claims to enforce "standards," which implies something both rigorous and clear, when in fact the standards are vague and dismally low. Another slogan is "critical thinking," which Common Core actually discourages in favor of rote answers to multiple-choice questions. (How can students think critically about a literary work if they have read only fragments of it—or none of it?) The only honest Common Core slogan is "Preparing for a twenty-first century competitive global economy," which forthrightly suggests that the curriculum has no priorities other than vocational training—and that if students don't learn their lessons and become obedient workers, their jobs will be offshored. From his own experience as a teacher, Moore concludes that, far from being shallow careerists, teenagers want a liberal education, if only schools will give it to them:

> A liberal education inspires young people because it speaks directly to their minds and souls. It calls on them to study the very human things they are already interested in. You do not have to convince a sixteen-year-old girl that she needs to learn about love. You do not have to convince a boy of any age to study the nature and causes of war. You do not have to trick teenagers into learning political and theological and economic and philosophical arguments. They are teenagers. They love to argue. It only requires a teacher who knows something and a book that has something in it worth arguing about. The things worth arguing about turn out to be the same things worth both working and fighting for, the great ends of human existence: truth, beauty, love, justice, liberty, prosperity, and so many other things both desirable and good. Devoting oneself to learning these things teaches young people how to bring about beauty and order and justice in the world...It should come as no shock that they are far more interested at age fifteen or eighteen with the passions of great men and women—who may be fictional, or who may have lived centuries ago—than they are in the "twenty-first century global economy."[13]

But Common Core architect David Coleman (an entrepreneur with no real training or experience in teaching) sees no meaningful value in students engaging in literary criticism or relating books to their own lives. "As you grow up in this world you realize people don't really give a shit about what you feel or what you think," he explained thoughtfully. "It is rare in a working environment that someone says, 'Johnson, I need a market analysis by Friday but before that I need a compelling account of your childhood.'"[14] And certainly, your boss doesn't want to read "I feel we may be doing something unethical here," or "I think one of our most profitable products is more toxic than we imagined." Of course, booklovers do care about what authors think, and politicians in a democracy should care about what citizens feel, but if Common Core aims solely at producing docile employees, then Coleman's remarks make perfect sense.

And the movement towards high-stakes literacy testing is global, taking in Common Core, England's National Literary Strategy, and Australia's National Assessment Plan—Literacy and Numeracy. On a worldwide scale, UNESCO has proposed a Literacy and Assessment Monitoring Program, "a global methodological standard for measuring reading and numeracy skills."[15] But in America there are growing protests against Common Core among parents, students, and teachers, including mass boycotts of standardized tests.[16] "Pearson's brand is politically toxic in the United States," warns investment analyst Ian Whittaker. Thanks to that grassroots resistance, plus the costly development of interactive digital courses that didn't work, Pearson is losing money handsomely on Common Core.[17]

Rather than throw huge sums of cash at Common Core textbooks, high-priced reading programs and consultants, and yet more standardized texts, we should turn to far cheaper and more effective strategies for encouraging reading. A reasonably well-stocked school library with competent staff is not terribly expensive. And in place of ponderous and costly anthologies, let me propose this three-part pedagogical strategy:

First, require all students to spend one session every day reading quietly in the school library. They can read whatever they choose (with some guidance from the librarian), but it has to be a book, not a screen. All the academic literature shows that this is the most effective means of enhancing reading comprehension and the reading habit.[18]

If principals protest that there is no room in the schedule for this, cut back drastically on standardized testing, and reallocate to quiet reading the time now devoted to tests and test prep. If they further object that Common Core doesn't permit them to do this, abolish Common Core. We have known for years that reading test scores correlate strongly with the amount of time devoted to daily reading, ranging from 90.7 minutes per day for fifth graders in the 98th percentile to 1.6 minutes for the 10th percentile.[19]

Second, let literature teachers teach pretty much anything they want. There might be very broad guidelines ensuring that all genres and historical periods are covered, but the aim would be allow teachers to teach whatever they feel most passionate about. That would attract passionate teachers to the profession, and if they communicate that infectious enthusiasm to students, then they have succeeded according to the only legitimate measure of success. This would resolve the sterile controversy over whether we should teach classics or ethnic literature: by the twelfth grade students would inevitably be exposed to a wide range of books taught by a wide range of teachers.

Third, once a teacher selects a required reading, the school would purchase paperback copies for students—and let them keep those books. They would become the property of the students, who could write in them and shelve them permanently in their home libraries. They wouldn't be more expensive than a huge slab of a textbook, and of course they would be far more portable. Decades after we graduate, we still have old copies of the novels and plays we read in school, and we still pull them off the shelves occasionally; but no one feels that kind of affection for a textbook. We know that poor children are less likely to have a nutritious breakfast or lunch than middle-class children, so we offer them free school meals. We also know that poor children are exposed to far fewer vocabulary words, have fewer books at home, and enjoy limited access to public libraries. By simply reallocating money from textbooks to real books, we could do much to correct those deficits.

Reading research consistently shows that we become hooked on reading when we experience it as a "flow," when we shut out the rest of the world and get "lost in a book," entering fully into the world created by the author:

"It's as if you are living completely inside the situation."

"I'm reading along and suddenly a word or phrase or scene enlarges before my eyes and soon everything around me is just so much fuzzy background."

"Reading was where I could always find friends."

"Even if dozens and dozens of people have read this same book, my experience of reading it is mine."

"I simply opened a book and shut myself in a different world."

"I just get completely absorbed and I'm there and I'm involved and I'm feeling all of the emotions and everything else."

"I'm convinced that, although reading is socially acceptable, it is an addiction."

Conversely, the most discouraging reading experiences, those most likely to turn students off books completely, involve a public humiliating failure at reading:

"I was always afraid and ashamed of my poor oral reading."

"Reading period was always a frightening experience for me."

"My friends were laughing at me and I wanted to cry—I was reading out loud in circle of students and I could not pronounce some of the words…I was a public failure."[20]

The sense of getting lost in a book can't happen if you know you're going to be tested on it. And if you constantly test children and flunk the majority, nothing is better calculated to make them hate the sight of a book. The No Child Left Behind Act of 2002 also emphasized high-stakes testing, and by 2006 the reading scores of American fourth-graders had actually declined relative to other countries. Meanwhile, Finland produces the most literate students in the world, though it has no standardized testing.[21] We should consider the possibility that Finns are superb readers *because* they have no standardized tests.

Proponents of Common Core robotically repeat that we must keep up with the Chinese (just as the post-Sputnik generation was warned that they had to keep up with the Russians). But China and other East Asian countries have lately come to realize that their traditional education systems (highly centralized, test-driven, emphasizing technical knowledge and skill) have not prepared their students to compete with Americans in terms of creativity and innovative thinking—the real core strengths of the US economy. That helps to explain why so many Chinese parents now educate their children (very expensively) at US universities. Shanghai, Hong Kong, South Korea, and Singapore have therefore moved to cut back on testing, allow greater breadth and flexibility in curricula, and promote the study of literature, the arts, and the humanities. As educational researcher Yong Zhao concludes, "If current efforts undertaken in Western education systems succeed, the outcome will be an obsolete version of Asian education, which the Asian systems themselves are eager to move away from."[22]

While literature in the schools is being undermined by behemoth foundations and corporations, on many college campuses it is under attack from another ideological quarter. At some of our best universities, activists warn that reading can create a psychological crisis in the mind of the reader, and therefore literature (like pharmaceuticals) should come with warning labels. According to this logic (if it can be called that), books can make readers uncomfortable, reminding them of traumatic episodes, and therefore they should be prefaced with "trigger warnings." It sounds like a first draft of *Fahrenheit 451*, though in more mundane terms it is yet another instance of adolescents ordering an adult to solve a non-problem that they could easily fix themselves. If a student sincerely wanted advance notice of any nasty bits in the required texts, he could simply (A) ask the professor or (B) look up the plot summary on Wikipedia. And given everything we know about the unpredictability of reader response, how can a teacher guess beforehand which readings will disturb which readers?

Yes, reading can be painful. In any given classroom, some students are struggling with demons that the instructor can scarcely imagine. I recall one student who, in the midst of writing an essay exam on the First World War, stopped and confessed that reading about the carnage on the Western Front had reduced him to tears. He was a soldier, about to be sent with his unit to Afghanistan. But if I had to list in the syllabus what parts of the course students might find triggering, I'd have to write: *Everything*. The class covers two world wars, several civil and colonial wars, mass terror across Europe, and more than one holocaust.

Nineteenth-century readers would have found this squeamishness inexplicable. Whether they were reading novels or newspapers, antebellum Americans expected them to be harrowing: respectable citizens murdered, ships lost at sea, factory explosions, epidemics, buildings burned by accident or angry mobs, war with Mexico, famine in Ireland, revolutions in Europe. As one factory girl ruefully wrote, "Each week brings the tidings of the death of...some acquaintance or friend," in this case a young woman killed by consumption. Given the slowness of the mails, you might first read of a death of a loved one in a newspaper, before any letters arrived. Even when the reader had no personal connection to any of the victims, diaries reveal that these reports still had the capacity to shock, whether they told of a fire ("I am...strongly impressed with the idea that every fire which occurs is a loss to every citizen of the country, and hate to read accounts of 'em"), a shipwreck ("it was shocking to read what must it have been to those on board!"), or lynchings ("awful murders...Woe to our country if a few years bring no change"). We had not yet grown accustomed to the deaths of millions, or the routine litany of crimes reported daily on television. Likewise, novels were supposed to trigger deep emotional disturbances, and might be considered insipid if they didn't. "Have you read & cried over *Uncle Tom's Cabin?*" a New England woman asked her sister. "I never read anything so affecting in my life."[23] If a book doesn't trigger something, what's the point of reading it?

The pain that reading provokes in troubled minds is a necessary part of the healing process. Bibliotherapy has been prescribed and practiced for the past 300 years, and for a long time it was probably the only form of psychotherapy that actually worked. Today it is used successfully to help refugees and asylum-seekers deal with the violence and persecution they have escaped, as well as the sense of exile that comes from living in a strange and not-always-hospitable host nation. In London, Marion Baraitser found that "Jane Eyre's story of survival in a cold northern country" resonated deeply with teenage refugees. "Jane Eyre was as maltreated and hurt as the young people sitting in the session with me who, through her story, imbibe her courage, self-determination and strength of will as a way of thinking about possible life solutions." One African girl, "abused and rejected by her family, then trafficked on her journey to England," recognized herself in *Great Expectations*. As she wrote, Pip "had no real kindness...He was lonely...It happened to myself. So I ask: who am I? Can I really become something? Dickens wants to make his readers know what it's like to be a teenager with no one to help you."[24]

Readers report that bibliotherapy helps them through identification with characters who have endured similar ordeals ("It just felt like this person experienced what I'm experiencing"). There may indeed be a wincing flashback to the original trauma ("as though I had been hit on the head with how I felt"), but the end result is catharsis: "You really do feel a healing. You feel a release . . . It's like a cleansing of the hurt, of the residual anger or whatever was there. And it's just a real lightening of your whole being." *Validated, comforting*, and *hope* are the words we hear from these readers, who come to realize that the burdens they face, though real, are also widely shared: "It was nice to read that other people felt the same way you did. Sometimes you'd say, why me and I must be the only one who feels like this and I'm going to lose my mind. But it's nice to hear that other people are losing their mind, too. You're not alone."[25]

The Reader Organisation in Britain sponsors a Shared Reading program which sets up reading groups for people at the bottom of the social scale: foster or at-risk children, the intellectually or physically disabled, the homeless or inadequately housed, the unemployed, ex-convicts, refugees, the elderly, and those struggling with drug, alcohol, health, or mental problems. (I provide these details to help university students check their privileges.) One group operated out of a mental health drop-in center in Bootle, a town with very high levels of poverty and mental illness, where 43 percent of the population had no educational diplomas. In fact, a prerequisite for admission to the class was a diagnosis of clinical depression, and most members were also dealing with other issues, including limited literacy. None had attended university. Readings were selected by vote, and this group chose *Great Expectations*. SR groups met in weekly ninety-minute sessions and read a common text far more closely than any college class would, just ten to fifteen pages a session. At that rate it took them thirteen months (April 2010 to May 2011) to finish the novel.

Great Expectations is a popular choice among SR groups, in part because of familiarity with film versions, but also because it is a recognized classic. That fact promises a special literary experience for readers with bleak lives, and reading it conveys a sense of accomplishment and self-confidence to individuals who have faced mostly failure. Oprah Winfrey successfully used this kind of appeal to persuade her book club to tackle *Anna Karenina* (all 838 pages). "This book has been on my 'must read' list for years, but I was scared of it," she admitted. "Let's not be scared of it. I'm going to team up with all of you, and we'll read it together . . . I believe we can do this. We can read the great literature of the world."[26]

Teachers today complain that students can no longer tackle long and complicated narratives, and it may be that the Internet and action movies have crippled our ability to pay attention. The problem was compounded for several SR readers, whose capacity for concentration was further eroded by mental issues. But because Dickens "knows how to construct a story," as one reader put it, *Great Expectations* was able to reverse some of this deterioration, exercising and recovering an atrophied ability to follow a long text. As a reader who suffered from dyslexia and attention deficit hyperactivity disorder (ADHD) explained it:

> I've found that my mind's starting everywhere and I want to be able to concentrate better. I want to learn more stuff than the stuff that I already know. And my memory's not so great so it helps my memory—putting more things in my mind all the time—you know like Pip, and Estella, Miss Havisham—well I've found I can remember all those . . . You see part of the thing about that *Great Expectations* is that it's a bit like solving a crime—there's a bit of detective work to do, you're trying to solve the plot . . . [And] there's so much in it, all those other characters, the style of writing and how they describe things, and how life was then in the 1800s and history and all that and it's like a chain reaction that takes place—it does inspire interest in other things.

Of course, there are numerous tragic turns throughout the novel, starting on the first page, but any trigger warnings would ruin the drama, and it was the drama that grabbed these readers from the start. They noticed that Dickens was brilliant at conjuring up the fears that plague small children, and that triggered disturbing memories of their own childhood phobias, but the story and the group discussion helped them work through the pain. "I think my body went umph and cringed my teeth," explained one reader, who had endured both learning disabilities and domestic violence. "I don't like hearing nasty things I know it's part of them days but . . .," she added, and confirmed that she recognized herself in Pip. "And is that painful at all? Or does it help?" asked the group facilitator. "In a way both," she answered. "It does help because you see in it something else, don't you? But it is painful as well because Pip's been through pretty harsh and rough things."[27] With trigger warnings, readers will never learn how to deal with life's sucker punches. Or, as Keats put it: "Do you not see how necessary a world of pains and troubles is to school an Intelligence and make it a Soul? A place where the heart must feel and suffer in a thousand diverse ways!"

In the 1990s, anthropologist of reading Shirley Brice Heath found that serious readers like to read unpredictable stories as a means of coping with unpredictability in life: "Therapists and ministers who counsel troubled people tend to read the hard stuff. So do people whose lives have not followed the course they were expected to: merchant caste Koreans who don't become merchants, ghetto kids who go to college, men from conservative families who lead openly gay lives, and women whose lives turned out to be radically different from their mothers."[28] And while elite university students demand trigger warnings, a high-school English teacher in Anaheim reports that the books that win over the "reluctant readers" in his classroom deal with the Holocaust, self-mutilation, abusive relationships, teenage parenthood, mental illness, jailed or dead parents, gang violence, school shootings, life-threatening illness, adolescent suicide, drug dealing, fatal car crashes, African civil wars, dystopian worlds, divorce, the murder of Emmett Till—in a word, the literature of trauma.[29]

It's telling that very average high-school pupils seem to be more willing to confront controversy than university students. Britain's National Union of Students has a "No Platform" policy, effectively a blacklist banning certain individuals and organizations from speaking on campus. Polls show that a clear majority of students think that the NUS is entirely right to ban "individuals they believe threaten a safe space" (meaning pretty much anyone they want).[30] Another 38 percent supported banning tabloids from student union shops: presumably they had no objection to posh papers. When asked whether instructors who address "difficult issues" should issue trigger warnings "so that those who wish to leave can do so," only 18 percent scoffed at the idea; they were far outnumbered by those who favored warnings "always" (25 percent) or "sometimes" (43 percent).[31] In the United States, in

2015, college students endorsed speech codes by 51 to 36 percent, and 63 percent favored making trigger warnings mandatory.[32] (In 1974, 78 percent of high-school pupils affirmed that "Censorship violates basic American principles of freedom of expression and freedom to read").[33] This seems to be a general pattern in Western countries: in a reversal of the 1960s, young people are less tolerant of dissent than their elders. In a 2015 Pew Research Center poll, 47 percent of 18-to-29-year-olds (and just 30 percent of the 50-plus generation) said that the government should ban statements that are offensive to religious beliefs, which has atheists understandably worried. What about the readers who find *The Origin of Species* offensive?[34] The philosophy underlying all this appears to be an extremely crude utilitarianism. A university education is conceived of as a four-year luxury cruise, with foodie food and some interesting lectures, but nothing should be done to vex the passengers.

While conceding that "political correctness" is guilty of plenty of excesses, Jonathan Zimmerman disputes that it poses a threat to academic freedom comparable to the McCarthy Red Scare, during which more than a hundred professors were fired or denied tenure for real or alleged Communist sympathies. He is right to argue that today political correctness isn't much of a danger to tenured professors—but there are fewer and fewer of them, as universities increasingly rely on adjuncts and short-term hires. As of 2014 they accounted for 76.4 percent of American college teachers, and they can be fired at will if they teach something that offends the left, the right, the university administration, or their students. The attacks can come from many points on the ideological compass and all ethnic groups (including, of course, whites). And that means itinerants have to be careful about the readings they assign: one part-time instructor was let go after students protested that his syllabus included "offensive" readings by Mark Twain. At Columbia University there were complaints that Ovid's *Metamorphoses* promoted a cavalier attitude toward sexual assault, and it was dropped from the university's required core humanities course.[35] In the McCarthy era you had to avoid any association with the Communist Party, but as far as we know, no one got into trouble for teaching Ovid. Professors could assign pretty much any readings they wanted, as long as they weren't too Marxist or too sexy. But today just about any book is a potential minefield. Though no campus has made trigger warnings mandatory (yet), adjuncts have good reason to fear that their students will complain to the dean that they were scarred by the required readings. Moreover, in the 1950s academia was a growth industry, opening up career opportunities for intellectuals of the non-Communist left like Irving Howe and Noam Chomsky—which is certainly not the case today. A 2010 survey by the American Association of Colleges and Universities found that, when asked if they felt free to express their views on campus, just 30 percent of seniors and only 16.7 percent of professors strongly agreed. If we factor in all these pressures, young academics may indeed enjoy precious little intellectual freedom or security.[36] In fact many of them are cutting back on controversial readings and assignments.[37]

And increasingly, they are teaching students who don't want intellectual freedom. Though the radical movements that germinated in the 1960s (feminism, gay rights, ethnic studies, environmentalism) are now entirely orthodox on campus, in one very important sense this generation of students has rejected what was perhaps the greatest virtue of that turbulent decade—dissent. William Deresiewicz has protested that there seem to be no more wild poets, anarchic iconoclasts, or existentialist lone wolves on campus, just "excellent sheep" who aim at careers in corporations or bureaucracies, where free expression is not valued.[38] (It is valued in academia and journalism, but now they offer extremely few job opportunities.) In the 1960s black and white students organized on their own initiative civil-rights demonstrations, often in the face of hostility from college administrators, and the protesters put their lives on the line. But in the most recent round of American college protests, the administrators anxiously assured the protesters that they agreed on all essential points, including the most important priority of all, the catchword repeatedly invoked by all parties—making students "comfortable." Recently, when Erika Christakis, a Yale University faculty member, circulated an email suggesting that "offensive" Halloween costumes were really no big deal, she found an angry mob of students on her doorstep. When her husband tried to calm the demonstrators by offering an intellectual space where reasonable people could discuss these issues, a student shouted, "It is your job to create a place of comfort and home for the students... It is *not* about creating an intellectual space. It is not! Do you understand that?"

M. R. James, who held a similar position at Cambridge University a century ago, once reportedly cut off a common-room debate between two undergraduates: "No thinking, gentlemen, please!" But the Sixties campus radicals were intensely committed to creating an intellectual space where they could criticize the larger society, and "comfort" was the dirtiest word in their vocabulary. For them it meant James Michener novels, the *Saturday Evening Post*, television, suburban complacency, and ignoring racism. We congratulate ourselves today on being environmentally aware and diverse and inclusive, but none of these movements would have gotten off the ground if an earlier generation had not repudiated comfort as an ideal. How can anyone, black or white, read an honest account of African-American history without feeling intensely uncomfortable? In 1968, when students at the University of California at Santa Barbara were asked which authors had most deeply influenced them, the top answers were Albert Camus, Hermann Hesse, and Jean-Paul Sartre, all of whom posed profoundly disturbing existential questions.[39]

The student leftists of the Sixties were also anti-authoritarian rule-breakers, contemptuous of their elders (including old leftists), and out to abolish restrictions of all kinds, particularly those policing sex. They rejected every form of bureaucracy (such as the administrative structure of the University of California at Berkeley) as oppressive and dehumanizing. But today, Yale English instructor Mark Oppenheimer regretfully admits that his students "think of themselves as somehow needing more control from above." The Black Student Alliance issued a list of demands, and almost all of them called for:

> an expanded, more active administration: "An email from Dean Holloway and/or President Salovey...," "[a] specific administrative team to collect data...," "the establishment of a formal space and procedure...," "mandatory diversity sensitivity trainings," encouragement for...students... "to read a series of Black feminist texts and report on what they have learned," and so forth. What's more, "[a]ll students must be required to take a certain number of classes" in ethnic and gender studies. In nearly every case, the students are asking to be controlled more, administered more, monitored more. They're even asking us to give them more required classes, more reading.

Oppenheimer observes that the same young people who vociferously squelch dissenting ideas about Halloween costumes are, in the classroom, fawningly deferential to their professors. He (and I) find it damnably difficult to provoke our students into disagreeing with us, or even offering an alternative reading of a set text:

> I know that my students have insights into literature that I don't, that they will often see things in an essay that I missed. I want nothing more than for them to claim their adulthood, challenge me, challenge each other. Yet they show obsequious fealty. I'm not sure which would be worse: if they actually think we teachers know everything, or if they are just pretending to think that because they think it will help their grade.

The assumption behind "diversity training" is that, if white students read black feminists, they will feed back all the right answers—and they probably will. Erika Christakis was slammed because she challenged (however politely) an administrator's advisory, and Yale students will inevitably take that lesson to heart. As Oppenheimer concludes, "They are adults who pay to be infantilized."[40] (Actually it is their parents who pay.) And the opinion editor of the *Yale Daily News* reported that, "Many students privately expressed their dismay at the protests, yet very few of these students were willing to express these views in the pages of the YDN when I reached out to them. They told me they were worried about being ostracized by their peers."[41]

If we have reached the point where students at a leading university are afraid to disagree about a point of literary interpretation (let alone Halloween costumes), then in an essential sense it has ceased to function as a university. In high-school English classes censorship pressures usually come from the political right, except for demands to ban or bowdlerize *Huckleberry Finn*.[42] That and "speech codes" on college campuses have normalized censorship for a generation, and there you have the "chilling effect" that civil libertarians had always predicted. A few years ago I saw on my campus something I never thought I would see again: an underground newspaper. Its politics were libertarian rather than New Left, and accordingly it published icons of F. A. Hayek rather than Che Guevara, but it was far more critical of our college administration (and society in general) than the tepid official student newspaper. Remarkably, every one of the contributors was anonymous. The reason became apparent when a professor wrote a letter to the editor advising against this policy—after all (he patiently explained), if we don't know who is writing for this paper, how can we take disciplinary action against them when they publish something offensive? I knew one of the editors, who as an undergraduate wrote (in his spare time) a book-length treatise on moral philosophy which was published by a major scholarly press. So this is what we are doing to the best minds of our generation: forcing them underground. Of course, you won't notice that if you only want your students to repeat back the formulas you have taught.

Given all that pessimism, one is tempted to conclude that we have, as a society, arrived at *Fahrenheit 451*. And if you read the book now for the first time, it is stunning to discover how much of the media dystopia we now live in—wall-sized television screens, interactive videos, earphones pumping noise directly into the brain, omnipresent advertising, omniscient computerized security systems (which often snag the innocent), liberal arts colleges and newspapers going out of business, Internet porn, speech codes, books banned because they "hurt" someone somehow, the media serving up a constant stream of gossip and factoids, the government pumping out propaganda about endless faraway wars—was predicted by Ray Bradbury in 1953. Between 2010 and 2016, as part of government "austerity" measures, 343 public libraries in the United Kingdom were closed, and a quarter of all paid library jobs were abolished.[43] Meanwhile, in Chicago and Los Angeles, school libraries have been shuttered as a cost-cutting measure.[44]

All the same, there are hopeful signs of a revival of liberated reading, though not necessarily in the university. Marjorie Perloff saw all too clearly how literary theory hemmed in the freedom of the reader: "I have seen job candidates, who are vying for the precious few tenure-track jobs available, actually apologize for discussing a novel or poem and hurrying through these same discussions so as to get on to some important theoretical point relating to postcolonialism or queer theory or globalization." But at the dawn of the twenty-first century she saw aesthetics, repressed in the academy, returning on the Internet. She pointed to the irruption of a host of websites devoted to the art of every author that inspired real passion among readers. "Poetics, we might say, abhors a vacuum: if the university doesn't offer courses on William Blake or Dante Gabriel Rossetti, on Ezra Pound or Samuel Beckett, the action moves elsewhere." Perloff correctly foresaw that digital humanities was not only the Next Big Thing, but also that it would refocus attention on literary art: "As such, poetics is attracting a new generation of students who are coming to aesthetic discourses by the circuitous channel of the digital media... The audience in question is primarily interested in how Beckett's radio plays or Apollinaire's *calligrammes* actually function and what younger artists and poets can learn from these examples." There is, then, no real "crisis in the humanities," only "a bad fit between an outmoded curriculum and the actual interests of potential students."[45]

Meanwhile, out in what we are pleased to call the "real world," there has been a revival of the kind of free reading circles that flourished a century ago. Recent surveys estimate that there are 500,000 book groups in the United States, 50,000 in Britain, 40,000 in Canada, and the phenomenon is also catching on in Australia, India, West Africa, and the Caribbean. Carrying on a tradition of plebeian self-education, UK participants identify themselves as 32 percent working-class and 36 percent lower-middle-class, but elsewhere book-clubbers are more likely to be professionals and college-educated.[46] When soundings were taken in around 2000, most reading groups were all-female: 69 percent in the United Kingdom, up to 85 percent in the United States, and 95 percent in Australia.[47]

Reading groups represent a return to the self-help ethos of the late nineteenth century. The revolt against mass prepackaged conformist culture, which began among dissident twentieth-century intellectuals, has now spread and triumphed throughout all levels of society. Consumers are determined to make up their own minds about the food they eat, they clothes they wear, the music they listen to, and the books they read. In book groups, participatory democracy is still the method of selecting readings, with the proviso that they must be "serious" literature. By this the members usually mean quality contemporary fiction plus some classics, and they recognize that the latter category is at least a notch above the former. As one group leader explained it, "We read across countries and historical movements; for instance, we might read something by Jane Austen, then something current, something by Henry James, and something current. We've read *Anna Karenina* and some French novels in translation..." The definition of "serious" does not generally include romances, westerns, science fiction, or thrillers, though exceptions were allowed for Dorothy L. Sayers and John le Carré.[48]

Jenny Hartley found that these groups are distinguished by a healthy lack of reverence for professorial authority. "We don't want it to feel like studying," said one, "It's deliberately not like school," said another, and for a group of English grammar-school teachers it offered "a chance to discuss something other than teaching and school!" Hartley concluded that, for these readers, "the academic was a comic figure," a pretentious snob.[49] And even earlier, before "theory" became fashionable, Elizabeth Long's readers dismissed academic "literary analysis as an arcane, demanding, and even manipulative game," if not something of a joke:

> At a September 1985 meeting, a CliffsNotes question about the meaning of the river in *Huckleberry Finn*, for example, led...to uproarious reminiscences about the tribulations of searching for symbols in English literature classes and everyone's favorite trick for getting A's. One member said that the ocean was his favorite symbol: "It could mean death, sex, rebirth—you could do anything with the ocean."

In another group, one reader had underlined every mention of windows in the book, and explained: "Oh, that was for a class. I wrote a paper on what windows might signify, but when I looked at it before the meeting, it seemed very odd, you know, sort of contrived." On the other hand, another group was "intrigued by the possibility that the main characaters in Lydia Telle's 1982 *The Girl in the Photograph* might all be aspects of one protagonist," and when they encountered in another novel a broken road-sign reading "[F]unfair," they got it. These readers were quite ready to do sophisticated literary analysis—provided they did it themselves.[50]

Book groups have their limitations, which capable leaders could help correct. They have difficulty relating to authors who evoke radically unfamiliar worlds (Nikos Kazantzakis, Ben Okri, Yukio Mishima, Naguib Mahfouz). They do read the standard classics: Jane Austen, George Eliot, Henry James, Virginia Woolf, Thomas Hardy, John Steinbeck, Anthony Trollope, Graham Greene, and E. M. Forster all made Hartley's lists of most-read authors. So (remarkably) did Arnold Bennett and Wilkie Collins. But long and difficult books (Cervantes, Walter Scott, Dostoevsky, Proust, Joyce) were less likely to succeed.[51] Book-club readers tend to look for characters they can identify with

("When I read something, I'm looking for me and my experience"), which can be shallow.[52]

With that qualification, most groups indulge in a varied literary diet, a mix of authors from different countries, contemporary and classic books covering a range of themes. In fact they are more varied than the typical college course, which focuses on a particular period, country, genre, or theme. Arguably, seminars must focus, because they are training students to master a coherent body of literature and write well-organized critical essays about them. But book-group discussions are more like the rambling *causeries* that late Victorian men of letters spun out. The book becomes a jump-off point for discussing politics, religion, philosophy, psychology, families, local affairs, personal reminiscences, morality, sex, death, and other (often apparently unrelated) books. One participant summed up these informal symposia quite simply: "We digress." Another said, "it's very casual and deliberately not like school," which is true in the sense that (as a third member put it) "There is nothing high-powered, competitive, or pretentious about the group. We are very ordinary everyday working women who enjoy a get-together to chat about books." A fourth says "We're not very intellectual," but that sells these groups short. What should the life of the mind be, if it isn't reading books and discussing all their implications?[53]

Amos Oz writes that "The game of reading requires you, the reader, to take an active part, to bring to the field your own life experience and your own innocence, as well as caution and cunning." And that, Jenny Hartley found, is precisely what happens in groups, "not just in terms of buying, reading, and discussing, but also in entering the literary arena. Groups write poetry, publish reviews in the local press, correspond with authors, and invite them to meetings." They will consider with open minds books recommended by reviewers, academics, or the Man Booker Prize Committee, but they see through puffery and hype. (Zadie Smith's *White Teeth* was the most selected book of 2001—and probably also the most disliked.) Though bookstore chains provide study guides and lists of suggested readings, groups generally don't use them. So if you're a postmodern academic who is looking for "subversive" readers who "resist commodification," Jenny Hartley has found them—outside the classroom:

> A sort of self-appointed fifth estate, reading groups enjoy taking on the fourth estate of the media. Their independence is

particularly important, given the recent controversy over the practice of publishers paying booksellers to recommend their books and display them prominently. To have this constituency of informed freethinkers, committed to reading yet standing at skeptical arm's length from the business of producing, selling, and reviewing books, is invaluable. They provide responsive audiences for writers; they help to keep mid- and backlists alive; and they can spot and pass on the good word for the one-offs from small publishers or unknown authors. Independent, maverick, unpredictable, and not to be bought off, reading groups are a treasure in the house of literature.[54]

Or as Oscar Wilde put it in "The Critic as Artist," these common readers have achieved the only meaningful goal of criticism, which is to compose "the record of one's own soul." For a liberal education, what other measure of success is there? If our students go on to spend their adult lives reading freely, then we as teachers have accomplished our mission, perhaps in spite of ourselves.

Notes

1. See Patrick Brantlinger, *The Reading Lesson: The Threat of Mass Literacy in Nineteenth Century British Fiction* (Bloomington: Indiana University Press, 1998); and John Carey, *The Intellectuals and the Masses: Pride and Prejudice among the Literary Intelligentsia, 1880–1939* (London: Faber & Faber, 1992).

2. Valerie Strauss, "Gates Gives $150 Million in Grants for Common Core Standards," *Washington Post* (12 May 2013).

3. Caroline Porter, "Common Core Contracts: A Fight is On," *Wall Street Journal* (24 Nov. 2014): A3; Loretta M. Gaffney, "The Common Core State Standards and Intellectual Freedom," *Journal of Intellectual Freedom and Privacy* 1 (Spring 2016): 5–15.

4. Mercedes K. Schneider, *Common Core Dilemma: Who Owns Our Schools?* (New York and London: Teachers College Press, 2015), ch. 11.

5. Bertrand Evans and James J. Lynch, "High School Textbooks in English: A Summary of a Report," in *Claremont Reading Conference: Twenty-Sixth Yearbook*, ed. Malcolm P. Douglas (Claremont, Calif.: Claremont Graduate School Curriculum Laboratory, 1962), 39–49.

6. *Literature: The British Tradition, Grade 12* (Upper Saddle River, NJ: Pearson, 2012).

7. Carol Iannone, "Experiencing the Common Core," *Academic Questions* 28 (Summer 2015): 184.

8. Deborah Meier et al., *Many Children Left Behind: How the No Child Left Behind Act is Damaging Our Children and Our Schools* (Boston: Beacon Press, 2004), 57.

9. E. D. Hirsch, *The Knowledge Deficit: Closing the Shocking Education Gap for American Children* (New York: Houghton Mifflin, 2006), 72.

10. Anya Kamenetz, *The Test* (New York: Public Affairs, 2015), esp. ch. 1; David Berliner, "Rational Responses to High Stakes Testing: The Case of Curriculum Narrowing and the Harm that Follows," *Cambridge Journal of Education* 41 (Sept. 2011): 287–302.

11. Terrence O. Moore, *The Story-Killers: A Common-Sense Case against the Common Core* (n.p.: privately printed, 2013), iii–xi, 6–13.

12. Carter Godwin Woodson, *The Mis-Education of the American Negro* (Washington, DC: Associated Publishers, 1933), 83–4.

13. Moore, *Story-Killers*, 262–3.

14. Mercedes K. Schneider, *A Chronicle of Echoes: Who's Who in the Implosion of American Public Education* (Charlotte, NC: Information Age Publishing, 2014), 168–9.

15. Beth Driscoll, *The New Literary Middlebrow: Tastemaking and Reading in the Twenty-First Century* (Basingstoke: Palgrave Macmillan, 2014), 91–3, 96–7.

16. Michael Rothfeld, "Cost Woes Plague Common-Core Rollout," *Wall Street Journal* (12 Nov. 2015): A1.

17. Michael Rothfeld, "Pearson's Bet on Common Core Fails to Pay Off," *Wall Street Journal* (22 Nov. 2016).

18. This literature is summarized in Stephen Krashen, *Free Voluntary Reading* (Santa Barbara, Calif.: Libraries Unlimited, 2011).

19. Richard C. Anderson, Paul T. Wilson, and Linda G. Fielding, "Growth in Reading and How Children Spend Their Time Outside of School," *Reading Research Quarterly* (1988) 23: 285–303.

20. Catherine Shedrick Ross, Lynne E. F. McKechnie, and Paulette M. Rothbauer, *Reading Matters: What the Research Reveals about Reading, Libraries, and Community* (Westport, Conn.: Libraries Unlimited, 2006), 147–79.

21. Kelly Gallagher, *Readicide: How Schools Are Killing Reading and What You Can Do About It* (Portland, Me.: Stenhouse, 2009), 43–4.

22. Yong Zhao, "Lessons that Matter: What Should We Learn from Asia's School Systems?," Mitchell Policy Paper No. 4 (May 2015).

23. Ronald J. Zboray and Mary Saracino Zboray, *Everyday Ideas: Socioliterary Experience among Antebellum New Englanders* (Knoxville, Tenn.: University of Tennessee Press, 2006), 252–8.

24. Marion Baraitser, *Reading and Expressive Writing with Traumatised Children, Young Refugees and Asylum Seekers: Unpack My Heart with Words* (London and Philadelphia: Jessica Kingsley, 2014), 27, 37, 51–2.

25. Laura J. Cohen, "The Therapeutic Use of Reading: A Qualitative Study," *Journal of Poetry Therapy* 7 (1993): 73–83.

26. Kathleen Rooney, *Reading with Oprah: The Book Club that Changed America* (Fayetteville, Ark.: University of Arkansas Press, 2005), 205.

27. Clare Ellis, "The Sharing of Stories, in Company with Mr Charles Dickens," in *Reading and the Victorians*, ed. Matthew Bradley and Juliet John (Fanrham: Ashgate, 2015), 143–57.

28. Jonathan Franzen, "Perchance to Dream: In the Age of Images, a Reason to Write Novels," *Harper's* (Apr. 1996): 48.

29. Gallagher, *Readicide*, 119–24.

30. <http://www.comres.co.uk/polls/bbc-victoria-derbyshire-no-platform-poll/>.

31. Nick Hillman, *Keeping Schtum? What Students Think of Free Speech*, HEPI Report 85, May 2016.

32. "Free Speech on Campus," *New Criterion* 34 (Nov. 2015): 3.

33. A. C. Erlick, "Adolescents' Views on Freedom to Read," *Social Education* 39 (Apr. 1975): 235–7.

34. "Don't Be So Offensive," *Economist* (4 June 2016): 60.

35. Mike Vilensky, "Columbia's Required Texts Challenged," *Wall Street Journal* (2 July 2015): A15.

36. Jonathan Zimmerman, *Campus Politics: What Everyone Needs to Know* (New York: Oxford University Press, 2016), chs. 2, 4.

37. Douglas Belkin, "Faculty's New Focus: Don't Offend," *Wall Street Journal* (28 Feb. 2017): A3. For a discussion in depth, see Edward Schlosser, "I'm a Liberal Professor, and My Liberal Students Terrify Me," *Vox* (3 June 2015).

38. William Deresiewicz, *Excellent Sheep: The Miseducation of the American Elite and the Way to a Meaningful Life* (New York: Free Press, 2014), ch. 1.

39. Josephine S. Gottsdanker and E. Anne Pidgeon, "Current Reading Tastes of Young Adults," *Journal of Higher Education* 40 (May 1969): 381–5.

40. Mark Oppenheimer, "Person Up, Yale Students," *Tablet* (10 Nov. 2015).

41. Aaron Sibarium, letter to the editor, *Wall Street Journal* (24 Oct. 2016): A14.

42. Elizabeth Noll, "The Ripple Effect of Censorship: Silencing the Classroom," *English Journal*, High School Edition 83.8 (Dec. 1994): 59.

43. "Libraries Lose a Quarter of Staff as Hundreds Close," *BBC News* (29 Mar. 2016), <http://www.bbc.com/news/uk-england-35707956>.

44. Teresa Watanabe, "Many L.A. School Libraries, Lacking Staff, Are Forced to Shut," *Los Angeles Times*, 23 Feb. 2014, <www.latimes.com/local/la-me-lausd-libraries-20140224-story.html#page=1>; Becky Vevea, "Librarians Are a Luxury Chicago Public Schools Can't Afford," National Public Radio, 2 Sept. 2014, <http://www.npr.org/sections/ed/2014/09/01/344905087/>.

45. Marjorie Perloff, "Crisis in the Humanities? Reconfiguring Literary Study for the Twenty-First Century," in *Theory's Empire: An Anthology of Dissent*, ed. Daphne Patai and Will H. Corrall (New York: Columbia University Press, 2005), 677–81.

46. James Proctor and Bethan Benwell, *Reading across Worlds: Transnational Book Groups and the Reception of Difference* (Basingstoke: Palgrave Macmillan, 2015), 5–7.

47. Driscoll, *New Literary Middlebrow*, 54.

48. Elizabeth Long, *Book Clubs: Women and the Uses of Reading in Everyday Life* (Chicago: University of Chicago Press, 2003), 116–30. Much the same pattern prevails in UK book groups: Jenny Hartley, *The Reading Groups Book: 2002–2003 Edition* (Oxford: Oxford University Press, 2002), 180–9, 205–28.

49. Hartley, *Reading Groups*, 34–5, 138.

50. Long, *Book Clubs*, 147–8.

51. Hartley, *Reading Groups*, 75–7, 180–2, 185–7.

52. Long, *Book Clubs*, 153–4.

53. Hartley, *Reading Groups*, 51–7, 99–101.

54. Ibid., 127, 155–6.

More Reading about Reading

Laurel Amtower, *Engaging Words: The Culture of Reading in the Later Middle Ages* (London: Palgrave, 2000).

Thomas Augst, *The Clerk's Tale: Young Men and Moral Life in Nineteenth-Century America* (Chicago: University of Chicago Press, 2003).

Deborah Brandt, *Literacy in American Lives* (Cambridge: Cambridge University Press, 2001).

Patrick Brantlinger, *The Reading Lesson: The Threat of Mass Literacy in Nineteenth-Century British Fiction* (Bloomington, Ind.: Indiana University Press, 1998).

Jeffrey Brooks, *When Russia Learned to Read: Literacy and Popular Literature, 1861–1917* (Princeton: Princeton University Press, 1985).

Matthew P. Brown, *The Pilgrim and the Bee: Reading Rituals and Book Culture in Early New England* (Philadelphia: University of Pennsylvania Press, 2007).

Allen Dwight Callahan, *The Talking Book: African Americans and the Bible* (New Haven: Yale University Press, 2006).

Andrew Cambers, *Godly Reading: Print, Manuscript and Puritanism in England, 1580–1720* (Cambridge: Cambridge University Press, 2011).

Mike Chasar, *Everyday Reading: Poetry and Popular Culture in Modern America* (New York: Columbia University Press, 2012).

Stephen Colclough, *Consuming Texts: Readers and Reading Communities, 1695–1870* (London: Palgrave, 2007).

Janet Coleman, *Medieval Readers and Writers 1350–1450* (New York: Columbia University Press, 1981).

Janet Duitsman Cornelius, *"When I Can Read My Title Clear": Literacy, Slavery, and Religion in the Antebellum South* (Columbia, SC: University of South Carolina Press, 1991).

Archie L. Dick, *The Hidden History of South Africa's Book and Reading Cultures* (Toronto: University of Toronto Press, 2012).

Frank Felsenstein and James J. Connolly, *What Middletown Read: Print Culture in an American Small City* (Amherst, Mass.: University of Massachusetts Press, 2015).

Jan Fergus, *Provincial Readers in Eighteenth-Century England* (Oxford: Oxford University Press, 2006).

Steven Roger Fischer, *A History of Reading* (Chicago: University of Chicago Press, 2004).

Kate Flint, *The Woman Reader 1837–1914* (Oxford: Oxford University Press, 1993).

Peter Fritzsche, *Reading Berlin 1900* (Cambridge, Mass.: Harvard University Press, 1996).

Kelly Gallagher, *Readicide: How Schools Are Killing Reading and What You Can Do About It* (York, Me.: Stenhouse, 2009).

William J. Gilmore, *Reading Becomes a Necessity of Life: Material and Cultural Life in Rural New England, 1780–1835* (Knoxville, Tenn.: University of Tennessee Press, 1989).

Carlo Ginzburg, *The Cheese and the Worms: The Cosmos of a Sixteenth-Century Miller*, trans. John and Anne Tedeschi (London: Penguin, 1982).

Jean Marie Goulemot, *Forbidden Texts: Erotic Literature and Its Readers in Eighteenth-Century France*, trans. James Simpson (Philadelphia: University of Pennsylvania Press, 1994).

Anthony Grafton, *Commerce with the Classics: Ancient Books and Renaissance Readers* (Ann Arbor, Mich.: University of Michigan Press, 1997).

D. H. Green, *Women Readers in the Middle Ages* (Cambridge: Cambridge University Press, 2007).

Ezra Greenspan, *Walt Whitman and the American Reader* (Cambridge: Cambridge University Press, 1990).

M. O. Grenby, *The Child Reader 1700–1840* (Cambridge: Cambridge University Press, 2011).

Wendy Griswold, *Bearing Witness: Readers, Writers and the Novel in Nigeria* (Chicago: University of Chicago Press, 2008).

Suman Gupta, *Consumable Texts in Contemporary India: Uncultured Books and Bibliographical Sociology* (London: Palgrave Macmillan, 2015).

Kevin J. Hayes, *A Colonial Woman's Bookshelf* (Knoxville, Tenn.: University of Tennessee Press, 1996).

Kevin J. Hayes, *The Road to Monticello: The Life and Mind of Thomas Jefferson* (Oxford: Oxford University Press, 2008).

David M. Henkin, *City Reading: Written Words and Public Spaces in Antebellum New York* (New York: Columbia University Press, 1998).

Konrad Hirschler, *The Written Word in the Medieval Arabic Lands: A Social and Cultural History of Reading Practices* (Edinburgh: Edinburgh University Press, 2012).

Barbara Hochman, *'Uncle Tom's Cabin' and the Reading Revolution: Race, Literacy, Childhood, and Fiction, 1851–1911* (Amherst, Mass.: University of Massachusetts Press, 2011).

James L. Huffman, *Creating a Public: People and Press in Meiji Japan* (Honolulu: University of Hawaii Press, 1997).

H. J. Jackson, *Marginalia* (New Haven: Yale University Press, 2001).

H. J. Jackson, *Romantic Readers: The Evidence of Marginalia* (New Haven: Yale University Press, 2005).

Cecile M. Jagodzinski, *Privacy and Print: Reading and Writing in Seventeenth-Century England* (Charlottesville, Va.: University Press of Virginia, 1999).

Clarence Karr, *Authors and Audiences: Popular Canadian Fiction in the Early Twentieth Century* (Montreal: McGill-Queen's University Press, 2000).

James T. Kloppenberg, *Reading Obama: Dreams, Hope, and the American Political Tradition* (Princeton: Princeton University Press, 2011).

Cheryl Knott, *Not Free, Not for All: Public Libraries in the Age of Jim Crow* (Amherst, Mass.: University of Massachusetts Press, 2015).

Denis Kozlov, *The Readers of 'Novy Mir': Coming to Terms with the Stalinist Past* (Cambridge, Mass.: Harvard University Press, 2013).

Amanda Laugesen, *Boredom is the Enemy: The Intellectual and Imaginative Lives of Australian Soldiers in the Great War and Beyond* (Farnham: Ashgate, 2012).

Elizabeth Long, *Book Clubs: Women and the Uses of Reading in Everyday Life* (Chicago: University of Chicago Press, 2003).

Stephen Lovell, *The Russian Reading Revolution: Print Culture in the Soviet and Post-Soviet Eras* (New York: St Martin's Press, 2000).

Elizabeth McHenry, *Forgotten Readers: Recovering the Lost History of African American Literary Societies* (Durham, NC: Duke University Press, 2002).

Robert McParland, *Charles Dickens's American Audience* (Lanham, Md.: Lexington Books, 2010).

Robert McParland, *Mark Twain's Audience* (Lanham, Md.: Lexington Books, 2014).

Martyn Lyons, *A History of Reading and Writing in the Western World* (London: Palgrave Macmillan, 2010).

James L. Machor, *Reading Fiction in Antebellum America: Informed Response and Reception Histories, 1820–1865* (Baltimore: Johns Hopkins University Press, 2011).

Alberto Manguel, *A History of Reading* (New York: Viking, 1996).

Molly Guptill Manning, *When Books Went to War: The Stories That Helped Us Win World War II* (Boston: Houghton Mifflin Harcourt, 2014).

Manuel M. Martin-Rodriguez, ed., *With a Book in Their Hands: Chicano/a Readers and Readerships across the Centuries* (Albuquerque, NM: University of New Mexico Press, 2014).

E. Jennifer Monaghan, *Learning to Read and Write in Colonial America* (Amherst, Mass.: University of Massachusetts Press, 2005).

Azar Nafisi, *Reading Lolita in Tehran* (New York: Random House, 2008).

Stephanie Newell, *Literary Culture in Colonial Ghana: How to Play the Game of Life* (Bloomington, Ind.: Indiana University Press, 2002).

David Paul Nord, *Communities of Journalism: A History of American Newspapers and Their Readers* (Champaign, Ill.: University of Illinois Press, 2001).

James W. Parins, *Literacy and Intellectual Life in the Cherokee Nation, 1820–1906* (Norman, Okla.: University of Oklahoma Press, 2013).

Iris Parush, *Reading Jewish Women: Marginality and Modernization in Nineteenth-Century Eastern European Jewish Society*, trans. Saadya Sternberg (Lebanon, NH: Brandeis University Press, 2004).

Christine Pawley, *Reading on the Middle Border: The Culture of Print in Late Nineteenth-Century Osage, Iowa* (Amherst, Mass.: University of Massachusetts Press, 2001).

Christine Pawley, *Reading Places: Literacy, Democracy, and the Public Library in Cold War America* (Amherst, Mass.: University of Massachusetts Press, 2010).

Jacqueline Pearson, *Women's Reading in Britain 1750–1835: A Dangerous Recreation.* (Cambridge: Cambridge University Press, 1999)

Glen Peterson, *Power of Words: Literacy and Revolution in South China, 1949–1995* (Vancouver, BC: University of British Columbia Press, 1995).

Leah Price, *How to Do Things with Books in Victorian Britain* (Princeton: Princeton University Press, 2012).

James Procter and Bethan Benwell, *Reading across Worlds: Transnational Book Groups and the Reception of Difference* (London: Palgrave Macmillan, 2015).

Janice A. Radway, *Reading the Romance: Women, Patriarchy, and Popular Literature* (Chapel Hill, NC: University of North Carolina Press, 1984).

Janice A. Radway, *A Feeling for Books: The Book-of-the-Month Club, Literary Taste, and Middle-Class Desire* (Chapel Hill, NC: University of North Carolina Press, 1997).

Gideon Reuveni, *Reading Germany: Literature and Consumer Culture in Germany before 1933* (Oxford: Berghahn Books, 2006).

Kathleen Rooney, *Reading with Oprah: The Book Club that Changed America* (Fayetteville, Ark.: University of Arkansas Press, 2005).

Jonathan Rose, ed., *The Holocaust and the Book: Destruction and Preservation* (Amherst, Mass.: University of Massachusetts Press, 2001).

Jonathan Rose, *The Intellectual Life of the British Working Classes*, 2nd edn. (New Haven: Yale University Press, 2010).

Jonathan Rose, *The Literary Churchill: Author, Reader, Actor* (New Haven: Yale University Press, 2014).

Timothy W. Ryback, *Hitler's Private Library: The Books that Shaped His Life* (New York: Knopf, 2008).

Paul Saenger, *Space between Words: The Origins of Silent Reading* (Stanford, Calif.: Stanford University Press, 1997).

Dana Sajdi, *The Barber of Damascus: Nouveau Literacy in the Eighteenth-Century Ottoman Empire* (Stanford, Calif.: Stanford University Press, 2013).

Elisabeth Salter, *Popular Reading in English c.1400–1600* (Manchester: Manchester University Press, 2012).

Katherine West Scheil, *She Hath Been Reading: Women and Shakespeare Clubs in America* (Ithaca, NY: Cornell University Press, 2012).

William H. Sherman, *Used Books: Marking Readers in Renaissance England* (Philadelphia: University of Pennsylvania Press, 2008).

Lisa Z. Sigel, *Making Modern Love: Sexual Narratives and Identities in Interwar Britain* (Philadelphia: Temple University Press, 2012).

Clarissa Smith, *One for the Girls! The Pleasures and Practices of Reading Women's Porn* (Chicago: University of Chicago Press, 2013).

Erin A. Smith, *What Would Jesus Read? Popular Religious Books and Everyday Life in Twentieth-Century America* (Chapel Hill, NC: University of North Carolina Press, 2015).

William St. Clair, *The Reading Nation in the Romantic Period* (Cambridge: Cambridge University Press, 2004).

Megan Sweeney, *Reading is My Window: Books and the Art of Reading in Women's Prisons* (Chapel Hill, NC: University of North Carolina Press, 2010).

Araceli Tinajero, *El Lector: A History of the Cigar Factory Reader* (Austin, Tex.: University of Texas Press, 2010).

Mark Towsey, *Reading the Scottish Enlightenment: Books and Their Readers in Provincial Scotland* (Leiden: Brill, 2010).

David Vincent, *The Rise of Mass Literacy: Reading and Writing in Modern Europe* (Cambridge: Polity, 2000).

Heather Andrea Williams, *Self-Taught: African American Education in Slavery and Freedom* (Chapel Hill, NC: University of North Carolina Press, 2005).

Ruth Clayton Windscheffel, *Reading Gladstone* (London: Palgrave Macmillan, 2008).

Ronald J. Zboray, *A Fictive People: Antebellum Economic Development and the American Reading Public* (Oxford: Oxford University Press, 1993).

Ronald J. Zboray and Mary Saracino Zboray, *Everyday Ideas: Socioliterary Experience among Antebellum New Englanders* (London: Routledge, 2005).

Index for *Readers' Liberation*